S0-AEQ-057

An Unexpected Minority

An Unexpected Minority

White Kids in an Urban School

EDWARD W. MORRIS

RUTGERS UNIVERSITY PRESS

NEW BRUNSWICK, NEW JERSEY, AND LONDON

LIBRARY OF CONGRESS CATALOGING-IN-PUBLICATION DATA

Morris, Edward W., 1973–
An unexpected minority : white kids in an urban school / Edward W. Morris.
    p. cm.
  Includes bibliographical references and index.
  ISBN-13: 978-0-8135-3720-7 (hardcover : alk. paper)
  ISBN-13: 978-0-8135-3721-4 (pbk.)
    1. School integration—Texas—Case studies. 2. Urban schools—Texas—Socio-
logical aspects—Case studies. 3. Children, White—Education—Texas—Case studies.
  4. United States—Race relations—Case studies. I. Title.
  LC214.22.T48M67 2006
  371.829—dc22   2005004839

A British Cataloging-in-Publication record for this book is available
from the British Library.

Copyright © 2006 by Edward W. Morris

All rights reserved

No part of this book may be reproduced or utilized in any form or by any means,
electronic or mechanical, or by any information storage and retrieval system, without
written permission from the publisher. Please contact Rutgers University Press, 100
Joyce Kilmer Avenue, Piscataway, NJ 08854-8099. The only exception to this
prohibition is "fair use" as defined by U.S. copyright law.

Manufactured in the United States of America

Chapter 4 originally appeared as "From 'Middle Class' to 'Trailer Trash': Teachers'
Perceptions of White Students in a Predominately Minority School." *Sociology of
Education* 78, no. 2 (April 2005): (99–121). ©American Sociological Association.
Chapter 5 originally appeared as "'Tuck in That Shirt!' Race, Class, Gender, and
Discipline in an Urban School." *Sociological Perspectives* 48, no. 1 (Spring 2005): 25–48.
© Pacific Sociological Association.

CONTENTS

TABLES

ACKNOWLEDGMENTS

Although my name is the only one that officially appears as the author of this book, its production was a collaborative effort. I have benefited greatly from the support of many friends, family, colleagues, respondents, and institutions (not necessarily mutually exclusive categories) throughout this process. Without these people and groups, this book would never have been written.

First, I would like to thank the administrators, teachers, assistants, and students at the school I call Matthews Middle School for allowing me into their lives. It was with great ambivalence that I began writing this study, because what comes forth as "data" to the reader—the anecdotes and statements of people at the school—I experienced on a very personal level. I got to know so many interesting and enjoyable kids and adults at the school that the experience itself could be considered valuable and rewarding even if it had not provided me with the basis for this book. Not only do their statements and actions form the data for this book, but, as the reader will see, the often insightful thoughts that kids and teachers shared with me were crucial to my own thought processes.

I thank the Annenberg Foundation, under the University of Texas guidance of Pedro Reyes, for funding my fieldwork for this study. This valuable financial assistance allowed me to select an ideal school for my study, funded my travel to the school, and facilitated my entrée into the school. Without this assistance, this study would look vastly different, and may not have been accomplished at all. I also thank the Department of Sociology at the University of Texas for awarding me teaching assistant, assistant instructor, and lecturer positions during the fieldwork and writing stages of this project.

I owe a huge debt to my mentors, who shaped not only this project, but also my overall progress as a graduate student. In my first semester of graduate school I took classes with Christine Williams and Christopher Ellison. Through their support and confidence in my intellectual ability, I learned more in a few months than it seemed like I had in all the years before. Craig Watkins taught me to think about race in an entirely new way, and this understanding has undergirded every project I have initiated since. Angela Valenzuela gave me crucial validation for some of my early hunches in this study and reinforced my excitement for ethnographic work. Chandra Muller has supported me in every aspect of this study, from finding me funding, to reassuring me of its merit, to shaping and honing its arguments. Chandra Muller and Christine Williams, in particular, have read countless drafts (some of which may have been quite painful to sift through) and given me extensive written comments. Christine always challenged me to think one step further and articulate even the most abstract thoughts in an accessible way (she was also not afraid to write "whoa!" on my drafts if I was getting off track). Chandra forced me to focus my thoughts in ways that related to "real-life" implications and, thankfully, identified when I was getting too "Pollyanna."

My friends and colleagues in our education research group at the University of Texas—Lisa Wyatt, Kathleen Nybroten, Lorena Lopez-Gonzalez, Jennifer Pearson, Belinda Needham, Ali Picucci, Eric Kinney, Amy Langenkamp, Jason LaTurner, and Kelly Goran Fulton—also had much to do with this project. Several discussions with this group were invaluable as I struggled through my ideas. Kathleen, Lorena, Ali, and Jason gave me thoughtful written comments. Kelly consistently lent her keen insight, moral support, and extensive knowledge to every stage of this study. Because Kelly was doing her research in a nearby school, we often drove many miles together between the research sites and home, and our conversations during this time gave me vital feedback on some of my hunches and concerns during fieldwork. In addition, my colleagues and friends at Ohio University have provided enormous encouragement and support in the closing stages of this project.

The staff at Rutgers University Press has expertly nurtured and guided this book. I thank Kristi Long for her early interest and support as well as her continued guidance through various stages of this project. I would also like to thank the external reviewers of the manuscript, who took time to provide thoughtful and helpful comments that improved the work substantially.

My family has always had a terrific, loving enthusiasm for whatever I have chosen to pursue. My parents, Waymon Morris and Deirdre Morris, and my sisters, Jennifer Morris, Melinda Morris Nichols, and Mary Morris Davis, have been there for me every step of the way—even when it started to seem strange that I was *still* in school.

Finally, this book absolutely could not have been finished without the help of my spouse and best friend, Jane Jaques Morris. She helped in every way imaginable: giving emotional support and technical expertise, reading over drafts, and critiquing my ideas from a teacher's perspective. But most importantly, she was just there for me when I needed it most—in the depths of writer's block or funding uncertainty. She kept my head above water through the entire process with her unwavering faith that I would finish and her unselfish help with whatever I needed (which even meant taking up cross-stitching and quietly working on it while I was consumed with sitting at the computer—a true sacrifice!). Her love and help were essential to this study.

An Unexpected Minority

1

Introduction

The wind began to swirl and turn slightly cooler that mid-November day, and it seemed that winter might finally arrive in Texas. As I walked from the doors of Matthews Middle School,[1] a predominately minority, urban school, I struggled to carry a massive stack of blue survey papers that flapped and twisted against the wind. The surveys came from students I had come to know during my past several months as a researcher at the school. My excitement and grip strengthened as I anticipated reading the responses. I was primarily interested in how these students would answer the portion of the survey asking them to name their racial identity. I provided several "standard" choices of racial/ethnic categories on the form, along with instructions that they could select any combination of these groups to describe themselves. I also provided a category called "Other" with a space for them to write in their own choice. Because of what I had begun to learn about race in this school setting, I wondered what the students would write. I got in my car and immediately rifled through the forms, looking in particular for responses from the few students at the school who might consider themselves "white"—according to school records, only about forty in this school of over one thousand. I soon came across the survey form of a boy named Jackson, whom school records designated as white and whom I had noticed from my earliest visits to Matthews. When I read Jackson's response, I paused momentarily and then laughed out loud. On his survey, Jackson had circled the category "White" and in the "Other" space had written in "white chocolate."

I think I laughed as much from a sense of relief and vindication as from the clever irony of Jackson's response. The term "white chocolate" seemed to perfectly capture so much of what I had observed, and would observe, about the meaning of being white in this predominately racial/ethnic minority setting.

White students such as Jackson, who lived and attended school in this nonwhite area, presented a white identity and style that embraced that of their minority friends and neighbors. It could be called, in many ways, a nonwhite, or "chocolate" form of whiteness. At Matthews, a working-class school where African American and Latino students dominated the population and peer culture, white kids did not interact and develop understandings from a central or normative position, as most whites generally do.[2] Many of these white youth aligned themselves with the nonwhite people and styles prevalent in their community, not the middle-class, suburban lifestyles and methods of interaction most people consider white. The term "white chocolate" impeccably described many of these students who, through their corn-rowed hair, baggy pants, rhythms of speech, and other styles, seemed to blur the line between white and nonwhite. Their thoughts, actions, and words have much to tell us about the meaning and future of whiteness and race relations in the United States. The experiences of this unexpected minority of white students, and the implications these suggest, form the basis for this book.

My focus on white students in the predominately nonwhite, urban setting of Matthews brings a new angle to the study of race, class, and gender inequality in education. During my period of research at the school I observed classrooms composed mostly of African American and Latino students with just one or two white students such as Jackson. Rather than overlooking these white students, I chose to make them a starting point for my analysis. As our school system continues to remain segregated by race, with white students and black students the least likely to go to school together (Reardon and Yun 2001; Reardon, Yun, and Eitle 2000), white youth who live in a predominately minority area and attend school in that area are certainly not typical. However, I think there is much we can learn from these students. Kids such as Jackson present a fascinating case for exploring how the meaning of race and whiteness alters when intersecting with social class, place, gender, and style.[3]

However, while being white tended to connote surprising meanings at Matthews, the typical rewards of whiteness remained largely intact. These included stereotypes that linked white students to high status and a high degree of self-discipline, as well as tracking and other processes, related to perceptions of ability and achievement, that disproportionately rewarded white students. Identity can tell us much about the meaning of race, but it cannot completely describe its impact on people as they go about their daily lives. Considering oneself white chocolate at Matthews did not fully translate into being seen as black and, thus, did not incur the typical assumptions and reactions associated with being black in U.S. society and schooling. This could make it difficult for many white students to fit in with their minority peers, but made it easier for them to fit in with the academic structure of the school. Even in this nonwhite, urban context, where white students lacked majority status as well as the advantages of living in a wealthy, suburban, safe area, whiteness retained many privileges and tended to aid white students academically.

This fact was apparent several months after I collected those survey responses on racial identity, at the very end of my two years of fieldwork at Matthews. It was late May, and I entered a cavernous gymnasium for the Matthews' eighth-grade graduation ceremony. Hundreds of families, most of them African American and Latino, crowded the bleacher seating, fanning themselves with graduation programs. I chose to stand just below the bleachers, near several parents and family members who did not want to sit. After the graduating students entered the auditorium, a teacher named Mr. Lang approached me and said that the principal, a black woman named Ms. Walker, wanted me to sit up front with the teachers. He said the principal considered me an honorary part of the school because of the volunteer work I had done tutoring students. I did not really want to take such a central position in the ceremony, but complied nonetheless, and walked with Mr. Lang to sit with the mostly African American faculty.

The graduation ceremony proceeded as one might expect, with speeches from the principal and head teachers, music and songs from students, and rousing cheers from family members. However, two aspects of this ceremony starkly demonstrated the resilience of white advantages in this mostly nonwhite context—one of which directly affected me, a white man. When Ms. Walker addressed the crowd in her opening speech, she began by thanking the faculty for their hard work all year. She mentioned the teacher of the year, a black woman named Ms. Johnson, and thanked her for her service. After this, to my utter shock and slight embarrassment, she announced my name to all those present and thanked me for volunteering to tutor students at the school! My face must have been quite red as I stood at Ms. Walker's request to acknowledge the applause from the crowd. I was certainly flattered by this, but also felt somewhat uncomfortable. I did not really think I deserved such an honor when educators at Matthews did so much more to help students than I thought I had.

As I grappled with my mixed emotions, I observed the next portion of the ceremony, in which teachers honored two students from each "team," or smaller grouping of students, as the best "all-around" students. This prize was not necessarily based on the strongest academic record, but on which students the teachers thought tried the hardest, performed the highest, and behaved the best. The school selected eight students that year for this elite award; and, to my surprise, two of them, a boy named John and a girl named Samantha, were white. Nineteen white students began the eighth grade that year, and, by my count, sixteen were slated to graduate. After the teachers called out the names of these white students, I thought back to the praise I received just moments earlier. A look around that gymnasium, crowded overwhelmingly with African Americans and Latinos, exposed the irony of white people such as

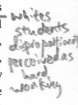
whites students disproportionately perceived as hard working

John, Samantha, and myself playing such a central role. In this context dominated by those with black and brown skin, it seemed strange that so many of
us with light skin were honored so handsomely.

Of course, I do not mean to imply that these students, or myself, did nothing to deserve this adulation. However, I use this example to show how white
people in this predominately nonwhite environment tended to be placed in
central positions academically, even as being white itself acquired very unique
meanings. Through the course of my study, I explored the meanings associated
with being white for youth in this nonwhite context, as well as the impacts
these meanings had on educational processes, such as the graduation honors I
described. I argue that schools serve as sites through which children learn
about race and build a sense of race for themselves. They accomplish this
through simultaneously constructing understandings of social class, social location, masculinity, and femininity. These constructions do not stand apart from
social life, rooted in individual psychology, but have real impacts on the structure of educational processes and how people approach educational organizations. White youth at Matthews did tend to demonstrate a unique sense of
white identity strongly influenced by black and Latino cultural style, but educational processes steeped in race, class, and gender assumptions continued to
link being white with educational success. Even as many of these students displayed a white chocolate persona constructed through their numerical minority status, they still enjoyed some of the larger benefits of membership in the
general racial majority.

Several valuable works have explored white identity formation—how white
people see themselves in terms of race—in various contexts (e.g., Chubbuck
2004; Frankenberg 1993; Gallagher 1995; Kenny 2000; Perry 2002). Much of this
research has been based on in-depth interviews, however, and does not closely
document the everyday work through which people develop understandings of
being white and the real-life impacts of these understandings. This book seeks to
broaden the analysis of being white beyond individual and group-level identities
and into everyday interactions, discourses, and educational processes. My focus
in this study is not on white identities per se, but whiteness more generally—what
I define as the meanings and processes associated with being white from various
perspectives and the consequences for white people and people of color.

Studying Whiteness

When I first encountered some of the early literature on whiteness in a graduate race and ethnicity seminar, I initially recoiled. I pictured departments and
programs of "whiteness studies" dominated by white researchers writing and
teaching about other white people. This vision of studying white people seemed
self-serving to me, and I critiqued the potential it had for perpetuating white

control over the production of knowledge. However, as I became more immersed in this work, I began to see its enormous potential to unearth and expose invidious notions of race and racial inequality. Studies of whiteness have transformed the question of race to critically examine how being white serves as a source of social privilege—a project crucial to developing a complete understanding of social inequality (Lewis 2004). We need to ask not only why groups defined as racial and ethnic minorities experience disadvantages in various settings, but also how those considered white experience advantages, because these compose two sides of the same coin (see Rasmussen et al. 2001 and Doane and Bonilla-Silva 2003 for further discussion of the potential benefits and pitfalls of studying whiteness).

Early in the development of this book, when I told several friends and colleagues about my topic, one of the first things they asked was often something like, Why would you want to study white people—isn't it African Americans and Latinos who experience most of the problems in education? At first, I responded to this question with some sort of rambling explanation about racial privileges and education. But as I have thought about it, two clear ideas answer this question for me and serve as the impetus for this book. First, although we often read educational data that separates groups according to race—the "black-white test-score gap" or the "Latino drop-out rate," for instance—we rarely try to understand how these broad racialized categories are interspersed with other important areas of difference such as social class, geographic location or "place," and gender, among others. We cannot understand race devoid of these other categories because they lend very unique and complicated meanings to race. Some African American and Latino students might experience different, and some might say lesser, problems in education than some whites, depending on economic resources, for example. Thus, we should understand racialized issues in education in relation to other educational issues and sources of inequality and difference, such as class and gender. This book explores the ways in which whiteness serves as a source of privilege as well as how class, gender, style, and location alter this privilege.

Second, when we speak about race in education, we should be clear that this does not only refer to groups commonly seen as racialized—Asian Americans, Latinos, and African Americans—but to whites as well, a group too often dismissed from race-based discussions and thereby framed as just "normal." White people have race, too; the main difference is that their race has been constructed as the norm from which all other racially identified groups have become "others." This means most whites do not have to think about their race. It does not confront them in their daily lives because other whites dominate most social spaces. By exploring race in the lives of white people, we can critique these advantages that ordinarily go unnoticed. We can ask why white people in general continue to disproportionately dominate in areas such as occupational mobility and educational attainment, and what this means for the disadvantaged groups we typically think of as "racial."

This second point leads directly into my reasoning for studying white people in the unusual situation where they compose the racial minority.[4] Most whites dominate public life just from sheer numbers. People claiming a European white identity still make up 70 percent of the population of the United States (U.S. Census Bureau 2000). This means that white people will have a certain numerical advantage in most areas of society. At the same time, according to data from census categories, racial/ethnic minority groups are growing rapidly and are projected to gain numerical strength (U.S. Census Bureau 2000).[5] This indicates that in the future white people in America will numerically dominate fewer and fewer public spaces. This raises some intriguing questions. What happens when whites constitute a numerical minority, as they might one day in the United States? How might the meanings of whiteness and white privilege change (and stay the same) in spaces dominated by people of color?

This book addresses these questions by exploring whiteness at Matthews, a school not dominated by white people in either the faculty or student body. This unique or exceptional case provides a new vantage point from which to examine white advantage and racial inequality in education (see Feagin, Orum, and Sjoberg 1991 for a discussion of unique cases). It shows how social class and gender complicate this advantage, but also how it persists, even in the presence of nonwhite authority figures and peers. In order to map the relations, interactions, and impacts built around racialized meanings at Matthews, I immersed myself in that environment, employing the research method known as ethnography: "the study of groups and people as they go about their everyday lives" (Emerson, Fretz, and Shaw 1995, 1). This method allowed me to understand and experience whiteness in this unique environment from a multitude of perspectives (see Lewis 2004 for a discussion of the benefits of ethnography in studying white people as racial actors). In the next sections, I briefly review the design of my study. For a more detailed account of my research, especially regarding various issues that arose, the reader should consult the appendix, "Research Methods."

An Ethnography of Matthews Middle School

As I became interested in the question of white students in a nonwhite school setting before I began this research project, I found that relatively little work had been done in this area. As I describe in the next chapter, some research had examined poor, "inner city" whites (e.g., Hartigan 1999) and some had examined urban racial/ethnic minority students bused to predominately white, suburban schools (e.g., Wells and Crain 1997). But nothing I could find specifically studied white youth living in a nonwhite, urban area and attending school in that area. Because little previous research had been done and the questions

TABLE 1.1

**Student Characteristics for Matthews Middle School,
2000–2001 and 2001–2002**

Race and economic background	Percentage of student body 2000–2001	Percentage of student body 2001–2002
African American	47	46
Hispanic (Latino)	40	43
Asian/Pacific Islander	9	7
White	4	3
Economically disadvantaged	60	66

Source: Texas Education Agency, www.tea.state.tx.us.

Note: Figures have been rounded.

that interested me pertained to meanings and interactive processes, I arranged to conduct a fine-grained ethnographic study of one school. I closely observed and documented the experiences of students, teachers, and administrators going about their lives in this educational context. I gathered as much information as I possibly could from this environment to answer my questions, including intensive participant observation, in-depth interviews, school documents, achievement test results, and census data. *methods*

Matthews Middle School, the site for this ethnography, is located in a low-income, predominately black and Latino area of a large Texas city (table 1.1 shows key characteristics of the school during both years of my study; I describe the school and neighborhood in greater detail in chapter 3).

I chose Matthews for several reasons. First, as the table shows, whites composed a numerical minority but still had significant enough numbers (around forty white students each year I conducted fieldwork) for me to observe and get to know different white students and to allow for the quantitative reporting of achievement test results. After I started research at Matthews I learned that the school also had a predominately nonwhite faculty—roughly two-thirds black and one-third white. This presented an additionally interesting situation where nonwhites dominated not only within the peer group, but also among authority figures.

Second, this school included a sizeable number of not only black students, but also Latino and Asian American students. Although black and white students remain the most polarized racial/ethnic groups in the United States in terms of achievement, a simple black-white focus downplays the recent growth of Latino and Asian American students in schools nationwide. I firmly believe that sociologists and other social scientists need to shift their paradigms of race and inequality to better incorporate the experiences of Latinos and Asian Americans. The racial and ethnic structure of the country is changing, and our theories explaining this structure should change with it. Matthews provided an opportunity to expand the study of white educational advantages beyond a black-white dichotomy, to reflect the reality of increasing diversity in the U.S. educational system and society in general.

Third, Matthews interested me because it was a middle school, composed of seventh and eighth grades. This interest might seem strange at first, because middle school for many of us (including myself) represents a time period we would rather forget! Similarly, most ethnographic literature demonstrates an avoidance of middle school, more often situating research in high schools or elementary schools. However, several factors intrigued me about the often-overlooked period of middle school. Middle school composes a liminal transition time during which children begin to learn the more adult roles and identities expected of them in society. This is a time when adolescents often begin to act out various social roles and anticipate where they will fit within the social framework in terms of race, gender, and class, for instance.

In addition, students in middle school tend to encounter formal educational stratification procedures, such as tracking and course sequencing, for the first time (Dauber, Alexander, and Entwisle 1996, 291; Stevenson, Schiller, and Schneider 1994, 187). Many high schools rely heavily on middle school track, or ability group placement, to determine high school placement (Gamoran 1992). This suggests that once a student is assigned to advanced courses in middle school, they should continue on an advanced track in high school, and those not considered advanced students in middle school will have difficulty moving up to advanced high school placement. Middle school often includes the formative stages of stratification procedures that structure future academic opportunities as well as future social positions. Thus, this period presents a crucial time for the development of social identities as well as trajectories for academic success.

Collecting Data

When I first entered Matthews as a researcher, the principal escorted me to a class taught by (of course) one of the best teachers in the school. The teacher introduced me to the class and explained to the students that I was there to observe. I sat quietly in the corner of this classroom, trying hard to detail my observations but feeling painfully aware of my own outsider presence. In this class, the teacher and students accepted my observer status and went about their business, which made things easier for me. But in other classrooms that I would observe over the next few months, teachers and especially students would express much more curiosity about my position in the classroom and the school.

To allay the concerns of students and teachers as well as my own inhibitions, I decided to inundate the school with the consistency of my presence. Over the course of two school years, from fall 2000 to spring 2002, and beginning most intensively in spring 2001, I visited the school from two to four times weekly. Soon, most teachers and students at Matthews grew very familiar with me. The principal eventually referred to me as "one of the staff," and many students came to know me as "Mr. Ed," a college student who was "doing a research project" at the school. After time, although people certainly noticed my distinct presence, most appeared to get used to it. I suspected that I had finally gained a decent level of acceptance among teachers when they began asking me to watch their classes while they ran an errand. I also suspected that the students began to accept me in the same situations, when I would only lightly discipline them and they would say to each other, "Don't worry—he's cool—he won't do anything."

During the course of my time at Matthews, I observed countless classes and wrote down detailed notes of what I observed. I volunteered as a tutor in many classes and also served as a writing tutor to prepare eighth-grade students for the writing portion of TAAS, the state assessment test, both during and after school. I attended after-school activities such as sporting events, club meetings, and various festivals and performances. I often just hung out with kids and teachers between classes, during lunch, and after school. I conducted semi-structured interviews with teachers and administrators, conversed with most of the teachers, and conversed with and tutored many students. I also conducted a student survey, mentioned at the outset of this chapter, that primarily served to assess student racial/ethnic identification. This survey asked students to circle all that apply from the following choices (which correspond to school and state racial designations): African American/black, Latino/Hispanic, Asian, white/Anglo, Native American, as well as the "Other" space Jackson so innovatively filled.

I used the results of this survey, along with teachers' perceptions, students' perceptions, and my own perspective, to understand students' "race." Most scientists now accept the notion that race is socially, rather than biologically, determined (Cooper 1984; Goodman 2000; Graves 2001; Omi and Winant 1994; Smedley 1993). In other words, our society (not nature) decides various ways to categorize groups within races and has even developed the concept of race itself. Based on this understanding, in this book I view race, social class, and gender not as characteristics that individuals inherently possess, but as socially constructed concepts that guide interaction and are negotiated through interaction (Schwalbe et al. 2000; West and Fenstermaker 1995). This view should not minimize the fact that social groups and structures often ascribe these characteristics to individuals in a way that profoundly constrains their actions (see Collins et al. 1995 for a critique of West and Fenstermaker 1995). Nor should this suggest that race is a mere illusion we can easily dispose of (see Winant 1994). However, it does indicate that people and institutions produce race through their interactions and understandings of this concept.

In recent work, Amanda Lewis (2003a) has traced the day-to-day processes through which people construct race. Drawing on ethnographic research in elementary schools, Lewis notes that race and racial categorization compose an important and persistent portion of school life, even for young children. In forming a sense of race, children and adults work to decide if others can be included or excluded from certain groups. People tend to rely on various cues such as skin color, language use, and neighborhood location in making racial assessments of others. At the same time, individuals also come to identify themselves within certain racial categories, often (but not always) based on how they think others see them (see also Cooley 1902). Such dynamics develop and provide structure to racial categories, but, as Lewis states, these are highly contextual and "influenced by local meaning systems, rules, demographics, relationships, and structures" (2003a, 300).

Similar to Lewis, I researched race at Matthews by trying to gain an understanding of how people in that context made sense of racialized categories—how they saw themselves and how others saw them. My goal in this process was not to gauge a student's "real" race, but to understand students' and teachers' perspectives on this concept. I then considered these along with my own perspective, as an "outsider within" (see Collins 1986) in this setting, which I consider an equally valid standpoint. Similarly, in studying the ways gender and social class interacted with race, I attended most closely to how people in the setting of Matthews developed meanings relating to race, class, and gender and reacted to others based on those meanings (see, for example, Blumer 1969; Mead [1934] 1967) rather than delineating particular individuals' backgrounds or identities per se.

In addition, as will become clearer throughout this book, students at Matthews actively "performed" or symbolically displayed race, class, and gender through ongoing face-to-face interactions (Bettie 2000, 2003; D. Foley 1990; West and Fenstermaker 1995). By tracing these interactions, I explore the continuing use and meaning of these concepts at the school. For example, students and educators at Matthews relied especially on interpretations of bodily displays and modes of interaction to develop their understandings of others' class backgrounds. What I call "street styles" (see also Dance 2002; Flores-Gonzalez 2002) served as especially important markers of class background, although these styles were also inflected with elements of race, gender, and personality. Students and educators at Matthews interpreted these styles as both representative of class origin and representative of class aspirations in the form of a student's orientation and attitude toward schooling. These styles were performed by particular youths to some extent intentionally and to some extent unintentionally (Bettie 2003), and I closely recorded how others interpreted and reacted to these various presentations.

Although much research underscores the importance of extra-school processes in parenting and home life on educational dynamics (e.g., Muller 1995; Lareau 1987, 2002), I focused primarily on the school environment at Matthews. Because I had a rather long commute to the school, as I explain further in the appendix, I had difficulty gaining a complete perspective from the students' families. This should not indicate that I view home life as insignificant to education. However, I found a great deal of complexity and depth among the interactions I recorded within the walls of this one school. I have simply chosen to concentrate on a few of the many stories enacted at Matthews to explore these in depth, and I have attempted to frame my research so I do not center issues of family life. These issues would form the subject of another study, and perhaps they should.

While my attention rested on the few white students at Matthews, I also sought the perspectives of many others. These groups included teachers, administrators, and nonwhite students. Although studying "whiteness" typically entails a relentless focus on white people and white identity, such an approach did not make sense at Matthews. African Americans, Latinos, and Asian Americans, not whites, dominated both student and teacher discourses at the school and contributed much to constructions of whiteness. This book tells their stories as much as those of individual white students because both inevitably intertwined. Asking how white students might retain advantages, for instance, also required asking how African American and Latino students might incur disadvantages, as we will see particularly in chapter 5. The contributions nonwhites made to definitions of whiteness were salient at Matthews because of the largely minority environment, but I believe these contributions should be further acknowledged and explored in general. White people are not the only ones who have proffered and maintained various definitions of "whiteness," and we should attend to the perspectives of African Americans, Latinos, and Asian Americans on this concept as well.

My analysis focuses on three main areas of school life at Matthews: disciplinary procedures, teacher perceptions of students, and student interaction and peer culture. These categories emerge largely from my study of day-to-day interactions at the school, and I concentrate on them because they represent the most important areas of this interaction regarding whiteness, class, gender, and schooling. Many works in educational research have highlighted the impact of curricular content (e.g., Asante 1987), pedagogy (e.g., Ladson-Billings 1994), and often some combination of both (e.g., Delpit 1995) in maintaining disadvantages in education. I do not deny that these are significant mechanisms that help reproduce educational inequality and white advantage, and that they remain important areas of study. But my interests, particularly because I maintained such a close connection to daily life in the school, lie less in the content of preexisting ideas about education (decisions of what to teach and how to teach it) and more in *how* educational processes unfold on the level of daily interaction—everyday decisions made by teachers; understandings formed and modified through continuing contacts; the adoption of certain styles of dress, behavior, and speech by students; the emergence of friendships, disagreements, and perceptions.

Because of this concentration on unfolding interaction, this study does not employ substantial analysis of student performance in terms of educational outcomes such as grades and test scores. I do use such data to set a context of achievement by groups of students at the school, but because this is a single case study, an extensive quantitative analysis of outcomes will tell us less than will understanding the processes that give rise to such outcomes. At Matthews, many processes related to race, class, gender, and schooling, but I have chosen three areas that I consider most prominent. The first, teacher perceptions of students, highlights how teachers interpreted white students at Matthews and how these interpretations mattered for students' educational experiences. The second area, disciplinary processes, composed the most palpable mode of daily teacher-student conflict. Contradictory expectations and resistance lay underneath proscriptions of student dress and behavior and imbued something as seemingly simple as tucking in a shirt with meanings pertaining to culture, upward mobility, and institutional acceptance. Through this, we can see the complicated ways in which whiteness, even in a minority context and differentiated by class and gender, can gain educational centrality. The centrality of whiteness did not persist, however, among the students themselves. Thus, the final area I examine consists of the interactions and culture formed by the kids at Matthews. These student dynamics often deviated from conventional notions of group boundaries and racial hierarchy (more apparent in the teachers' discourse), which pointed to important possibilities for change and equality in our increasingly multicultural future. However, even these progressive youth dynamics still exhibited many stereotypical, hierarchical notions of race and whiteness.

All these themes emerge from patterns of interaction at the school, and all interconnect through the web of these interactions—youth culture and identity influenced students' projection of styles of dress and behavior, which influenced teacher perceptions of appropriate, academically inclined students, which influenced disciplinary and other treatment that mediated student educational experiences, which influenced student perceptions of connections between culture, style, identity, and educational acceptability. And as we shall see, understandings of class, gender, and whiteness seeped through all threads of this interactional web, shaping notions of which kids fit in with the educational framework of the school and which kids did not.

In my final write-ups of interview and field note excerpts, which appear in the remainder of this study, I have occasionally purposefully deleted or obscured certain details. In making these decisions, I had to balance the need to provide necessary information about individuals, settings, and situations against my promise and conviction to protect participant confidentiality. Unless it was absolutely crucial to understanding a situation, for example, I have deleted references to the exact subject matter taught in a class or by a particular teacher. Matthews employed about sixty teachers, but certain subject areas were small enough that identifying the area would basically identify the teacher. Similarly, because few administrators worked at the school, I refer to them as administrators, rather than identifying their particular area or title (except the principal, whose position I found it necessary to identify). These decisions have caused me to sacrifice some more precise details in my data excerpts, but I attempt to compensate for this by supplying detail in descriptions that would not necessarily identify a particular school, classroom, or individual.

Organization of the Book

In chapter 2, I develop the theoretical framework for this book. I review the important research recently produced on race, whiteness, and education and consider the contributions and gaps this literature presents for understanding inequality and privilege. I propose a theory of understanding whiteness as a hegemonic system that marginalizes nonwhites as well as white people who do not fit the hegemonic ideal. Readers may want to skip this chapter if they have little interest in sociological theories. Chapter 3 provides an overview of the historical background and context of the neighborhood and school environment of Matthews. It tells the interesting story of how the school changed from predominately white to predominately minority virtually overnight and how adults at the school interpreted these changes. It also describes the school environment of Matthews during my fieldwork.

Chapter 4 concentrates on how teachers perceived and interacted with the white students at Matthews. I show how perceptions of race, class, and neighborhood combined to influence how teachers reacted to these unique white students. Further, perceptions of these students varied according to teachers' racial backgrounds in counterintuitive ways. In my observations and interviews, black teachers typically described white students as middle class and as good students. Most white teachers, by contrast, interpreted these students as low-income, unremarkable students—"trailer trash," as one teacher described them. Whiteness in this predominately minority setting represented very different things to these different teachers. I examine why this was the case and what this means for our understanding of white privilege in education.

Chapter 5 explores an important process for centralization and marginalization at Matthews: disciplinary procedures, especially in terms of dress and manners. I explore how school officials tended to view the behaviors of African American girls as not "lady-like" and the behaviors of Latino boys as especially threatening. Members of these groups tended to receive strict and persistent discipline in how they conducted themselves. By contrast, the behaviors of white students, along with Asian American students, tended to be viewed as nonthreatening and gender appropriate. Most school officials focused less disciplinary attention on these students. Such processes, I will argue, tended to make nonwhite students appear problematic, while white students, although modified somewhat by class-based perceptions, appeared docile and normal.

Chapter 6 examines the meanings and boundaries of whiteness for white youths and racial/ethnic minority youths at Matthews. In contrast to conventional patterns of white centrality, which the previous chapters demonstrated to inhere in schooling processes at Matthews, in the peer culture of the school whiteness had little currency. I explore how white youths at the school consistently enacted styles, consciously or unconsciously, that distanced them from normative or stereotypical whiteness, using the examples of Jackson and other intriguing white students. In the peer culture of Matthews, being "white" had few advantages for white youths or minority youths. Thus, white kids often, with the help of minority kids, constructed notions of race that eroded much of the power from whiteness and blurred the boundaries typically separating whites and nonwhites. I consider what these findings imply about the future of being white in the United States.

In chapter 7, I conclude the book by reviewing the ethnography and delineating what this study tells us about theories and practices in education. I stress the importance of viewing whiteness as it intersects with class, gender, and social location, positioning this understanding within a framework of hegemonic whiteness. I consider what the study suggests about the nature and resilience of white advantages in education. Finally, I explore implications for future educational practice.

2

Understanding White Advantages in Education and Society

Education is frequently seen as the great equalizer in society. Many view schooling as the means through which people can succeed and work their way to a higher social position based on sheer determination and energy. While this certainly remains the goal of education in society, it does not yet represent the reality. The disparities and disadvantages that exist between groups in society as a whole are mirrored in the educational system. Educational inequities in terms of race provide an important example: of major racial/ethnic groups, African American and Latino children are most likely to drop out of high school, least likely to go to college, and most likely to score relatively low on standardized tests (Jencks and Phillips 1998; U.S. Department of Education 2001). In addition, African American and Latino children are more likely to attend public schools in racially segregated, high-poverty areas that have lower overall test scores, fewer advanced placement course offerings, more special education students, and higher dropout rates than predominately white schools (Kozol 1991; Orfield 1996).

What accounts for these disadvantages that continue to appear in education? A welter of explanations exists, but scholars continue to argue over the ultimate source of educational inequality. I suggest that we should not focus on finding a single or most important source of inequality, but instead attempt to comprehend multiple sources as they combine and interrelate. In this book, I study the complicated factors underlying educational disparities, such as race, class, and gender, as they interact with each other. I do this by using race as a starting point. I examine how race, in particular, being white, can function as a type of advantage in schooling, even though this advantage can be altered by meanings and disadvantages of class and gender.

It might seem strange when discussing inequalities in education to focus on white people. After all, white kids in general go to some of the best schools, have low dropout rates, tend to matriculate to and graduate from college, and score highly on standardized tests (Blau 2003). But it is precisely through examining why white youths overall maintain such advantages that we can understand why others might experience disadvantages. Too often, we have turned the spotlight on "underachieving" minority students, and this scrutiny has encouraged suggestions that these kids (or their families) are responsible for their own struggles. Many continue to entertain consistently debunked and stereotypical ideas that the educational troubles of minority students stem from racial differences in innate intelligence. Still more people attribute educational disparities to a family or culturally based devaluing of education—an equally false and stereotypical assumption. If we accept either idea, we suggest that educational inequalities are virtually impossible to overcome, because these notions blame families and individuals rather than critiquing the particular structure of education and society. Such ideas will flourish if we relentlessly focus on those who are disadvantaged in education, but they could be challenged if we finally ask how those on top protect their advantage. For this reason, I propose that we momentarily turn the spotlight away from minority students and attempt to illuminate the educational experiences of white students.

This chapter establishes a framework for understanding educational privileges and inequalities of race, class, and gender as interconnected positions. I foreground the often unacknowledged privileges linked to being white, but emphasize that meanings and consequences of whiteness may be altered by other modes of inequality such as gender, class, and residential location. I propose conceptualizing whiteness as a "hegemonic system" that produces and maintains advantages in two main ways. First, through positioning whites as separate from and implicitly superior to nonwhites, and, second, through marginalizing ways of being white that do not exemplify the hegemonic ideal. As I will explain, this hegemonic reproduction can be seen in schools through hidden assumptions about cultural capital and procedures of normalizing discipline. These processes have consequences for racial minority students as well as white students who might face nonracial forms of inequality and difference.

Theories of Whiteness

The conceptualization of race as a socially, rather than biologically, determined category is central to my perspective and to most theories of whiteness. Despite popular assumptions, race does not have an inherent "essence" rooted in biological or cultural constants. Rather, race is formed through social interactions shaped by political and power relationships, a process Omi and Winant (1994) call "racial formation." Thus, society constructs the ideas and consequences

linked to particular racial groups, including whites. Currently, as well as historically, being white tends to involve separation from those defined as racialized
minorities, in terms of where people live and with whom they interact as well
as how they see themselves (Lewis 2001; Lipsitz 1995; Warren and Twine 1997).
In this way, white people often elide any racial identification while implicitly
benefiting from their race (Frankenberg 1993). As Ruth Frankenberg writes in
one of the earliest studies of whiteness, "White stands for the position of racial
'neutrality,' or the racially unmarked category" (1993, 55). Being white is often
seen and experienced as a lack of race, just as in artistic terms the shade
"white" represents a lack of color. As long as being white avoids a racial connotation or marking, it remains the norm—in contrast to racialized "others," who
remain different and marginalized (Dyer 1997). Indeed, as Pamela Perry (2002)
has cogently documented, white people, particularly those in homogenous race
and class settings, tend to view themselves as just "normal." For this reason,
many whites hesitate to invoke race when describing themselves and fail to see
it as an advantage in their lives.

This discursive formation of whiteness as a nonracial, central position *does*
have important implications for people's lives, however. In pioneering work,
Peggy McIntosh ([1988] 1996) argues that the tacit normativity of whiteness
leads to various forms of "white privilege": the unacknowledged advantages
white people have because of their race. This privilege, for example, allows
people considered white the luxury of surrounding themselves with others of
their race and seeing others of their race widely represented in television,
movies, and newspapers. White privilege can also appear in education, where
many argue that teaching and curricula tend to favor a white cultural perspective, although this perspective is never called "white" (Delpit 1995; Fine, Powell,
and Wong 1997). Students considered white invariably benefit in educational
situations compared to their minority peers primarily because of this unstated
white bias. In fact, although few people see education in this way, schools can
exemplify modern, institutionalized forms of racial bias that perpetuate white
advantages while posing as neutral meritocracies (e.g., Blau 2003; Bonilla-Silva
2001; Van Ausdale and Feagin 2001). In her book *Race in the Schools: Perpetuating
White Dominance?* Judith Blau argues that schools and other social institutions
"are racialized settings and hierarchies that reproduce white advantage" (2003,
1). For all the talk about schools as potential vehicles for upward mobility, white
children in general appear to experience greatly enhanced opportunities in
education, to the detriment of their minority peers.

This unstated educational bias manifests in several ways. One form
involves segregation by race across schools and concomitant lack of funding,
lack of qualified teachers, and lack of other resources besetting predominately
minority schools (Bankston and Caldas 1996, 2000; Kozol 1991; Orfield 1996;
Roscigno 1998). White students overall are much more likely to attend schools

with greater resources and lower levels of student poverty (Blau 2003; Kozol 1991). Other processes favoring whites occur within schools. White students, for instance, tend to receive disproportional placement in higher-level courses or tracks (Oakes 1985, 1995; Oakes, Gamoran, and Page 1992; Oakes, Selvin, Karoly, and Guiton 1992). White students, compared to African American and Latino students overall, also tend to "get in trouble" in schools less frequently (Blau 2003; A. Ferguson 2000). Many minority youths may experience education as an alienating or "subtractive" experience, in the words of Angela Valenzuela, while their white counterparts easily connect to white-oriented curricula and testing (Delpit 1995; Ogbu 1978; Valenzuela 1999).

Thus, advantages for whites inhere in the educational institution itself, at the same time that the dominant discourse frames this institution as neutral, unbiased, and even helpful for disadvantaged minority students. The educational system tacitly insulates and distances white students from racialized others through de facto segregation across schools and segregation within schools through ability-group placement. White-oriented curricula and testing make white history and ways of life appear as the norm, while disciplinary procedures tend to frame white students as unproblematic. Hence, schools allow for the exclusion and normalizing that predicate white advantage but wrap this up in a neutral package of meritocracy. Evidence from schooling appears to corroborate existing theories of whiteness and white privilege quite well—white people seem to have distinct, unspoken advantages in education.

However, not all white people experience *similar* advantages in education. Stratification according to race exists in U.S. society overall, but it also exists within white people as a particular social group—some whites certainly experience tremendous disadvantages. To illustrate, I recently gave a talk at a university in rural Kentucky. The concept of white privilege in education—the subject of my talk—made little sense to people in this part of the country. They did not see whites necessarily tied to positions of privilege and dominance, but instead saw them living in situations of poverty and isolation. It appears perplexing to describe these rural white Appalachians, living in horrendous conditions, battling poverty, inadequate education, and discrimination, as basically advantaged compared to racial/ethnic minorities.

Thus, to understand white advantage in education, we must consider how other modes of difference and inequality (such as class, gender, and geographic location) intersect with whiteness. I propose that these areas of intersection might alter the very meaning and impact of being white. For example, social class and geographic location make the experience of being white very different for a poor, rural Appalachian kid than for a wealthy kid from the suburbs. Similarly, white kids who live and go to school in predominately minority, urban areas, like those I got to know at Matthews, experience their race differently than kids who live and attend school mostly with other whites. Following this line of thought, some intriguing ethnographic studies have explored the various ways white people experience and interpret whiteness when not surrounded by other white people. These studies, discussed next, suggest new directions for understanding whiteness and white privilege.

Differences within Whiteness

In his ethnography of poor, inner-city whites in Detroit, John Hartigan (1999) argues that these whites seemed to have few racial advantages over their minority neighbors. His research shows that poor whites in Detroit, a predominately African American city, tended to recognize their racialness rather than ignore it and saw themselves as more structurally similar to urban blacks than suburban whites. These white, urban hillbillies (so-called because of their Appalachian origins) appeared to see racial categories as existing along a continuum and placed themselves somewhere between whiteness and blackness on this scale. Hartigan argues that this view stems from social class position as well as the context of African American political and social power: "Whiteness, as an ideological order, requires material supports. In Detroit's core, these supports—segregated residential areas, race-conscious political and social institutions, racially selective employers—gradually deteriorated over fifty years. . . . The means for assuring white privilege and for maintaining the illusion of its supremacy were undermined in Detroit. For whites who remained in the city, especially those in decimated inner-city areas, the significance of race has drastically altered" (1999, 20). Hartigan suggests that in those rare contexts in which whites do not benefit from numerical and structural power, whiteness becomes no longer hegemonic, but exposed and challenged. This compels white people in those contexts to view race and whiteness in complicated ways.

Pamela Perry (2002) has also explored the complexity and malleability of whiteness—applying this more specifically to education. Perry studies white youth identity at two California high schools, one predominately white and the other predominately minority (12 percent white). At the predominately white school, white students did not often question their race, and when they did, they tended to see it as a disadvantage (see also Gallagher 1995; Olsen 1997). At the predominately minority school, by contrast, Perry finds that white students were more aware of their whiteness and even tended to see how race created advantages for them and disadvantages for others, expressed, for instance, in support for affirmative action. Perry attributes this to the influence of students of color in this context: "[face-to-face negotiations] were power-*inverted* in that black and other youth of color were the ones defining the terms of the negotiations and wielding considerable cultural weight over whites" (2002, 183, emphasis in original). Based on this evidence, Perry concludes that identities of white youths become more complex and visible the more they interact with racial/ethnic minority youths. This interaction influences them to see their race from the perspective of others and exposes it as a source of advantage.[1]

Perry suggests that whiteness was not normative and unquestioned in the predominately minority school setting, and this mitigated the blind acceptance of privilege for white youth, especially in the peer culture of the school. This underscores the impact of proximity to people of color in forging variations in white identity and understandings of privilege. However, as Perry notes, the tracking system of the predominately minority school still over-represented white students in higher academic tracks; she describes this as visibly striking. According to this finding, schooling processes, even in the predominately minority context, contributed to the repositioning of whiteness as dominant and normative in the academic arena. Perry's overall analysis (understandably) focuses on white identities, however, and does not elaborate on how schooling processes might construct and maintain advantages associated with whiteness. Nor does it examine how social class and gender might alter how others perceive whiteness and the advantages resulting from these perceptions. As I will discuss, it is schooling processes (rather than identities per se), along with intersections of whiteness with perceptions of class and gender, that I intend to analyze further in this book.

The path-breaking studies by Perry and Hartigan make a strong case that important differences exist among white people and that local contexts can alter the meanings of whiteness. Based on these works, it makes sense that a white kid such as Jackson (mentioned in the previous chapter), who grows up and goes to school with mostly African American and Latino kids, would call himself "white chocolate." The meaning of being white to him is quite distinct from, for example, the respondents in Ruth Frankenberg's study mentioned earlier, who tended to experience their whiteness as a cultural and racial void. The meanings and consequences of being white can shift to fit realities of class, gender, and social location. But as Perry suggests, the rewards of whiteness, in general, might remain. Still, examining white privileges potentially imbedded in education requires understanding how other characteristics might shape being white. In this book, I want to build on the important works that reveal differences within whiteness but move further toward understanding intersections of whiteness, class, and gender within a hegemonic framework.

Intersections of Race, Class, and Gender

Race, class, and gender are, of course, common areas of inequality in education and society. Although each characteristic certainly holds importance in its own right, I, along with other scholars, am particularly interested in studying combinations or intersections of race, class, and gender (see, for example, Collins 1990, 1998; Glenn 2002; Zinn and Dill 1996). To these (and of particular importance for this study), I would also add the factor of "place"—some-one's regional and residential location. According to an individual's position in society, based on various combinations of race, class, gender, and place, we might expect them to experience an array of simultaneous advantages and dis-advantages. For any one individual, some characteristics might provide him or her with social benefits, while others might entail social costs. Patricia Hill Collins notes, for instance, that in current U.S. society "white women are penalized by their gender, but privileged by their race" (1990, 225). By placing various white people within a conceptual framework of intersectionality, we can understand that while they might have power in terms of race, some might have less power in other areas, such as gender or class. Thus, the white stu-dents I studied at Matthews could be viewed as advantaged through their membership in the dominant racial group in society, but disadvantaged through living in a working-class area of town with relatively high crime and poverty.

However, in this book I want to explain not only various differential impacts of race, class, and gender, but also how these concepts combine to alter one another. I argue that positions of intersection represent not only where one might be simultaneously advantaged and disadvantaged, but where we might suspect the existence of an entirely unique position whose status could not nec-essarily be inferred from knowledge of the particular intersecting modes of inequality. For example, I suggest that a white woman not only has the privilege of race and the disadvantage of gender, but her race fundamentally affects the way her gender is socially perceived (and vice versa). This could be compared to an interaction effect in statistical terminology: sometimes two variables, when combined, produce an effect one would not suspect based solely on the additive effects of these variables.

Several examples can illustrate how particular combinations of race, class, and gender alter meanings and impacts of these social positions in education and other social fields. For instance, we might suspect black men and boys to experience racial oppression but gender advantage. This does not always seem to be the case, however. In *Unequal Freedom*, Evelyn Nakano Glenn observes that historically, "(black women) were seen as less threatening than black men and therefore could go where black men couldn't" (Glenn 2002, 130). Today, the particular combination of blackness and masculinity instills stereotypical fear in many, creating negative interactions for many black men with strangers, store proprietors, and the police (Anderson 1990; Feagin 1991; Feagin and Sikes 1994). This association of blackness with dangerous masculinity even pertains to young black boys, who often receive harsh and strict discipline in school (Dance 2002; A. Ferguson 2000). Black women and girls tend to provoke less fear, thereby experiencing less negativity in interactions with strangers, the police, or school officials (Anderson 1990; Grant 1984).

Thus, it seems that the particular combination of blackness and masculinity creates a unique social position whose effects do not necessarily logically follow from our knowledge of gender and racial inequality in general. Blackness can shape masculinity such that it becomes almost disadvantageous in certain settings. I witnessed this at Matthews, where many black boys endured constant monitoring and reprimands by teachers. Educators certainly disciplined and regulated the black girls in my observations, but less severely than the black boys, who (along with Latino boys) tended to be seen as instigators of classroom disruptions. This differs markedly from research showing white boys to have advantages over white girls in education because of the aggressive, attention-demanding behavior of these boys (e.g., Sadker and Sadker 1994). It appears that while whiteness makes the forceful behavior of many boys seem normal and acceptable, blackness makes similar behaviors seem problematic and hazardous. Interpretations of masculinity and femininity, as I explore further in chapter 5, are read through understandings of race and cannot be separated from such understandings.

Similarly, race can shape the way people perceive social class. Although we often think about social class as directly determined by economic resources, in everyday life people tend to use more visual cues, including race, to assess class background. Joe Feagin (1991), for example, reports that several middle-class African Americans he interviewed complained of situations where white strangers assumed they were lower-class solely because of their skin color. Joleen Kirschenman and Kathryn Neckerman (1991) have detailed parallel findings, describing how inner-city employers in Chicago frequently confounded race, class, and residential location in their assessment of job applicants. According to their interviews, many employers immediately perceived black (and to some extent Latino) applicants as lower-class, inner-city residents and, therefore, undesirable workers. Black applicants would have to somehow signal to these employers that they did not belong to these class-based categories, something not required of white applicants (Kirschenman and Neckerman 1991, 231). In contrast to blackness, whiteness immediately connoted a middle-class, suburban resident and, therefore, a desirable worker.

In addition, we can also consider ways social class shapes the understanding of race. For example, the common Brazilian phrase "money lightens," referring to the effects of class on race, seems relevant here. Perhaps achieving a lofty class standing, or coming from such a standing, makes one seem lighter skinned, or whiter. Obversely, perhaps having a lower class standing makes one seem less white. In U.S. history, social class and social location appear to have done just that—studies have shown that groups we now consider indisputably white, such as the Jews and the Irish, were once considered ambiguously white at best (Brodkin 1998; Ignatiev 1995; Roediger 1991). This ambiguity stemmed largely from the predominately working-class, immigrant status of members of these groups during the particular historical periods of their greatest influx. Only through gaining social, political, and cultural power (achieved in part by distancing themselves both socially and spatially from African Americans), along with the loss of salient ethnic characteristics in the second generation, did members of these groups become unequivocally white.

Although the history of white ethnics in the United States demonstrates a journey from the margins to the center of whiteness, many whites continue to occupy the outskirts of this racial category. Poor whites, sometimes referred to as "trailer trash" or "white trash," historically and presently represent to the popular imagination an anomalous, "polluted" form of whiteness (N. Foley 1997; Hartigan 1997; Newitz and Wray 1997). The eugenics movement popular in late nineteenth- and early twentieth-century America directed its primary concern onto poor whites, fearing that these "inferior" whites might eventually corrupt the white gene pool (N. Foley 1997; Graves 2001; Zuberi 2001). In some cases, zealots even called for sterilization of poor white people to end the progression of what they considered "bad genes" (N. Foley 1997; Rafter 1992). Although such fanaticism has thankfully ended, Hartigan (1997) shows that it remains popular to invoke the term "white trash" to indicate an aberrant, backward, and lowly form of whiteness. Thus, it seems that class standing has the ability to shape the perception of whiteness. It is not only that a lower-class white person might be privileged by their race and deterred by their class, but that class standing (in the case of white trash, perhaps coupled with southern origin) shades the particular projection of whiteness. For this reason, some scholars have even referred to poor white people as "off whites" (N. Foley 1997).

Such examples show that perceptions of class can impact perceptions of race, including whiteness, and, in turn, perceptions of whiteness can impact perceptions of class. Social and historical context, as seen through the historical changes in the meanings and boundaries of whiteness, appears important for highlighting class markers or racial or ethnic markers. Similarly, as Elijah Anderson (1990) notes, residential context, or place, also influences the perception of race and class meanings. At Matthews, I observed the importance of such contextual factors, especially understandings of neighborhood demographics and history, in perceptions of whiteness. In addition, the social standpoint of the perceiver held particular importance in framing interpretations of white students. As we shall see, teachers had different perceptions of the class background of white students, largely based on how they made sense of the atypical social positioning of white kids living in this predominately nonwhite environment. While some teachers interpreted white students at Matthews as middle-class, others invoked a common pejorative term in describing these students: "trailer trash." The perception of a denigrated, "trashy" form of whiteness connoted by this term lends further credence to how social location and social class mediate the interpretation of race, including whiteness.

Yet, even in the case of off-whites and white trash at Matthews and in other contexts, such castaways from the center of whiteness are still considered white. This provokes important questions for the role of whiteness when considering intersections with class and gender. Does being white not provide poor and working-class whites such as the kids at Matthews with certain advantages in social institutions, including education? Does the system of whiteness continue to privilege all whites, albeit in different ways, or does social class and location strip virtually all advantages from being white? To answer these questions, I propose a framework for viewing whiteness, in schools and other social settings, as a hegemonic system, borrowing from the theory of "hegemonic masculinity" developed by R. W. Connell (1995). In this way, we can understand the current racial hierarchy as a system that benefits whites generally, but also positions them differently vis-à-vis whiteness—particularly those considered socially and stylistically close to nonwhites, like so many of the white students I came to know at Matthews.[2]

Hegemony and Whiteness

The sociological concept of hegemony has its roots in the theories of Antonio Gramsci (1971). Writing in an Italian prison in the 1930s, Gramsci developed a fragmented, but astoundingly complex, theory of inequality that applies well to modern complications of race, class, and gender (Hall 1986). Many scholars have subsequently adopted Gramsci's ideas to form their own theories of inequality. One such theory, applied specifically to gender inequality, is the concept of "hegemonic masculinity," developed by R. W. Connell. In his book *Masculinities*, Connell (1995) argues that theories of gender relations should account for differences among men and forms of masculinity. His theory of hegemonic masculinity suggests that multiple masculinities exist simultaneously and are stratified in relation to the hegemonic, or most dominant, ideal (Connell 1995).[3]

According to Connell, within this broad system of gender relations, some men, because of sexual orientation, race, class, etc., might find themselves marginalized. These men have their masculinity interpreted differently than the white, middle-class, heterosexual norm and therefore do not accrue the full dividends ordinarily linked to masculinity. Such alternative forms of masculinity may openly or indirectly challenge the hegemonic, or dominant, form, suggesting competing ways masculinity may be defined and embodied. However, those embodying these forms may also follow the lead of most other men, who do not always represent paragons of dominant masculinity, but accept the existing system of hegemonic masculinity nonetheless. In this sense, they can be called complicit with the hegemonic project—consenting to the dominant definition of masculinity in hopes of receiving some reward from it, or because they accept the "common sense" of hegemonic preeminence.

Thus, in Connell's system, men might be positioned differently depending on various forms of masculinity. But most to some degree frame themselves as different from women, and most derive some benefits from the overall system of masculinity, which attempts to maintain power over women. I suggest adapting this theory to understand the current system of white advantage and how whites might profit from it differently. Whiteness, like masculinity, consists of a hegemonic form and other forms that, because of areas of difference such as class and gender, stratify whites in relation to the hegemonic ideal. The hegemonic form of whiteness currently stresses material success, suburban residence, a nuclear family structure, basic intelligence, and other stereotypical qualities associated with white people in America. Yet, as I have mentioned, not all whites exemplify this model. Poor white people obviously face constraints in realizing this vision of material, suburban success. Other whites, based on sexual orientation or gender, might also experience subordination from the hegemonic ideal. Gay and lesbian white people, for instance, are shut out from the heterosexual nuclear family ideal. Women tend to earn significantly less than men in the same jobs, hindering their ability to achieve material success in relation to men (U.S. Department of Labor 2003). But although these groups might not accrue the same rewards as those who embody the gender-specific, successful model of hegemonic whiteness, they might consent to the aspect of this model they can all profit from—the notion that whiteness is different from nonwhiteness and should maintain a certain power over those not considered white.

Such consent may come in the form of blatantly racist calls for the rights of white workers (more common historically, see Roediger 1991) or subtle complicity with and reproduction of daily forms of white privilege (McIntosh 1998; Haney Lopez 1996). Each case exhibits an elevated sense of "group position," to use Herbert Blumer's (1958) terminology, a stated or unstated sense that whiteness should protect them and place them in a superior position. This consent echoes Anthony Chen's (1999) notion of a "hegemonic bargain," in which men embodying marginalized masculinities emphasize aspects of their manhood that come closest to the hegemonic ideal. A man framed as physically weak and unathletic, for example, might emphasize material and occupational success to bolster perceptions of his masculinity. Similarly, various white people tend to overtly or covertly seek support from the system of racial hierarchy that places whiteness on top—even if they might experience subordination within it. Thus, adapting the theory of hegemony to whiteness allows us to conceptualize differences among white people while considering how most whites bolster and support the hegemonic formation of whiteness that is based on maintaining advantages over nonwhites. Further, it allows us to consider race, class, gender, and other modes of inequality as interwoven in such a way that they alter the meaning and impact of each other.

For example, as Glenn notes, nineteenth-century concerns over maintaining the supposed integrity of the white race placed a special responsibility on women: "white womanhood was the central symbol and guarantor of white racial purity" (2002, 122). Social class, however, tended to frame middle- and upper-class white women as more pure, and poor white women as potentially tainted because of their presumed tendency to perpetuate the production of "bad" (and racially suspect) genes (Rafter 1992). Thus, gender altered understandings of whiteness, elevating white women as exemplars of racial purity, but burdening them with a special reproductive responsibility that also required control and protection from white men. Social class further altered understandings of white womanhood, as poor white women were seen as especially problematic and potentially less racially "pure."

The positioning of poor white women according to gender and class changed the meaning and impact of being white for them. These women became subordinated compared to whites in general because of this particular understanding of their whiteness. At the same time that a sense of privilege and superiority stemmed from being white, the control and fear directed at poor white women (sometimes, as mentioned earlier, in the form of forced sterilization) presented uniquely *racialized* problems for them. While whiteness did confer privileges, these came with significant costs for these women. The concerns directed at them echo the larger concerns of the hegemonic project of whiteness. These surfaced in the ideology that whiteness should remain pure, meaning that it should maintain distinction and superiority (genetic, in this case) over nonwhiteness.

The concept of hegemony allows us to articulate these various embodiments and strata of whiteness, both historically and currently. It complicates our understanding of white privilege, but in ways that better fit social reality. We can think of poor white women as not just privileged by their race and penalized by their class and gender, but as a group that represents a particular meaning and embodiment of whiteness—one that might serve to maintain the overall illusion of white superiority while simultaneously exacting subordination within it. As long as whites accept the core premise of hegemonic whiteness—that being white is different from being nonwhite and should result in privileges over nonwhites—they become implicated within the hegemonic project and often consent to it.

As Gramsci argued, hegemony endures primarily through the ruling groups winning the consent of subaltern, lower-strata groups. Hegemony is always tenuous because the hegemonic groups must convince others of their legitimacy, even as subaltern groups struggle to resist their own marginalization. Hegemonic domination occurs when dominant groups convince others of a certain commonsense view of social reality that supports their position but masquerades as neutral and natural. In terms of whiteness, many have struggled to make the hegemonic ideal appear natural, particularly through positioning it as normative—racially neutral, "American." This normalizing—which subordinates nonwhites as well as whites that do not fit the hegemonic ideal—can occur especially within educational processes. As Gramsci wrote, "Every relationship of hegemony is necessarily an educational relationship" (1971, 350). Education can produce and continue the common sense that connects inequalities of race, class, and gender into a larger structure of hegemonic control.

Reproduction Theory

Thus, we can turn to education to consider how hegemonic whiteness maintains its dominant position. But what are the educational processes through which this might occur? "Reproduction theory" provides an excellent way of understanding the practices in education that preserve such inequalities. Reproduction theory, broadly defined, argues that schools tend to reproduce and even exaggerate inequalities of race, class, and gender (e.g., Bowles and Gintis 1976; Bourdieu and Passeron 1977; Willis 1977). In current educational research, the most widely used reproduction theories stem from the work of the French theorists Pierre Bourdieu and Michel Foucault. Although they do not refer specifically to white advantage, these theories can illuminate the processes through which schools might perpetuate the hegemonic model of whiteness.

Pierre Bourdieu's reproduction theory is based largely on the concept of cultural capital. According to Bourdieu (1977, 1984), social status in various fields or social settings is strongly tied to what he calls "cultural capital"—a certain set of cultural tastes, skills, preferences, and knowledge. People who understand and appreciate cultural norms held by those with societal power have a greater ability to obtain this power themselves. As I will explore further in chapter 5, clothing styles, for example, can function as one rather visible aspect of cultural capital. It is often repeated that to succeed in the white-collar business world one must learn to "dress for success"—wear appropriate attire to convey the impression of neatness, order, and ambition. In this case, occupational success relates strongly to a particular set of cultural norms surrounding clothing style. People tend to have differing abilities to understand such norms or differing amounts of this particular cultural capital, depending on their class position growing up.

Much research in education has utilized and examined Bourdieu's version of reproduction theory (e.g., Farkas 1996; Lareau 1987; Lareau and Horvat 1999; Lewis 2003b; Roscigno and Ainsworth-Darnell 1999; see Lamont and Lareau 1988 for a review). These studies find that the cultural capital students bring with them to school can affect their success within that institution. However, many students are perceived to lack the cultural background and skills that schools reward, which often leads to the alienation and marginalization of these students (Delpit 1995; Farkas 1996; Gilmore 1985; Ogbu 1978). Because those in power define cultural capital, it often reflects their interests and tastes. In the context of the United States, for example, the "proper" or standard ways of speaking and interacting tend to be white and middle class. African American students who speak "black English" or working-class white students whose styles of interacting are perceived as aggressive or rude are likely to struggle in school compared to their white and middle-class counterparts because they do not display the valued forms of cultural capital.

A second version of reproduction theory stems from the work of Michel Foucault ([1977] 1995). This line of thought examines how schools discipline and regulate students, identifying those who fit the norm of the proper student and, in particular, those who do not. Foucault argued that modern control is enacted through techniques of surveillance and physical regulation, or "discipline," aimed at the body. According to Steven Best and Douglas Kellner, "The ultimate goal and effect of discipline is 'normalization,' the elimination of all social and psychological irregularities and the production of useful and docile subjects through a refashioning of minds and bodies" (1991, 47). Although Foucault focused his analysis on prisons, he claimed that an array of modern institutions, including schools, utilize similar disciplinary techniques aimed at normalization. Subsequent research in education has pursued this claim and documented how schools attempt to discipline students into embodiments of compliance (A. Ferguson 2000; Martin 1998; McLaren 1986; Noguera 1995). Schools use this discipline to rework the behavior and appearance of students so their bodies display acceptable, normative comportment.

One of the most compelling recent works to utilize Foucault's theory in education is the book *Bad Boys*, by Ann Arnett Ferguson (2000). Ferguson focuses on disciplinary procedures aimed at black boys. She finds that the school she studied considered most of these boys recalcitrant and oppositional. Ferguson argues that culturally based assumptions about black males made these boys appear as "challenging, oppositional bod[ies]" requiring constant surveillance and discipline in dress, behavior, and speech. This regulation stemmed from a perception of black masculinity as not normal and potentially resistant and dangerous. The disciplinary procedures aimed at black boys attempted to normalize them, but also identified them as problematic, particularly compared to white students. In this way, disciplinary regimes constructed white masculinity as the norm and black boys as a distinct deviation from this.

Ferguson also emphasizes the importance of cultural capital in these disciplinary procedures—particularly outward or visible forms of cultural capital such as dress, language, and personal style. In this way, she aims to show "how manners, style, body language, and oral expressiveness influence the application of school rules and ultimately come to define and label African American students and condemn them to the bottom rung of the social order" (A. Ferguson 2000, 51). But her analysis suggests more than how students are treated differently based on race alone. Ferguson shows how race and gender intersect to promote distinct stereotypes and expectations. Language, clothing, and style acquire different meanings depending on the perceived race and gender of the student. This suggests different expectations of cultural competency from students and different procedures of discipline.

The value of cultural capital and the disciplinary goal of normalization do not, of course, appear within the official curriculum of what schools should teach. Instead, schools teach most lessons about appropriate behavior, dress, and speech as part of a "hidden curriculum" (Giroux and Purpel 1983; Snyder 1971). A key concept within reproduction theory, the hidden curriculum suggests that schools tacitly teach students unspoken lessons about race, class, and gender (Anyon 1980; Orenstein 1994). Hidden curricula reinforce the position of dominant groups through implicitly gearing schooling to their interests, and thereby conferring educational privileges to members of these groups. Presumptions about what counts as cultural capital, and which students adequately fit the norms of the school, fall under this area of unspoken bias. Through this curriculum schools and students also actively construct ideas and embodiments of race, class, and gender (Lewis 2003b; Martin 1998; Thorne 1993). School organizations are embedded with ideas and practices pertaining to race, class, and gender, and these sculpt students (albeit not without their consent or resistance) into particular understandings and personifications of these concepts.

The hidden curriculum, through subtle molding and regulation, teaches these assumptions and embodiments as natural and taken for granted, similar to Gramsci's notion of the "common sense" that bolters hegemony. To merge the concept of the hidden curriculum with hegemonic whiteness, we can see how such commonsense ideas and practices tend to favor the hegemonic model of whiteness. This can foster disconnection for nonwhites in particular, but also white students who (largely because of class or geographic location) do not display the cultural capital and comportment valued by schools. It can also work to elicit consent and acceptance, even among potentially resistant groups, of knowledge and behaviors common to the white middle and upper class. Thus, this framework provides a way for us to conceptualize differences and inequalities within and without whiteness and focus on the practices through which schools may actually reproduce these various inequalities.

However, this perspective also requires considering the important role youths might play in accepting hegemonic definitions of race, class, and gender or resisting them. We must understand kids as active agents in schooling and social processes, not just passive victims. Moreover, youths, including kids at

Matthews, often demonstrate unique behaviors and progressive, edifying perspectives that deviate from acceptance of hegemonic notions of whiteness. Kids can display very flexible ideas about race and racial distinctions (Chin 2001; Harris and Sim 2002; Lewis 2003b; Moore 2002). A study conducted by Valerie Moore (2002), for instance, shows that kids from six to twelve years old can construct creative definitions of whiteness and who might be considered white. One black kid at a multiracial summer camp Moore studied insisted that a white counselor he confided in was "not white," even after the counselor explained to him that she was, in fact, white (Moore 2002, 69). It appears that whiteness for this boy stemmed more from social location and association than from physical characteristics. He placed this counselor, perhaps because she worked in a multiracial setting and cared for him, a black boy, outside the boundaries of whiteness—as simply "not white." This indicates how children can develop racial concepts that move beyond rigid boundaries based on outward appearance and merge race, including whiteness, with social and interpersonal factors.

Similarly, as the studies of Hartigan (1999) and Perry (2002) suggest, white youths in multiracial settings might view themselves as outside the boundaries of whiteness and perhaps resist consenting to the hegemonic rewards promised for separation from their minority peers. Indeed, at Matthews Middle School I observed white students who genuinely valued the opinions, styles, and friendships of their nonwhite peers. It may be within multiracial settings such as Matthews that we can witness white and minority youths creating new ideas about race and whiteness, ideas that transcend invidious distinctions and demonstrate resistance to hegemonic white privilege. As I discuss further in chapter 6, I saw white and minority kids at Matthews doing just that through the many friendships they formed across racial boundaries. Within these friendships, hegemonic meanings of whiteness changed greatly, even allowing minority students to view some white students as "white and black"—a mark of an integrated and egalitarian whiteness. These ideas and interactions suggest possibilities for resisting and changing the social reproduction of white advantage.

Educational Advantage at Matthews Middle School

The remaining chapters of this book explore the reproduction of hegemonic whiteness at Matthews Middle School. It might seem odd to examine a middle school for something as sinister sounding as "reproducing hegemonic white advantage"—and I certainly do not intend to cast "blame" on particular teachers, students, families, or others through this analysis. However, it is within school organizations overall that we can see why the educational inequalities mentioned at the outset of this chapter persist. Such ideas and practices permeate virtually all schools, as they do society more generally, and the reader should not consider them peculiar to Matthews. As we shall see, most of the ideas and practices that linked being white to educational privilege and capital at Matthews were not stated by particular individuals, but existed as part of a hidden curriculum. I aim to unearth this curriculum through documenting the ways kids and adults at the school implicitly practiced, embodied, and occasionally resisted it. In the context of Matthews, being white could entail educational advantages or disadvantages, depending on how people interpreted this concept and related it to hegemonic notions of whiteness. Interpretations tended to associate whiteness with educational privilege, but varied depending on how being white interacted with perceptions of class—often interpreted through "street styles" and residential location—as well as gender. While many white students themselves tried to attain distance from stereotypical, hegemonic ways of being white (thereby creating pockets for resistance), the hidden curriculum tended to pull them into the hegemonic project, in which whiteness was framed as normal, intelligent, powerful, and distinct from nonwhiteness.

The theory of hegemony makes historical and spatial context central to the development of particular configurations of advantaged and disadvantaged relationships.[4] As I have indicated in this chapter, context is also important in understanding the complex interplay of race, class, and gender and how these concepts might alter the meaning of each other. Thus, to analyze the ways whiteness, class, and gender combine to elicit certain patterns of privilege and disadvantage at Matthews, we first need to establish the organizational, residential, and historical context of the school. I introduce this context in the next chapter, which provides the reader with a general view of Matthews Middle School as I saw it during my time there. This will set the background for important themes and perceptions (including my own) at the school, from which I will more specifically analyze schooling processes in the subsequent chapters.

3

Matthews Middle School in Historical and Contemporary Context

I first entered Matthews Middle School with an unsteady mix of excitement and apprehension. In driving through the streets that led to the school, I observed a landscape scattered with vacant lots, apartment complexes, and convenience stores. From the outside, the school appeared like the stereotypical image of an under-financed "urban school," with dingy, stained bricks and an unremarkable façade and courtyard. However, the inside of the school presented a dramatic shift in atmosphere, exuding brightness and cheer. Student artwork hung on the walls and appeared in two prominent display cases outside the front office. An administrator named Ms. Delaney greeted me warmly that first day. In the future, I would typically see Ms. Walker, the charismatic principal, welcoming students as they entered in the morning.

In this chapter, I introduce the reader to Matthews Middle School, the site where I spent countless hours observing, tutoring, and interviewing. This chapter outlines the contemporary and historical context of Matthews. This context is critical for understanding schooling processes and student experiences, including those pertaining to white students. The contextual areas I review here—the framework of school structure, including tracking and state-standardized testing, the history of race and class-based change in the neighborhood, and the diversity among students and student groupings at the school—all profoundly influenced the circumstances of white students as well as nonwhite students at Matthews. I will draw from many of these contextual themes to further analyze facets of the hidden curriculum and the perspectives of students and educators in subsequent chapters. Through this chapter I also intend for the reader to acquire a general sense of the school and its surroundings, as I developed this sense from my first day there to my last day, over twenty months later.

Ms. Delaney, the administrator I met on my initial visit to Matthews, ushered me through a tour of the school during my first day. Matthews had two main hallways that led to a cafetorium, which served as a combination cafeteria and auditorium. The small gymnasium lay on the other side of the cafetorium, in a separate building. Networks of classrooms honeycombed out on either side of each of the main hallways. The interior of the school followed an "open concept" plan, with classrooms connected by mutual corridors, separated only by small walls, some only temporary. During the tour we would pass by corners of the building with desks but no walls surrounding them, which Ms. Delaney described as "classrooms." The open concept created a challenging teaching situation, especially for middle school, as any commotion in one classroom could easily spill over into others.

And at Matthews there were many commotions. The students, I noticed early on, seemed to alternate between extremes of emotion and behavior. Kids appeared ebullient or despondent, excited or lethargic, angry, happy, depressed, all at once. This reminded me of my own middle school feelings and actions, which changed constantly as I moved through time. Challenging authority and disrupting mundane, seemingly boring situations served as part of this movement. Middle school often allows many students their first taste of brief freedoms, which kids tend to relish and extend as much as they possibly can. For example, I observed kids at Matthews, allowed to throw something away without asking, who could stretch this into an extended interpretive dance involving several attempts to throw the item into the trash can and then retrieve it, alternating between sluggish and rapid motions. Many kids also immediately seized any opportunity to shift their focus away from the classroom and onto something else—and this something else often involved me.

When I first, somewhat hesitantly, stepped into classrooms at Matthews, I entertained the idea that I could remain detached—observe this new world of change and restlessness from the background. In one of my first observations, an eighth-grade math class, I sat in the corner of the room near a flimsy, portable partition that separated that classroom from the one next to it. During the class, kids in the classroom next door proceeded to yell and bang on the partition so hard it started to move and hit me on the shoulder. Soon, the entire structure swayed as if it would tip over, and this was accompanied by vigorous guffaws next door. The teacher noticed this quickly, went next door to stop it, and apologized to me. But this quickly disabused me of any notion that my study could consist of quiet and detached classroom observation. Thus began my indoctrination into the sometimes turbulent, but always exciting, environment of Matthews Middle School. The more I became a part of this world, and not detached, the more I came to understand it from different perspectives.

School Structure

Indeed, while students craved freedom and excitement, teachers, composing an entirely separate perspective, craved discipline and order. School officials tended to react sternly to youthful energy and limits-testing. Rules and regulations abounded at the school. This structure appeared primarily in two forms: first, procedures stemming from policies of the State of Texas and the Maplewood School District, which Matthews was a part of, and second, rules generated by the school and teachers themselves. In my overview of organizational structure at Matthews, I will briefly discuss the shape of state and district policies first, followed by an examination other rules and regulations particular to the school.

Matthews, like any public school, followed state and district policies that set certain structural conditions for both students and teachers. Among the first things teachers discussed with me about the school was the Texas Assessment of Academic Skills (TAAS) exam, the state's standardized test, which seemed to constantly lurk in the back of the minds of students and teachers.[1] The Texas system of school accountability utilized the TAAS assessment test to "hold schools accountable" for student achievement. At the time of my fieldwork, the state required students from third through eighth grade and tenth grade to take the TAAS exam each year. The TAAS exam has been called a "high stakes" test because the scores students receive on it are used to rate schools and districts and are reported to the public. The state also groups these publicly available results by race, gender, and economic disadvantage (defined by free- or reduced-lunch eligibility). Hence, Texas schools faced considerable pressure at the time of my research to improve student achievement as measured by the TAAS. Many Texas schools implemented strategies such as TAAS "cheers" and devoted entire weeks to practice testing to motivate and prepare their students for the exam (McNeil 2000). Matthews was no different in this regard. The school even staged a TAAS pep rally before the exam, intended to boost student motivation to score well on the test, which included music and skits about TAAS and a cheer urging students to "attack" the test.

Matthews earned an "acceptable" performance rating each year I conducted fieldwork there (the Texas accountability system ratings include, in order from lowest to highest, "low performing," "acceptable," "recognized," and "exemplary"). But the overall passing rates fell behind state and district averages for students in general (these passing rates appear in table 3.1 and table 3.2).[2] Achieving the next step up to "recognized" would have required the school to have 80 percent of its test-taking students pass in each subgroup (delineated by race and economic disadvantage) as well as in the school overall. This would have entailed substantial improvement, especially in certain subgroups of students at the school.

TABLE 3.1

Percentage of Matthews' Students Passing the Texas Assessment of Academic Skills Test (TAAS) in 2001, by Race/Ethnicity

	African American	Hispanic (Latino)	Asian/Pacific Islander	White
Grade 7				
Reading	82	69	91	88
Math	75	74	88	67
All tests	68	63	85	67
Grade 8				
Reading	91	74	89	100
Writing	76	53	77	86
Math	79	81	95	92
Science	87	73	95	100
Social studies	62	44	81	85
All tests	52	34	66	79

Source: Texas Education Agency, www.tea.state.tx.us.

Note: Figures have been rounded.

The logic behind reporting TAAS passing rates by subgroup holds that schools must focus efforts on all students to attain certain minimum standards, rather than relying on the most advantaged students to lift the average for the school. In looking at the performance of racial subgroups, we can see that the TAAS passing rates for Hispanic students at Matthews remained the lowest overall. Similarly, in my classroom observations, Latino students tended to be the ones most disconnected from classroom activities, often with little notice from teachers. School officials tended to perceive Latino boys, in particular, as potentially threatening and oppositional; this I discuss further in chapter 5. A lack of Latino- and Spanish-speaking teachers may have contributed to the marginalization of many Latino students. The school only employed one educator identified by records as Hispanic in the first year of my research, and just two the second year. This probably hindered the school's ability to communicate to Latino students that it cared about them and valued their cultural background (see Valenzuela 1999).

TABLE 3.2

Percentage of Matthews' Students Passing the Texas Assessment of Academic Skills Test (TAAS) in 2002, by Race/Ethnicity

	African American	Hispanic (Latino)	Asian/Pacific Islander	White
Grade 7				
Reading	86	77	96	82
Math	79	83	92	100
All tests	73	71	88	83
Grade 8				
Reading	91	85	91	92
Writing	84	66	94	85
Math	88	86	97	77
Science	83	87	94	93
Social studies	71	58	77	86
All tests	58	43	71	71

Source: Texas Education Agency, www.tea.state.tx.us.

Note: Figures have been rounded.

As I have mentioned, white and Asian students in the United States tend to score the highest on standardized tests in general, and this remains true for TAAS statewide. Interestingly, at Matthews this was not necessarily the case, especially for white students. As tables 3.1 and 3.2 show, white students' passing rates at Matthews, although relatively high, did not consistently outpace their minority peers. These passing rates also substantially trailed the overall rates for white students in the state. This echoes other studies which suggest that white students attending schools with a higher percentage of nonwhites tend to perform lower than those attending schools with a lower percentage of non-whites (Bankston and Caldas 1996, 2000). Despite this, however, although educators often discussed strategies to boost the performance of black and Latinos students, they did not often perceive problems with white students, generally assuming that they performed adequately. For example, teachers rarely described white students as needing academic assistance. As I have mentioned, I volunteered as a tutor in several classes, where teachers would often choose for me a student or students who could benefit from extra help. Although I

often attended classes with white students, some of whom I knew did not perform well, no teacher selected a white kid in these classes as a student that
needed extra help. I will discuss these perceptions of white students academically, along with their performance on TAAS, further in chapter 4.

State policies such as the TAAS test placed certain strictures on academic
life for the students as well as the teachers. Teachers continuously criticized
TAAS, viewing the test as anywhere from racially biased to just plain annoying.
TAAS made many students somewhat nervous, but made teachers more so and
dominated much of the teacher discourse at Matthews. Many teachers viewed
the test as an unwelcome intrusion into their instructional purview, one that
placed too many restrictions and guidelines on their teaching. One teacher
criticizing TAAS, for example, viewed the test as a mechanism for surveillance
and mind control: "The government is trying to control how teachers and students think." Few teachers viewed this test positively, but regardless of this,
most put forth considerable effort to prepare their students for it.

A second major organizational policy at Matthews, encouraged by the district leadership for all middle schools in the school district, came in the form of
"tracking," or grouping students according to ability. Core subjects such as English, science, and social studies all had "pre–advanced placement" courses,
"regular" courses, and "resource" courses. Pre-AP classes were considered the
highest level, and resource classes the lowest. Math progressed in a course
sequence, with students deemed higher ability taking algebra in eighth grade
(or, with one student, geometry), other students taking regular, or grade-level
math, and still others taking below-grade-level resource math. The school left
entrance into accelerated pre–advanced placement and higher-level math
courses relatively open, only asking for a parent's signature and proof of meeting minimum requirements on the TAAS exam. However, teachers and counselors often informally urged certain students to move up to pre-AP or drop out
of pre-AP.

In my observations, vast differences existed between pre-AP and regular
classes. Pre-AP classes tended to be taught by extraordinary teachers who often
led their students in thought-provoking discussions and in solving challenging
problems. Although entrance into these classes remained relatively open at
Matthews, eighth graders not taking pre-AP, especially advanced math and science, would almost certainly not be enrolled in high school advanced placement courses, which are eventually important for college eligibility (see
Gamoran 1992).

Much research suggests that school stratification mechanisms such as
tracking tend to result in white students dominating the upper-tracked classes
(see, for example, Oakes 1985, 1995; Perry 2002). At Matthews, however, this was
not the case. Interestingly, according to my observations and school records,

African American girls were the most prevalent race and gender group in pre-AP courses at Matthews. The prevalence of black girls in the classes was certainly not overwhelming, however. In my observations of higher-tracked classes I typically saw students from an array of racial and ethnic backgrounds, virtually all of them engaged in the class, as in the following example:

> Ms. Hamm, pre-AP U.S. History, eighth grade. The class contains eighteen students: one white boy named Kevin, who I've seen before, three Asian American boys, two Asian American girls, two Latino boys, two Latinas, two black boys, and six black girls. The black girls are all sitting together on one side of the room. The boys are all pretty dispersed. The white boy, Kevin, who is somewhat quirky, sits in the front and center of the room.
>
> The "warm up," which Ms. Hamm, a black woman, gives the students at the beginning of the class, instructs the kids to write about their moral standing regarding the underground railroad. It asks them the comment on whether breaking existing laws to support a "higher law" is permissible in certain cases. After the students reflect and write down their answers, Ms. Hamm invites them to share their thoughts with the class. Brina, an Indian or Pakistani girl, comments first that she thinks you should never break the law. Ms. Hamm accepts her opinion, but argues against it. Javier, a Latino boy, follows Ms. Hamm's argument and says that it is acceptable to break laws sometimes if you are being discriminated against. Brina, who appears very outspoken, continues to challenge this view. Tanya, a black girl, speaks up to disagree with Brina. Things are getting a little heated, so Ms. Hamm reminds the class that Brina has a right to her opinion. Rodney, a black boy, and Abdul, an Indian/Pakistani boy, also offer comments. (Field notes, May 11, 2001)

As the excerpt also indicates, students of all racial and ethnic backgrounds at the school took pre-AP level courses, and white students certainly did not dominate them. The racial diversity present in these courses appeared to stem from two factors. First, educators made commendable efforts to attract minority students to upper-tracked classes. Many black teachers at the school, for example, taught such classes, which probably gave less of an impression to minority students that taking upper-level coursework was akin to "acting white" (see Fordham and Ogbu 1986). Second, the racial composition of the school, having only around 40 white students, meant that whites could not statistically dominate upper-level classes. That said, however, white students were still *overrepresented* in pre-AP courses. According to school records, for example, during the first year of my fieldwork they composed 8 percent of the enrollment for these courses, but only 4 percent of the Matthews' student body. I will discuss

over-representation of whites in upper level courses

the implications of the tracking system in influencing meanings and boundaries of whiteness at Matthews further in chapter 6.

In addition to larger organizational procedures such as tracking and TAAS, Matthews' administrators and teachers also implemented numerous rules and regulations of their own. The most evident local rule enforced at Matthews was the uniform dress code policy. Matthews required students to wear uniforms based on the school colors, with navy blue, red, or white shirts (not T-shirts) and navy blue or khaki shorts or pants. Girls could wear navy blue or khaki skirts or skorts (half skirt, half shorts) that were required to fall below the knee. Most sneakers and dress shoes were allowed, except sandals and boots. The school expected students to have their shirts tucked in at all times. According to teachers, the movement for uniforms at Matthews started about eight years before my fieldwork began. Teachers told me that this was a collaborative effort between parents and the school, and the few parents with whom I spoke supported the uniforms. Similar to many urban schools, the uniform dress code at Matthews was intended to decrease gang activity (to rid the school of the "flying colors," according to one teacher) and make student poverty less visible. As I will examine further in chapter 5, this uniform dress code policy often served as a source of conflict at Matthews, with educators perceiving it as necessary for a sense of order and students finding it stultifying.

Rules, regulations, and adult monitors also structured how the students moved through the space of the school. Virtually all student activity was structured, including lunch. During lunchtime, classes of students led by their teachers came into the cafeteria and sat, by class, at specific tables. Once they sat, students were supposed to remain silent. When a class of students achieved complete silence, an assistant principal selected them to go get their lunch, and this proceeded until all tables were eating. During this time, students could get up and move around only briefly. They could not wander around the cafeteria and certainly could not walk through the doors that led to an outside courtyard. Assistant principals patrolled throughout the lunch period—little more than thirty minutes—before the teachers came back to collect their classes. This tableau of students in uniforms being lined up and put at specific tables in a lunchroom patrolled by stern-looking assistant principals with walkie-talkies evoked an image of prison films. This seemed contradictory, considering that many educators sincerely wanted to create a caring atmosphere at the school.

Indeed, most educators at Matthews emphasized that the school should function like a caring family, although "tough love" was part of this goal. Educators at Matthews thought that most students could benefit from, above all, discipline and "structure." When I asked a black teacher named Ms. Lewis about characteristics that are helpful or harmful to students academically, she described the type of student who struggles in school in the following way: "Well, one that is not used to structure. Our job is teaching them how to make it outside of school. But it's hard when they are not growing up in a household with structure. There are some that are not used to structure but are willing to conform. Others, though, are not used to it, but they don't want to do it either. They want to do it their way. . . . The biggest problem is not knowing structure" (Interview, February 22, 2002). A white teacher named Mr. Simms described a similar view of struggling and disruptive students, a view he thought characterized most students at Matthews: "It's mostly coming from the children's homes; they're just not taught discipline or rules at home. But the school is not consistent either; we've got to stick by the rules" (Interview, May 8, 2002).

I will discuss the teachers' perceptions of which students lacked a sense of structure and required discipline from the school later in the book. For now, though, I want to describe this as a general concern and interest of most educators at Matthews. As these quotes suggest, teachers' interest in teaching the kids "structure" and their frustration that many students come to school without knowing how to follow rules emanated from their perceptions of the students' families. Such perceptions of students and their families at Matthews tended to have their roots in perceptions of the surrounding community. Many educators considered strictness and discipline particularly important in general for the current student population of Matthews, who were mostly minority and from lower-income backgrounds. To further understand processes within the school, then, we need to look closer at the community surrounding Matthews and its history.

The Neighborhood

Matthews Middle School opened its doors in 1974 on the edge of a large suburban school district called Maplewood School District. Matthews sat on the edge of this district, closest to the central part of a teeming, busy Texas city named Balcones City. At the time of my research, the neighborhood around the school consisted largely of busy roads, sprawling apartment complexes, and strip malls. The most evident businesses in the area were fast-food chain restaurants, convenience stores, liquor stores, "all items 99 cents" stores, and a few small, local Mexican, Indian-Pakistani, and African food shops. Although certainly an urban area, the density of the neighborhood was uneven, with a scattering of vacant lots interspersed between strip malls and multilevel apartments. The area had no recognizable parks and evoked little sense of serenity. Two major highways nearby added to the traffic and noise level, although few drivers ventured down neighborhood side streets, which wound past the relatively old, low-rent apartment complexes and modest, occasionally dilapidated houses.

The neighborhood only recently came to acquire such building and population density. The Maplewood School District was established in the early 1900s to serve a then small rural community. Eventually, Balcones City began to increase in population and area, and in the later part of the twentieth century much of this growth spilled over into Maplewood. This caused Maplewood to change quickly from rural to suburban to urban within a few generations. According to district records, even as late as the early 1970s, when Matthews first opened, the area of Maplewood consisted mostly of farmland and open spaces. Many of the multilane roads, which at the time of my research overflowed with heavy automobile traffic, were still unpaved in the 1970s. Urbanization spread briskly across Maplewood in the 1980s, however, increasing the density of businesses, homes, and traffic, beginning in the area of the Matthews attendance zone (the boundary from which Matthews draws its students). Balcones City incorporated the then-popular suburban area of Maplewood into the city limits beginning in the late 1970s. By the early 1980s, the city expanded bus routes to the area, and developers turned the once empty spaces of pastureland into large, low-rent apartment complexes. According to district records, the population of Maplewood almost quadrupled from 1970 to 1985. Seemingly overnight, the area had changed from a sleepy patchwork of rural grassland to a bustling urban neighborhood within a burgeoning city.

Portions of the Maplewood district lying on the outskirts, relatively far away from Matthews, still had many suburban characteristics at the time of my research, such as quiet roads that wove through tree-lined neighborhoods, connecting volumes of large, virtually identical houses. The area surrounding Matthews, by contrast, had much more of an urban quality, with a density of small businesses (especially convenience stores and fast-food chains, as I have mentioned) and residences connected by busy, multilane roads. Few home owners remained when I conducted fieldwork, and in the year 2000 the area consisted of over 75 percent renter-occupied housing (U.S. Census Bureau 2000). The Matthews attendance zone lay on the edge of Maplewood closest to the central city area of Balcones City, and at the time of my research it appeared as part of a seamless connection of growth outward from that city.

Local History and Neighborhood Change

The history of Matthews and the surrounding community has little importance apart from how people in this context interpret, share, and utilize it in guiding their perceptions and future actions (see Berger and Luckmann 1966; Bird 2002). Themes of race, social class, place, and change were very important to how educators forged an understanding of the reality of the Matthews neighborhood and their place within it. They constructed this reality in two ways. First, and most obviously, educators discerned this through continuing interaction in the school and neighborhood. Second, they developed and shared a local history of the area, guided by their perceptions of the neighborhood's current social characteristics.

An important part of the historical lore at Matthews involved the story of how the school changed rapidly from white and middle class to minority and working class during the late 1980s and early 1990s. Teachers at Matthews often described how "the demographics have changed" in the school and neighborhood, and one teacher even characterized this as "white flight." Officials referenced these changes as an important reason why the school sought help for reform from the Annenberg Foundation (which I discuss in the appendix). They did so, many claimed, because the old ways of proceeding did not work with the new student population. A document I collected from the school shows the way that many educators there interpreted the history of change in the neighborhood. It states, "Our once vibrant, middle class [Maplewood] neighborhood has become an area of concentrated poverty, unemployment, lower education levels, poor housing, substance abuse, and crime." This statement encapsulates how adults at the school viewed the neighborhood—as "once vibrant" but now riddled with poverty and other social problems.

For many educators, this perception stemmed from working and (for some) living in the area of the school for a long time (some teachers had worked at the school since it first opened). For others, however, this history and perception was learned from other teachers. Newer teachers and administrators, for example, tended to informally receive this historical perspective from more experienced ones. I was even informed of this history early in my research at Matthews by a new teacher named Ms. Cohen. Ms. Cohen, a white woman, asked me one morning if I had ever looked at the class pictures in the main hallway of the school (Matthews displayed class pictures in the hall from every eighth-grade class since the school opened). I told her I had noticed them, but had never taken a good look, so she showed me all the pictures as they progressed from the 1970s through the 1980s and 1990s and into the year 2000. As Ms. Cohen pointed out, the racial change represented in these pictures was dramatic. In the early years of Matthews until the mid-1980s, the students were almost entirely white—there were no black students at all in some of these pictures. In the mid-1980s some more nonwhite faces started showing up, until the early 1990s, when the pictures became mostly nonwhite and predominately African American. Towards the end of the 1990s, more students that looked Latino appeared in the pictures, along with more that appeared to be Indian or Pakistani. The white faces dropped dramatically from these pictures over time, appearing in recent pictures only here and there, as black faces did in the school's early years. We often read about white flight and trace it demographically, but here was an actual pictorial documentary of this process, represented through the smiling faces of real students.

Aside from serving as a visually compelling example of rapid racial change, Ms. Cohen's story also shows how quickly teachers learned and incorporated the lore of this historical transition at the school. Here was a first-year teacher showing me, a researcher who had been at the school only a few months, this demonstration of racial change and framing it as an important part of how she understood the school, the students, and her relationship with them. This same story was undoubtedly passed on from teacher to teacher and gave teachers a shared sense of the historical and social position of the school and its current students. However, teachers did interpret this story differently, especially teachers of different racial backgrounds, and this related to different perceptions of the neighborhood and students, which I explore further in chapter 4.

Racial and Economic Context and Change According to the Census

As several researchers have documented (e.g., Lipsitz 1995; Massey and Denton 1993; Oliver and Shapiro 1995), changes in neighborhood racial composition tend to accompany metropolitan outgrowth. The Matthews area was no exception to this. As the area became more urbanized, more minority residents, especially African Americans and Latinos, moved in and more white residents moved away. These racial changes began to take hold in the mid-1980s and intensified through the 1990s, as the school pictures displayed. Census data from 1990 and 2000 also demonstrate these changes. Tables 3.3 through 3.6 compare four census tracts that fell approximately within the attendance zone of Matthews in 1990 and 2000.[3] (I do not use the tracts' actual identification numbers in these tables because I do not want to identify the specific area of Matthews, which I promised to keep confidential.[4]) Overall, the figures for race across these two censuses match the educators' discourse of historical neighborhood change. The racial categories represent a dramatic shift toward increasing numbers of Latinos and African Americans.[5] Within a period of ten years, whites went from being the most populous group in the Matthews attendance zone, nearly double that of the next largest group, to being the least populous group—a numerical minority.[6]

As tables 3.5 and 3.6 show, economic changes are also apparent from 1990 to 2000, although not as drastic as the change in racial composition. In 1990, two of the four census tracts had median household incomes slightly above the median income for the nation that year ($30,056). These tracts also had poverty rates (as reported for individuals) substantially below the national rate of 13 percent that year. In 2000, all the census tracts in the school attendance zone had median incomes below the national median ($41,994) and poverty rates above the national rate (12 percent). Although the income and poverty changes do not show as dramatic a shift as race, they do show that poverty and lower incomes dispersed across the area since 1990. Further, they provide a view of the economic situation of the area surrounding Matthews during my fieldwork

TABLE 3.3

Racial Characteristics for Matthews' Attendance Zone, 1990 (N = 41,912)

	African American (%)	Hispanic (Latino) (%)	Asian/Pacific Islander (%)	White (%)
Tract 1990 A (N = 10,897)	39	25	5	30
Tract 1990 B (N = 12,746)	23	16	13	47
Tract 1990 C (N = 12,023)	13	14	22	51
Tract 1990 D (N = 6,246)	37	16	7	39
Total	**27**	**18**	**14**	**43**

TABLE 3.4

Racial Characteristics for Matthews' Attendance Zone, 2000 (N = 25,436)

	African American (%)	Hispanic (Latino) (%)	Asian/Pacific Islander (%)	White (%)	Multi-racial (%)
Tract 2000 A (N = 6,199)	67	15	6	10	3
Tract 2000 B (N = 7,133)	49	28	9	13	4
Tract 2000 C (N = 2,271)	44	13	31	10	4
Tract 2000 D (N = 9,833)	28	35	21	15	4
Total	**45**	**26**	**15**	**12**	**4**

TABLE 3.5

**Economic Characteristics for Matthews'
Attendance Zone, 1990**

	Median income	Poverty (for individuals) (%)
Tract 1990 A	$19,151	27
Tract 1990 B	$30,070	9
Tract 1990 C	$30,561	9
Tract 1990 D	$22,676	13

Source: U.S. Census Bureau 1990.
http://factfinder.census.gov.

there, with few adults earning incomes above the national median and many living below the poverty line.

Although I can track changes and current estimates of racial and economic composition in the Matthews area, I unfortunately lack the data to compare across race and income. In other words, I do not know the income level of whites,

TABLE 3.6

**Economic Characteristics for Matthews'
Attendance Zone, 2000**

	Median income	Poverty (for individuals) (%)
Tract 2000 A	$26,616	20
Tract 2000 B	$26,591	20
Tract 2000 C	$28,633	20
Tract 2000 D	$36,322	18

Source: U.S. Census Bureau 2000.
http://factfinder.census.gov.

Note: Tracts do not precisely match those in table 3.5.

African Americans, Latinos, and Asian Americans within each group. Similarly, within the school population, I did not have access to data that disaggregated free- and reduced-lunch recipients (60 percent of the school the first year of my study, and 66 percent the next year) by race. This brings up an interesting question of whether the small group of white students at Matthews came from higher-class backgrounds than the others. The school understandably restricted my access to free- or reduced-lunch data, which named specific students, so it was difficult to obtain a firm statistical answer to this. However, an administrator familiar with these statistics told me that about half of the white students at the school received a lunch subsidy and half did not. The attendance zone (Matthews was a neighborhood school, with no students bused in from other areas) did have some neighborhoods that appeared higher income than others, primarily based on whether houses or apartments predominated, but I did not observe vast differences in wealth across the community as a whole. Moreover, I did not observe that white students and their families all lived in the more comfortable areas—although some did live in these locations, many also lived in low-rent apartments and struggled to make ends meet like many of the other students. For example, a teacher once showed me a paper written by one white student named Samantha, who, as described in chapter 1, was honored by the school as an outstanding student. In the paper, Samantha describes her mother as her hero because, as a single parent, she worked late hours at an area liquor store to support Samantha and her five siblings. Samantha, similar to many other white students at Matthews, did not come from a wealthy background.

Race, Class, and Gender at Matthews

Matthews succeeded admirably in creating a sense of racial harmony among students and teachers. While Matthews had difficulty attracting Latino and Asian American teachers, it did attract many African American teachers, who actually composed the majority of teachers at the school. According to school records, Matthews had approximately one-half white teachers and one-half African American teachers the year before I began my research, and this proportion shifted to approximately one-third white and two-thirds African American during my fieldwork. Many black educators, women especially, held leadership positions at the school, including administration (the principal, Ms. Walker, was a black woman). This predominately black staff, along with the predominately minority and poor student population, set Matthews apart from the other middle schools in the district, which tended to have a slightly higher proportion of white students and overwhelmingly white staffs.

This was strikingly apparent one day when counselors and a few principals from a high school that Matthews' students feed into came to the school. Matthews' students did not all feed to the same high school, but several different ones, and the counselors came to meet with groups of eighth graders at Matthews and help them select their high school classes. Virtually all these counselors and principals were white women. This appeared rather intimidating for many minority students at Matthews, for whom the transition to high school undoubtedly signified a transition to a white-dominated arena. I recall observing an interaction with one of these counselors, a young white woman, and a Latino student named Daniel, whom I had tutored before. Daniel, an amiable, laid-back kid, seemed eager to please the counselor, who had given a stirring account of her high school's greatness. I recorded their interaction in my field notes:

> The counselor asks who is taking algebra currently and passing it. Three students, a Hispanic boy, a Pakistani or Indian girl, and an African American girl raise their hands. After a slight delay, Daniel also raises his hand. Jawad, a black boy sitting next to Daniel, whispers to him, "You ain't taking algebra, are you?" Daniel nods that he is and then asks the counselor, "Miss ——, I'm taking algebra. What do I do?" The woman seems reluctant to believe Daniel. She says, "Well, if you *know* you are taking algebra—and *passing* it—then sign up for geometry." A little later, Daniel tells the counselor that he wants to sign up for the schools' drill team, which she had mentioned was very prestigious. She smiles and asks him, "Now are you *sure* you want to join the drill team?" Daniel nods adamantly. The counselor says, "Now, that's like a bunch of girls marching around with flags." Daniel grins sheepishly and admits that he actually does not want to do that. (Field notes, March 6, 2002)

Daniel, along with many students at Matthews, interacted with the high school counselors in a rather awkward and shy way. Students I knew as boisterous and self-assured suddenly became quiet and hesitant around these counselors. Of course, the transition to high school alone would provoke this in most eighth graders, but the fact that virtually all of these counselors were white, while the majority of adults at Matthews were not, appeared to accentuate the distance of the step from Matthews to high school.

Perhaps because of its proximity to the central city area of Balcones City, many teachers said that Matthews had a reputation as a "bad" school in the district. Indeed, once when I spoke with a district substitute teacher at the school, he described Matthews as a bad school and the students as unruly. Many Matthews teachers interpreted other schools and the district leadership as subtly, or even blatantly, hostile to Matthews. This annoyed these educators because they perceived the school as very good and thought the district did not adequately recognize its accomplishments. Some claimed that this stemmed directly from the racial composition of the student body. A black teacher named Mr. Caldwell, for instance, stated, "Matthews has a reputation since I've been here as becoming a blacker or, quote, 'diverse' school, so people thought that was bad. Let me put it this way—if we were doing the same things we're doing, but the school was lily white, it would be different" (Interview, April 24, 2002).

Thus, the racial composition of Matthews set it apart from most other middle schools in the district, according to teachers, perhaps because of outright racism. Further, as Mr. Caldwell implies, the white flight away from Matthews as it increased in minority enrollment underscored the distance many who lived in other parts of the district wanted to establish from Matthews. According to several teachers at Matthews, this fueled the refusal of many in the district to acknowledge the school's achievements. This sentiment, and awareness of racism, appeared most acute among African American teachers. This makes sense especially when placed in the historical context of Texas, which includes a southern legacy of overt racial conflict (N. Foley 1997; Glenn 2002).

As I mentioned in the introduction, the student body of Matthews was indeed mostly African American and Hispanic, followed by Asian and white students. Considerable diversity existed within these broad categories, however. Many of those students included in the "African American" category were recent immigrants from Africa or, less often, the Caribbean. Hispanics consisted mostly of Mexican-Americans, but many also had roots in El Salvador, Guatemala, Cuba, Brazil, Argentina, and other Latin American countries. Asians consisted about equally of those from East Asian origin, especially Chinese and Vietnamese, and those of South Asian origin, especially Indian and Pakistani. Even some students considered white by school records had Spanish surnames or recently emigrated from non-English-speaking countries. Within each of these categories, students differed based on their generation of immigration— generally marked by whether they took English as a second language (ESL) classes or not. Also, based on my student surveys, several students identified themselves with more than one of these racial categories.

I was fascinated at times to watch the mix of students from such diverse social and cultural backgrounds fuse into the framework of a single class. Often students borrowed cultural elements from each other, but at the same time used culture to restrict the behaviors of themselves and others. The following excerpt from my field notes gives an indication of the type of cultural and social diversity typically present at Matthews and how kids negotiated this:

> Ms. Klein, art class. The students are working on various projects at their own pace. Ahmed, a Pakistani boy I recognize from another class, is acting pretty rambunctious and is play-boxing with a group of Latina girls and a black boy named Robert. He then goes to the front of the room and practices hip-hop dance moves.
>
> A quiet boy sitting by himself who, judging by his accent, seems to be African keeps staring intently at a map of the world hanging on the wall

near his table and points toward a West African country. Ms. Klein comes over to see if he needs help and he silently points the country out to her. She acknowledges this and he continues his work.

One of the Latina girls (whom I later learn is named Luisa) eventually accuses Ahmed of pinching her, which Ms. Klein ignores. Seeing that she is getting no response from the teacher, Luisa walks up to Ahmed, feigns a punch in his direction, laughs, and then continues to Ms. Klein's desk to get some supplies.

The girl then goes back to the group of girls and tells the story of what she did the past weekend in a mix of Spanish and English. I overhear the word "mall," for instance, followed by "con mis hermanos." During this conversation, a small black boy in the back of the room (whom I later learn is named DaMario) mocks her. He starts shouting, "Odelay, holmes!" "Quit talking Spanish, holmes!" and "Ay Chihuahua, holmes!" He continues these exclamations periodically for the rest of the class, seeming to be entertained by the way the words sound coming from his mouth. He sits at a group with two black boys and a Latino boy, but the Latino boy doesn't seem to care. DaMario eventually takes his clay roller (he and other students have been working with clay) and starts to bang it around, still repeating his new Spanish phrases. He turns to a black boy at the table behind him and, without a pause, smashes a clay sculpture of a small dog that boy had been working on. "Ay Chihuahua!" DaMario exclaims, looking at the pile of clay that used to be a dog. The boy working on the dog says, "Man, why'd you do that?" DaMario can offer no explanation, but apologizes. (Field notes, April 5, 2001)

I relay this passage at length because it conveys a good sense of how students at Matthews managed the mix of cultural backgrounds present in most classrooms. Ahmed, a Pakistani boy, practices African American–based dance moves and flirts (in the middle school style of attempting to inflict pain) with a group of Latina girls. The Latinas speak using Spanglish, a mix of Spanish and English, while an African American boy at first mocks their speech but eventually appears fascinated by it and incorporates it into his own lexicon. Meanwhile, a quiet boy, whom I learn has recently emigrated from Africa, appears homesick and isolated from the social interchange of the other students. (African students, many of which took ESL classes, straddled ESL/immigrant and African American social groups at the school. See Waters 1999 study of black Caribbean immigrant youth.) Cultures often fused together in the peer interactions at Matthews, but at the same time subtly competed for dominance. African American culture, especially in the form of music such as hip-hop and rhythm and blues (R and B), held the most popularity among students, and in my observations black students tended to set the cultural norms at the school, which I describe in more detail in chapter 6.

While the school made genuine efforts to encourage the recognition and expression of all cultures, African American cultural forms remained the most prevalent. This stemmed from both the popularity of these forms in the larger youth culture and the predominately African American staff of the school. The excellent band at the school, for instance, was led by a young African American man named Mr. Harris. This band patterned itself after historically black college bands and featured a strong base drumbeat and various physical movements from the players to embellish the songs. The band composed a salient and popular presence at virtually all assemblies and played many R and B songs, including some sung by a vocalist. It interested me to watch the few white students and Asian students in this band, who stood out visually but whose playing blended right in. During such assemblies, African American students, especially girls, were the most involved, often clapping with the band and standing up near their seats to dance.

When I first talked to teachers at Matthews, I asked them about the main social groups among students at the school. These teachers surprised me by saying that few distinct social groups really existed. They claimed that students separated themselves somewhat by race and somewhat by popularity or "coolness," but not into distinctively observable groups. I interpreted this view critically at first, but after continued participant observation, I was inclined to agree that only vague student groupings existed. In contrast to ethnographic studies of high school students, I did not find an array of distinct, crystallized social groups among students at Matthews (see, for example, Bettie 2003; Eckert 1989; D. Foley 1990; Perry 2002). Like any school, Matthews had kids considered cool ("tight" in the kids' vernacular) and kids considered nerdy or uncool ("hatin'" or "haters" in the kids' vernacular). This did not necessarily relate to school performance—a nerd could be found in a regular class just about as easily as in a pre-AP class. But it did relate to interactive style, including what the student chose to wear, how they spoke, and who they hung out with.

Although student groupings were rather vague, race and gender composed the most apparent distinctions among students at Matthews. Girls tended to group with girls and boys with boys, often under the instruction of school officials (see Schofield 1989; Thorne 1993). However, particularly towards the end of eighth grade, these gender distinctions began to erode, and more boys and girls interacted with each other. In most classes, such as those in my field note excerpts above, students of different racial backgrounds tended to interact and share friendships with each other. However, it remained most common for students to socialize, especially in closer friendships, with others of their same race. Interestingly, white students formed somewhat of an exception here. As I discuss further in chapter 6, these students did not tend to socialize exclusively with other white students at Matthews. However, I did observe more social connections between white and Asian American and Latino students than white and African American students.

Student dress and display marked subtle differences in student groupings and indicated where students aligned themselves vis-à-vis schooling. This system was complex and functioned rather clandestinely within the uniform restrictions. Boys tended to prefer oversized pants and shorts, worn substantially below the waist so that they bunched at the bottom. The pants and shorts boys wore were often Dickies, a brand marketed as durable, blue-collar work clothing. Students who wore Dickies tended to take regular or resource classes—in my observations of pre-AP classes I saw few students wearing this brand. However, many boys in pre-AP classes, especially those considered popular, still wore their pants or shorts (often a generic version of the Dockers brand marketed for white-collar work or leisure) baggy and below the waist. Boys also tended to wear oversized polo shirts with T-shirts underneath (even in hot weather), which gave many the illusion of bulkiness. Boys who wore tighter, more fitted clothing tended to be seen as nerdy. By contrast, girls at Matthews preferred tighter-fitting clothing, especially with pants, shorts, and skirts. Girls also occasionally wore Dickies pants, but less often than boys did because at the time of my research this brand did not make clothing specifically designed for women and girls. Girls who wore longer, looser skirts (which the dress code actually called for) tended to be seen by other kids as nerdy.

Some differences in student stylistic presentation appeared along racial as well as gender lines. Latina girls and some white girls, especially those in regular or resource classes, wore liberal amounts of makeup. These girls often devoted the few minutes before the bell in many classes to elaborate makeup application rituals, meticulously checking their appearance using compact mirrors and their girl friends (see Bettie 2000). Some of these girls wore very thick, dark eyeliner and lip liner that some teachers told me they interpreted as a mark of gang affiliation. African American and Asian American girls rarely wore thick makeup and tended to not apply makeup openly in classrooms. For boys, some subtle differences emerged over footwear. Black boys tended to prefer high-top basketball shoes similar to the popular Air Jordan line from Nike, worn with ankle length socks. Latino boys tended to prefer "old school" leisure-type tennis shoes, especially brands such as Nike, Adidas, and Puma. I also noticed differences in which students wore Dickies brand pants. I only occasionally observed East Asian students wearing Dickies, and I almost never saw white students wear them (I only saw one white student wear Dickies—Lisa, whom I will mention later—but only on one occasion toward the end of the school year). As I explore later in this book, some teachers interpreted Dickies pants, especially when worn baggy and oversized, as representing opposition to schooling.

Many aspects of student life at Matthews, such as the importance of dress and fitting in with a desired social group, reminded me of my own middle school experience. However, my observations also reminded me of how the lives of these students differed substantially from my middle-class adolescence. It was not unusual, for example, for students at Matthews to talk to each other about crimes committed near their residences the night before. In one pre-AP class I sat next to two African American girls discussing a shooting at their apartment complex the night before in an almost blasé manner, dryly rehashing the details of the shots and the police arriving while simultaneously filling out their science worksheets. I occasionally viewed police making arrests and handcuffing people on the same sidewalks Matthews' students walked on to get home. After school one day I observed police officers frisking a group of boys lined up against an outside wall of the school. Crime and the police composed a prevalent, almost mundane presence in the school and the neighborhood.

Further, as I mentioned above, the neighborhood consisted almost entirely of rental properties, many of them run-down and poorly managed. A black boy named Charles articulated this reality in a deceptively whimsical way in a class I observed:

> Ms. Cohen's class. The assignment is for the students to write a business letter to appropriate parties. Ms. Cohen asks for volunteers to read their letters to the class. Charles volunteers to read his letter. It is a business letter addressed to the apartment complex in which he and his mother used to live. Charles reads: "Dear [Fifth Avenue Apartments], my mother and I used to live at your apartments and it was awful. First we had ants, then we had cockroaches that would fly all around the kitchen. Then we had lizards, and I even found one under my bed. You never did anything about any of these problems. Therefore, I am suing you for one hundred million dollars and nineteen cents. Sincerely, Charles. P.S., I have ten lawyers and one of them is [a local lawyer with popular television advertisements]." This letter brings roars of laughter from the class. Ms. Cohen asks, "Charles, I've got to know what the nineteen cents is for." Charles replies, "So I can buy some extra candy," which prompts further laughter. (Field notes, April 6, 2001)

Charles's experience was humorous and relatively benign, but it exemplifies the typical existence for most students at Matthews, who came from poor or working-class backgrounds. These kids often lived in crowded and exploitative rental conditions, and many were forced to move around in search of better locations. The high mobility rate of the school (26 percent) demonstrated this, as did my often frustrated attempts to get to know students and learn their names, only to have new ones arrive at the school and old ones leave. Interestingly, in my experience, this occurred relatively equally among all races of students at the school and hindered my association with white students just as much as other students.

The Importance of Context

This chapter has set the historical and contemporary context of Matthews Middle School. I view this context as crucial to understanding the more specific school discourses and actions addressed in the chapters that follow, including the educators' understandings of the local history of racial change, the importance educators placed on discipline and dress, and the prevalence of cross-racial student groupings and interactions at the school, among others. Such contextual understandings were also vitally important in guiding teachers' perceptions of students at Matthews. This emerged especially in educators' perceptions of the numerical minority of white students at Matthews. The following chapter explores how educators perceived and reacted to this atypical minority of students. Teachers tended to perceive this group of students in two divergent ways, which stemmed largely from different interpretations of the neighborhood context and history of Matthews as well as from different interpretations of how whiteness interrelated with class background in this context. As we will see, such perceptions mattered for the educational experiences of white students as well as students of color.

4

From "Middle Class"
to "Trailer Trash":
Teachers' Perceptions
of White Students

There was an advertisement several years ago that compared the importance of teaching and practicing medicine. At the end, the ad asked, "Without teachers, where would doctors come from?" I agree with this suggestion that teaching composes one of the most important jobs in society and that teachers are vitally influential for guiding young people into the adults they will become. Teachers' perceptions and interactions with students shape kids' schooling experiences, profoundly impacting their educational and emotional growth. I observed this vitality and importance of teaching at Matthews Middle School. Many teachers there approached their jobs in a dedicated, generous way, intending to teach and guide their young students in the best way they knew how. Matthews' teachers were aware of educational issues related to race and class, and most discussed these issues with me in a cooperative (albeit, for many, rather guarded) way. As the reader will recall, the school had a relatively high percentage of students from poor or working-class backgrounds and a student body composed primarily of African American and Latino students. However, most teachers appeared somewhat off guard when the discussion of minorities turned to white students. These students obviously composed a minority in the school and neighborhood, but a minority that was uncommon and unexpected. So, how did teachers interpret and react to this unexpected minority of white students in the racial/ethnic context of Matthews? How did the teachers' understandings of these students matter for their educational experiences? This chapter sets out to answer these questions by examining how teachers perceived and interacted with students at Matthews.

I mentioned in the previous chapter the importance of context and interpretations of local history at Matthews. On the foundation of such contextual understandings, teachers built understandings of the backgrounds of the students they taught. Interpretations of whether families were deficient, unfortunate, or helpful; whether students were unruly, lacking social skills, or appropriate; whether the student body was improving, striving, or becoming more troublesome; all referenced interpretations of neighborhood context and history. I have mentioned that most teachers received some knowledge of the neighborhood and its history from other teachers; however, their interpretations of this often diverged. Teachers' social backgrounds appeared to relate to some of this divergence. One's personal history and past encounters undoubtedly guide present interpretations and actions (see, for example, Mead [1934] 1962). For teachers at Matthews, this mattered for how they understood race and class, including for white students.

Indeed, the more I observed at Matthews, the more I noticed differences in how educators there interpreted and interacted with white students. Interestingly, these differences related especially to the racial background of the teacher. When I saw white students overlooked in classroom discussions, or reprimanded because of infractions, this came especially from white teachers. African American teachers, by contrast, often called on white students to give answers in classrooms and rarely disciplined them. This chapter explores these different reactions to white students at Matthews, which, I argue, stem from different perceptions of the neighborhood in which these students lived and different perceptions of the white students' class background. Teacher perceptions were very significant in guiding the experiences of white kids at Matthews—the classroom advantages of these students depended largely on how teachers perceived their race, class, and academic ability.

In tracing the interpretations of whiteness in the teachers' discourse, I demonstrate how race and class work in combination. In ethnographic studies, as well as survey-based research, scholars tend to position race or class as having a more important effect on educational processes. Some tend to assign primacy to social class (Bourdieu and Passeron 1977; Bowles and Gintis 1976; Willis 1977) and others to race (Delpit 1995; Ogbu 1991; Fordham 1988) in shaping educational experiences.[1] Such perspectives, although valuable, do not account for how race and class interact in everyday life, including within schools. People do not experience these characteristics in isolation, and they develop understandings of others based on their perceptions of both at once. As I mentioned in chapter 2, it may be helpful heuristically to separate race from class, but these concepts often interrelate in complex ways and tend to defy a clear division. Frequently, in social interaction, one of these concepts symbolizes the other. This view is important when considering the potential privileges of whiteness because being white undoubtedly produces more social rewards when symbolizing a hegemonic, higher-class position.

My observations from Matthews show how whiteness symbolized a particular class background to teachers. Different teachers expressed polarized views of the family and class backgrounds of white students in this setting, views which ranged from "middle class" to "trailer trash." Such divergent perceptions of social class stemmed from how teachers interpreted whiteness within this predominately minority context and shaped how teachers reacted to these students academically. Interestingly, teachers interpreted whiteness differently based on their own racial background. Black teachers typically saw white students as middle class and as good students. White teachers tended to interpret white students as low income and unremarkable students. These perceptions of class background and academic ability corresponded to how these different teachers made sense of the atypical situation of white students in the predominately minority setting of Matthews and influenced how they reacted to these students.

Perceiving Students

Much compelling ethnographic work in education has explored how youths develop race- and class-based identities that impel them to either embrace school or disengage from it (Bettie 2000, 2002; Flores-Gonzalez 2002; MacLeod 1995; Fordham and Ogbu 1986; Willis 1977). But little of this research thoroughly examines how educators actually *perceive* these identities. Several studies suggest that teachers' perceptions of students play a profound role in shaping educational experiences (Alexander, Entwisle, and Thompson 1987; R. Ferguson 1998; Muller, Katz, and Dance 1999; Rist 1970). To more fully understand the impact of race and class in the schooling of white students at Matthews, it is important to analyze how educators, the gatekeepers for students' educational trajectories, interpret these characteristics.

In interaction, observers appear to rely especially on visible cues and social context to develop interpretations of those they interact with (Anderson 1990). In chapter 2 of this book, I described how these cues are often highly interwoven so that some can imply others. Because of its high social visibility, race often signals a range of characteristics, including social class position. However, social class carries its own identifiers, and the perception of these can perhaps alter the perception of race, including whiteness (West and Fenstermaker 1995). An urban, predominately minority residential location, along with certain styles of speech, dress, and behavior are often interpreted as lower class, for example (Anderson 1990; Kirschenmen and Neckerman 1991). Teachers and administrators most likely draw on understandings of neighborhood location and context, along with attention to styles of interaction, to develop their interpretation of a student's social background. Such interpretations have real consequences—educators may react negatively to students exhibiting perceived "lower-class" and "street-based" markers (Bourdieu and Paseron 1977; Dance 2002; Valenzuela 1999). Most research in the United States, however, has concentrated on racial/ethnic minority students who carry such markers. Few have considered how teachers might view white students who live in predominately minority areas and display these street-based styles. How might educators interpret and react to these white kids?

Exploring these perceptions and reactions has important implications for understanding white privilege in education because these might mediate and perhaps alter this privilege. Indeed, I observed the process through which educators interpreted whiteness and social class at Matthews to be critically important in shaping white students' educational experiences there. Several factors influenced the way teachers interpreted white students in the predominately racial/ethnic minority setting of Matthews. These factors consisted of a complex interplay of perceptions relating to school and neighborhood type, social class, and race. In the remainder of this chapter I discuss these factors, beginning with teachers' perceptions of students in the school generally and then narrowing this focus to how teachers perceived and interacted with white students specifically. This discussion shows how perceptions and context play crucial roles in the social construction of whiteness. These factors influence ways that being white might acquire powerful, hegemonic connotations on one hand, or anomalous, marginalized connotations on the other. Such divergent interpretations of whiteness at Matthews also incurred consequences for how white students were viewed and treated academically.

Teachers' Perceptions of the School and Their Role as Teacher

Educators at Matthews saw the school and their role in it in various ways. White teachers tended to see themselves in somewhat of a missionary role to help disadvantaged kids. Ms. McCain said, "I chose to teach these kids because I think they deserve a quality education. Not that I'm like the greatest teacher or something, but they deserve the same education as rich kids" (Interview, April 26, 2002). Mr. Wilson said, "I was driving down the street one day and I saw a group of young black males in a ghetto type area with nothing to do than pitch pennies. I decided then that I wanted to go into education so these kids could grow up and have more opportunities and more to do than just sitting around pitching pennies" (Interview, May 15, 2002).

Many white teachers saw Matthews as a very disadvantaged inner-city school, whose students they wanted to help. Black teachers, however, seemed reluctant to characterize the school as "inner city," or even particularly disadvantaged. Ms. Lewis said, "I worked over in [another school district] through a computer company for a while. People say this school is an inner-city school, and I guess it is, but over there they had a lot more problems" (Interview, February 22, 2002). Ms. Boyd said, "I guess this is the inner city, but not like where I taught before). These kids need to learn that they have opportunities" (Field notes, February 22, 2001).

Few teachers, white or black, lived in the immediate vicinity of the school. Most African American teachers, however, lived closer to the school than most white teachers (many white teachers said they drove more than an hour to get to the school). Some black teachers even had children in nearby schools and told me they would see their students at area supermarkets. Thus, the school for many black teachers was less a distant or "other" reality than for many white teachers. This appeared to shape the way each group of teachers saw the students in the school. White teachers saw most students as having serious educational and social needs, whereas black teachers stressed that most students actually had "opportunities" for learning and upward mobility.

Many African American teachers saw themselves as helping disadvantaged kids, similar to white teachers, but when they described this role they connected it more specifically to race and combating racism. Mr. Caldwell said, "My parents and schools gave me the tools for how to deal with racism. One of the things I try to teach these kids is how to survive in a racist society . . . but not to hate. Sooner or later they find out that education is the atomic bomb for dealing with racism" (Interview, April 24, 2002). Black teachers such as Mr. Caldwell tended to direct this racial focus especially at the black children in the school. Black teachers sometimes mentioned that Latinos also suffered from racial discrimination, but emphasized this discrimination far less in conversations and teaching. One black teacher named Ms. Taylor thought that Hispanic kids at the school tended to come from stable family environments which valued education, and she gave the following example: "Like the book fair we just had, the kids who bought something there were basically Hispanic kids. Our kids were buying candy bars and soda pop with their money. There are no books in the house in these families—they come here hollow" (Interview, March 27, 2002). Interestingly, Ms. Taylor referred to "our" kids in this excerpt. She implied throughout the context of the interview that this meant black children. Ms. Taylor connected how families viewed education to race—with Hispanic families at the school being more supportive of education and black families less so. In contrast to Mr. Caldwell, she attributed problems faced by African American students more to their families than to racial discrimination. Similar to Mr. Caldwell, however, she distinguished students primarily by race and directed much of her concern at African American students. This concern was also reflected in a poem, celebrating black identity and pride, that Ms. Taylor displayed in her classroom.

Thus, black teachers expressed an acute consciousness of race, especially in terms of disadvantages faced by African American students. This consciousness shaped their teaching style and influenced the way they perceived students of different racial backgrounds. African American teachers tended to be more aware of the variations and needs of African American students. In addition, race itself acted as a primary organizing principle for black teachers in

their stated perceptions of students in general. I suggest that this race-based
focus attuned African American teachers to the importance of race for racial
minority students as well as other students—for whom they often interpreted
race to be an advantage (or less of a hindrance). By focusing on the race-based
disadvantages of black students, black teachers often constructed other groups
of students as comparatively better off. Ironically, as exemplified by Ms. Taylor,
this often led African American teachers to be most critical of African American
students.

White teachers, by contrast, denied that race played much of a role in shaping social processes in the school (see Lewis 2001; Pollock 2001). Mr. Wilson, for
example, responded with the following when I asked what he thought about the
white students at the school: "I've never thought about it really. I don't think
about race when I teach—when I look in [the classroom] I don't see black, white,
Asian—I just see kids, and that's the way I treat them. And with my coworkers I
don't see that either. . . . When we look in that classroom we don't look at skin
color" (Interview, May 15, 2002). White teachers such as Mr. Wilson often
couched their discussion of educational inequalities in class-based rather than
race-based terms and espoused a "color-blind" perspective. Perhaps because
they experienced their race as a form of advantage, white teachers downplayed
its potential significance (Frankenberg 1993). With some exceptions, white
teachers I spoke with tended to see all the students at the school as disadvantaged and related this especially to class background. A white teacher named
Ms. McCain, for instance, stated that "the kids here are all on the same SES
[socioeconomic status] anyway" (Interview, April 26, 2002). This did not mean
that race was unimportant to white teachers, however. Rather, racial consider-
ations came in more coded forms, such as racial residential composition. Residential segregation typically inhibits wide interaction between members of
different racial groups in the United States, especially white people and black
people (Massey and Denton 1993). These different racialized residential and life
experiences influence how people perceive and assign meaning to race. Whites
who live in predominately white suburban areas tend to view predominately
black areas as dangerous, poor, and exotic (Farley et al. 1994; Lewis 2001).
African Americans tend to view predominately black areas less negatively,
probably because they have often had closer physical and emotional connections to such areas (Collins 1990; Farley et al. 1994). I find a similar pattern of
perceptions at Matthews. White teachers characterized the school and the area
as particularly poor, although it had a lower proportion of students receiving
free or reduced lunch (60 percent the first year of my research, 66 percent the
second) than several other middle schools in the same city (a nearby middle
school on the edge of a district adjoining the Maplewood district had 97 percent
of the students on free or reduced lunch, for instance). The predominance of
black and Latino students at the school appeared to influence white teachers to

see Matthews as very poor, which was not necessarily the perception of black teachers. However, although race may have been a factor in their perceptions of the school, white teachers did not highlight it in their descriptions of educational processes, which led them to downplay race per se as a potential source of educational disadvantage or advantage.

Social Class and Academic Ability

While black and white educators held different views of the importance of race at Matthews, neither group attributed a causal role to race per se in student academic ability. By contrast, they did tend to relate ability to social class. Teachers used the term "middle-class" to imply a good student. Many would point out a student whom they considered intelligent and then tell me that their parent(s) had some middle-income occupation such as police officer, teacher, or, in one instance, lawyer, implying that the parental occupation explained the student's intelligence. "Poor," by contrast, indicated that the student faced greater obstacles in academics. For instance, Mr. Reed, a black teacher, described the practical challenges faced by poor students: "It's hard to think about academics if you're just worried about surviving" (Interview, April 5, 2002).

Living in rented apartments served as a key indicator of poverty to many teachers. A white teacher named Ms. Phillips, for example, mentioned this when talking about her perceptions of the class background of white students at Matthews: "I'm pretty sure most of the white kids who go here live in apartments and are poor like a lot of the other kids" (Interview, November 26, 2001). Ms. Phillips, along with other teachers, used "living in apartments" as synonymous with "poor." Many educators considered students from such residential backgrounds to have low academic ability. Ms. Taylor, for instance, connected parental reliance on public assistance and living in apartments to a lack of student motivation. In describing some students whom she considered troublesome she said, "[They] live in apartments—and they don't want to live anywhere else. It just shows you how much motivation they have" (Field notes, March 25, 2002).

This should not imply that teachers were necessarily *wrong* in their assessment of the connection between social class and academic competence (see, for example Lareau 2002), but that in the teachers' discourse social class corresponded to academic ability more directly than race. Thus, how teachers perceived a student's social class was the most proximate factor in how they perceived that student's academic potential. Because social class did not have the same immediate visual impact of race, and teachers did not reference school records of those students classified as "economically disadvantaged," determining social class was a rather complicated process in which teachers relied on various cues. As mentioned before, parental occupation and residence served as some of these cues. Teachers gleaned other cues from more direct interaction with the students, such as how students' spoke and especially how they dressed.

As I mentioned previously and will discuss more in the following chapter, Matthews enacted a dress code that was intended in part to make income differences less visible. However, even within these strictures, a student's dress—the brands they wore, the cleanliness and newness of their clothing—could still indicate class background. As I will describe further in chapter 5, students displaying noticeably neat and clean clothing tended to gain more positive reactions from teachers and less disciplinary action. Teachers often interpreted such neat dress to indicate a middle-class background or upward mobility—a symbolic representation of cultural capital.[2] In my conversations with teachers, some would even intertwine dress, family income, and being a good student so that one would imply the others. For example, one white teacher named Mr. Simms stated that one of his students was wealthy, and he further explained this by saying, "He wears nice clothes and is a good student" (Interview, May 8, 2002). For Mr. Simms and other teachers, wearing "nice clothes" and being a "good student" indicated a relatively wealthy background. Thus, teachers linked perceptions of academic performance and potential largely to perceptions of class background, based on certain cues gleaned from interacting with the students.

School History and Perceptions of Students

How teachers perceived the social class of students also stemmed from their understanding of the history of the school. Recall from chapter 3 that teachers shared among themselves an oral and local history of the school, which most participated in learning and teaching to new staff. This history related especially to the socioeconomic and racial changes the school had experienced since it first opened in the 1970s. These changes represented a classic case of white flight—many white residents near Matthews had moved away as more racial/ethnic minority residents moved in (Farley et al. 1994). Ms. Delaney, a white administrator, described this white flight and its affect on the school: "When Matthews first opened it was a white middle-class school. Can you believe that? . . . Maplewood was once a suburb of Balcones City. Then, as minorities started wanting to get out of rough areas, a lot moved here. Then the whites said, 'We don't want to live next to *them*,' and moved even further out. . . . Matthews was one of the first schools [in the district] to feel this change, and we've been through it. Now we've got these other middle schools calling us up, saying, 'Help—we don't know what to do!' [*laughs*]" (Interview, October 1, 2001).

Teachers at the school tended to associate this change, either implicitly or explicitly, with a more problematic student population. Ms. Delaney, in the excerpt above, for example, implied that the poorer and minority student population presented new and different problems for Matthews. Other teachers were more explicit and saw the current students as more troublesome—"wilder" in the words of one teacher. In either case, the history of the school framed a perception for many teachers that the most economically advantaged and stable families had left the area of the school. According to this view, Matthews was currently populated with poorer and more difficult to manage students. Corresponding to teachers' association of apartment dwelling with impoverished and difficult students, mentioned before, many teachers attributed this change to the growth of apartments in the area. Ms. Phillips, for instance, described how and when apartment complexes came to dominate the area: "Around the mid-1980s they sold off a lot of the empty land near the school. The developers came in and they turned it all into apartments because that was the way they thought they could turn the quickest profit. The apartments started advertising one dollar move-ins, and this brought a lot of low-income people in" (Interview, November 26, 2001).

Black teachers also described the changes at the school and linked these to the proliferation of apartments. Interestingly, however, African American teachers such as Mr. Caldwell more directly described apartment dwelling families as black and Hispanic: "They moved out here in Maplewood—a bunch of whites— to get away from everyone else. But the mistake they made was building a bunch of apartments. So, people who could only afford to rent moved out here. So now, if you look at the schools, all the students are black and Hispanic" (Interview, April 24, 2002). While Ms. Phillips connected apartments to low-income families without specifying race, Mr. Caldwell specifically cast apartment dwellers as black and Hispanic. Mr. Caldwell also described the previous population of the neighborhood as white, without clarifying class background. White teachers tended to stress that the previous population was white and wealthy or middle class. This discrepancy reflects how white and black educators at Matthews talked differently about race and class in this context, especially regarding white residents. White teachers tended to emphasize class differences more in their discussion of white people in the history of the neighborhood, whereas African American teachers tended to characterize whites especially in terms of race.

In previous research on the impacts of race and class in schooling, Julie Bettie (2002) compares white working-class students with Mexican American working-class students in a mixed-race school. Although Bettie notes that the class background of white working-class students hindered their upward mobility through education, she argues that these students still benefited from their race. For instance, she states that "white working-class students can escape tracking more easily [than Mexican American working-class students] because their class does not as easily appear encoded onto the body" (Bettie 2002, 420). Thus, according to Bettie, the whiteness of students may signal a relatively high class status regardless of their actual class background. But do educators with different social backgrounds and in different social contexts interpret the links between whiteness and class in the same way? My findings from Matthews suggest that in this context educators held very different views and interpretations of whiteness and class background.

Perceptions of the Class Background of White Students

Context and past experiences thoroughly influence our perceptions and understandings of social characteristics. How we view others in terms of race, for example, is strongly patterned by social interaction and contact between those groups we consider racial. The less contact people have with those they consider to be from a different racial group, the more likely notions of basic racial distinctions and stereotypes will persist (Allport [1954] 1958). Perhaps because of infrequent and fleeting white/nonwhite social interaction, people often perceive others very differently depending on if they consider them to be from their own racial group or a racial "out-group" (Hill 2002). In this way, "race," along with the particular ideas it might represent, becomes part of how we organize our social experience. Our past race-based experiences congeal into what Mark Hill calls "a powerful social prism" that "filters" our perception of those we consider racially different from ourselves (2002, 106). For teachers, such a prism could refract different understandings and interpretations of the class background and academic ability of their students. Indeed, racialized experiences and understandings appeared to tacitly guide black teachers and white teachers at Matthews, who expressed discrete perceptions of white students in this predominately minority context.

In particular, black and white educators tended to view the class background of white students at Matthews quite differently. White educators I talked to thought most or all of the white students at Matthews were poor, whereas African American educators thought they were middle class. Recall from earlier in this chapter that Ms. Phillips, a white teacher, described the white students as poor and noted that she thought most of them lived in rented apartments. Mr. Wilson also thought that white families in the area had low incomes and were drawn to the area because of affordable housing:

EDWARD MORRIS: Now, the few whites that are still here—what do you think their income level is? Are their families sort of holdouts from before the change, or . . . ?

MR. WILSON: Well, this is a predominately low-income area, and those that are here, whatever race, are probably of that group. So, I don't think they are holdouts, but just for those families the availability of housing in the area is what they can afford. (Interview, May 15, 2002)

Ms. McCain expressed a similar view:

EDWARD MORRIS: What about the few white and Asian students who are here? Do you think they're from the same SES as the others, or . . . ?

MS. MCCAIN: The school once had a large Asian population, but they moved. Most white students—yes, they're from the same SES as the other students. I have some of these [white] students. One young man I know—they have like five kids, and the girl the same way, just like the other kids. For the most part I think their parents probably bought a house here in like 1978, when it was real hot. And then they were blue-collar, so they didn't have the same opportunities to leave like the other whites when it started changing. (Interview, April 26, 2002)

Thus, white teachers thought that white students at Matthews came from economically disadvantaged families who could not find better housing elsewhere. This perception indicates that many white teachers at Matthews understood white families in the area as a particular type—those who lacked the resources or ambition to live in a "better" neighborhood and were therefore particularly unfortunate. These families could not or would not seize opportunities to live in wealthier and whiter areas, which made their competence suspect to many white teachers. Mr. Simms, who possessed a rather candid style, expressed his perception of the white students and their families very directly:

EDWARD MORRIS: What do you think about the white kids who are still here— like we were talking about [a white student] before—do you think they're just middle-class holdouts that don't want to move, or . . . ?

MR. SIMMS: No, they're from low-income families, too. . . . To say it bluntly, they're what you would call "trailer trash" [laughs]. (Interview, May 8, 2002)

Although Mr. Simms was the only white teacher to actually use the term "trailer trash," the other white teachers' comments, albeit more careful, express a similar perception of these students as poor and unfortunate.

White educators' perceptions of the families of white students at Matthews as poor, or "trashy," contrasted sharply with the perceptions of African American teachers and administrators. Black educators, such as Ms. Remier, assuredly told me that the white students at the school came from middle-class backgrounds:

MS. REMIER: Yes, [the white families] have been here for a while [interruption— telephone]. What was I saying? Oh yes, they've been here—if we have thirty, maybe five have moved in recently.

EDWARD MORRIS: What do you think their income level is then?

MS. REMIER: Oh, they're middle-class. (Interview, May 16, 2002)

Ms. Boyd also thought the white students were middle class and used their performance on the Texas Assessment of Academic Skills (TAAS), the state achievement test, as evidence:[3]

EDWARD MORRIS: What do you think the SES of [white and Asian] students is?

MS. BOYD: I would say—the Asian kids, probably upper middle. The white kids, middle to upper middle. You don't see the poverty as much with those students. And I know, like if you look at the TAAS scores, the white kids and the Asian kids here score phenomenally on TAAS. (Interview, May 10, 2002)

In this quote, Ms. Boyd describes the primary way teachers assessed student class background—through what the students looked like. As I have described previously, teachers at Matthews remained acutely aware of student appearances. Based on Ms. Boyd's assessment, it seems that the perception of race, a highly socially visible characteristic, shaped the perception of social class. White (and Asian) students did not *appear* poor to Ms. Boyd or other African American teachers. Instead, African American teachers thought white students looked middle class. This perspective contrasts sharply with Mr. Simms's perception of these same students as poor "trailer trash." For white teachers, the perception of race also shaped the perception of class, but in the completely opposite way regarding white students. Most of these white teachers thought that white students attending this predominately minority "inner-city" school must come from especially disadvantaged backgrounds.[4]

Also in this quote, Ms. Boyd, similar to other teachers, connects class background to academic performance and uses one as proof of the other. She links race to class and achievement through the presumption that whites and Asians at the school were middle class in part because of their achievement test scores. However, as I have noted, the TAAS performance of white students at Matthews was not outstanding. For example, as table 3.1 in chapter 3 shows, in 2001 white eighth graders did have the highest passing rate overall on TAAS, but seventh graders had one of the lowest passing rates.[5] In addition, the passing rates of white students at Matthews were considerably lower than the state average for whites in virtually every subject. In 2001, for example, 67 percent of white seventh graders at Matthews passed all TAAS tests for that grade, versus 92 percent of white seventh graders statewide.

Directly after my interview with Ms. Boyd in which she described the performance of white students as "phenomenal," I met with Ms. Delaney to look at the school's TAAS scores, which presented an interesting contrast:

After I finish my interview with Ms. Boyd, I go to Ms. Delaney's office and discuss the TAAS scores, which have just come in. She has only the overall scores at this point as well as the math scores broken down by subgroup—race, economic disadvantage, etc. She tells me that the only subgroup that went down [from the last year, 2001] was white students, and they are actually the lowest scoring racial subgroup in math. Ms. Delaney appears surprised by these results and says, "Yeah, the weird thing is, if we're just looking at math scores, it's our white student subgroup that's actually keeping us from 'recognized' [a relatively high designation within the Texas system of accountability]." She adds [*with some hint of irony*] that the school needs to think about how to raise their white students' scores. I find this particularly interesting because, in my interview just before, Ms. Boyd told me white students performed very highly at the school. (Field notes, May 10, 2002)

I do not mean for this analysis to criticize Ms. Boyd for being "wrong" in her assessment of the academic performance of white students. Rather, I want to highlight that this was her perception, despite the fact that white students at Matthews appeared to only achieve average results on TAAS. In fairness to Ms. Boyd, as I discuss next, white students did marginally outperform others in many subject areas. In my observations, however, teachers at Matthews continued to have very different perceptions of white students academically and interacted with them differently in classrooms.

How Teachers Evaluated and Interacted with White Students

White students at Matthews exhibited marginally higher achievement than their minority peers in some areas. In the 2000–2001 school year, eighth-grade white students at the school did have the highest passing rate on TAAS for "All Tests" of any racial subgroup (see table 3.1). However, seventh-grade whites did not perform substantially better than their peers and were even the lowest performing subgroup at the school in math. In 2002, white students' passing rates for "All Tests" improved somewhat in both grades but were still among the lowest in certain subjects (see table 3.2). According to my observations and school records, white students were overrepresented in accelerated "pre-AP" courses,[6] but plenty took "regular" courses, and some, who were classified as special needs, took remedial "resource" courses as well. Student academic behavior at Matthews ranged from complete disengagement from classroom activities to active "ability shows" (Tyson 2002) to gain teachers' attention and demonstrate aptitude. White students, like other students at Matthews, displayed behavior across this continuum.

While white students did not appear particularly unique compared to other students academically, I found that teachers of different racial backgrounds perceived the white students differently in terms of their academic ability.[7] Interestingly, the African American teachers I spoke to evaluated the white students more highly than the white teachers did. During my classroom observations, white teachers never described a white student to me as intelligent or talented. African American teachers, by contrast, did this with frequency, such as in the following examples from my field notes:

> Ms. Boyd's class. Students are writing a murder mystery from different angles. They are brainstorming in groups to come up with a story. Ms. Boyd, a black woman, sits down next to me and points out Damien, a black boy, whom, she says, "just can't sit down" and gets in trouble a lot. She also talks to me about Greg, the lone white student in the class. Ms. Boyd contrasts Damien with Greg, whom she sees as a good student. She says, "That boy over there, Greg, he's always saying something funny. He's real bright." (March 8, 2001)
>
> Ms. Taylor's class. There are twelve students, including one blonde white boy named Jeremy. Jeremy yells out answers to all the questions. He is very persistent and keeps trying to get the correct pronunciation for the word "caricature." He demands a lot of attention from Ms. Taylor. Jeremy wears his pleated khaki pants pretty high up over his hips, and his shirt is tightly tucked in. (March 30, 2001)

After class I talk to Ms. Taylor, a black woman, about Jeremy, who is relatively new to the school and whose family has moved around a lot. I ask, "Is his family in the military or something? I can't believe he has traveled that much." Ms. Taylor answers, "I don't know, but something like that. I joke that his dad is a spy. He knows a lot, though. . . . He knows a lot about other cultures. . . . But his family thinks he will stay here until the end of the semester, and maybe even until he finishes high school, which is good because he is very *bright*—smart as a whip."

African American teachers also called on white students frequently in classes, even when African American students were also eager to answer:

> Mr. Kyle's class. There are twenty-two students in the class, including one white girl named Valerie. Valerie is very petite, with light brown hair tied back in a loose ponytail. She sits with a black girl and a Latina girl, both of whom are pretty quiet. During the course of the lesson, the teacher, an African American man named Mr. Kyle, calls on Valerie the most of any student, and she provides the most correct answers. Despite her diminutive size and quiet voice, Valerie is not afraid to volunteer—her hand shoots into the air like a rocket at every question. She has tough competition from an African American girl named Chartrice, though, who also seems very bright and is eager to answer. But Mr. Kyle calls on Valerie the most, and he calls on her frequently early on in the class. After a while he seems to realize that only a few students have been talking, and he tries to spread the questioning around more. (Field notes, October 10, 2001)

Black teachers tended to give white students very positive feedback in the classes I observed. As with Mr. Kyle in the example above, they often called on white students first and with regularity. They also often responded positively to the remarks and schoolwork of many white students in classrooms. In my observations, African American teachers regularly described the work of white students as exceptional, such as in the following excerpt from my field notes: "Ms. Lewis' class. The class is doing power-point presentations on careers. Ms. Lewis, a black woman, has invited parents to come see the presentations for extra credit for their child. She asks John to go first, because his mother is there, and he completes his presentation with no errors. Ms. Lewis seems to think it was one of the best presentations. She tells his mother, 'Now, I used John's as a model for other students to look at because he did everything I asked for and even finished it early. He did a very nice job'" (November 14, 2001).

I observed several of Ms. Lewis's classes with parents present, but this was the only time that I heard her directly praise a student in front of his or her parent. She was very cordial to the other parents, all black and Latino, and thanked them for coming, but did not give them any evaluation of their child's work, as she chose to with John.

I observed the student mentioned above, John, in several other classrooms during my time at Matthews and will discuss him more in the chapter 6. He appeared to be a fairly good student who took regular classes in seventh grade and pre-AP classes in eighth grade. In my conversations with white teachers, however, they never described him as an exceptional student. For example, a white teacher named Mr. Lang taught a pre-AP English class that John took. Mr. Lang once picked a few students to do their English presentations for me. He claimed that these students—all African American girls—had developed the best presentations. Although he mentioned that John's presentation was good, Mr. Lang did not consider it one of the best.

The racialized difference in teachers' evaluations of white students was also evident in the end-of-year honors announced at the eighth-grade graduation ceremony, which I described in the introduction. Matthews, like many middle schools, organized its teachers into teams made up of teachers of different subjects who all taught the same group of students. At the end of the year, each team selected two students whom they considered to be the best all-around students. Although whites composed only 3 percent of the student body that year, two white students were selected among this group of eight elite students: John, mentioned above, and Samantha. There were only eight white students out of 258 total students on the teams that selected John and Samantha as exceptional students. Interestingly, black teachers predominated on each of these two teams. In contrast, a team of predominately white teachers chose two Asian American students as their best students.

Indeed, unlike black teachers, white teachers did not appear to perceive white students as academically distinguished. Overall, the white teachers I observed almost never singled out white students to me for praise, even if these students took pre-AP classes or other teachers considered them good students. Instead, white teachers tended to mention African American girls as exceptional students. On occasion they also mentioned Asian American students—in my observations, East Asian boys were the only students teachers described to me as "geniuses" (Ms. Cohen, for instance, once described a Chinese boy named Jamie to me by saying, "He's a genius—Mensa material"). The few times a white teacher did mention a white student to me, they implied that the student was organized, but not necessarily bright, such as in the following example from my field notes:

> Ms. Scott's class. Ms. Scott, a white woman, sits down next to me and goes through all the students in the class, loudly proclaiming their strengths and weaknesses. Among those she thinks are the better students, she seems to describe many of the boys: Pablo, a Latino boy; Ricky, a tall black boy with glasses; and Tony, an Asian boy whom she sent to the office are described as "bright." Many of the girls are described as "conscientious" or "hard workers," except for an Indian girl wearing a head scarf. She is described as "very bright," and Ms. Scott mentions that she went to school in India last year because her parents wanted her to become more enriched in Indian culture. Ms. Scott tells me that Martha, the lone white student, is the oldest of seven children. She describes Martha as organized and says that she likes to make sure that things get done, "like an oldest child would." (April 5, 2001)

In this example we can see some intersections of gender and whiteness, with the white girl described not as "bright," but as well organized and conscientious, reflecting institutional perceptions and rewards for girls to exhibit neatness and self-control. This example is one of the only times, however, that a white teacher told me of the academic strengths of a white student in any way. In contrast to black teachers, white teachers seemed to overlook these students academically. In my observations white teachers did not call on white students frequently and tended to not discuss them with me.

Discipline of White Students

As I will discuss in more detail in the following chapter, black and Latino boys were the most persistently and harshly disciplined groups at Matthews. White girls and boys tended to avoid much scolding and punishment, but certainly not entirely. The discipline of white students appeared to follow certain patterns, and adults at Matthews differed in how they disciplined these students. Specifically, in my observations, white teachers and administrators tended to chastise white students for behaviors that black teachers tended to ignore. Sometimes, this discipline took the form of minor scolding or reprimands in classrooms: "Mr. Wilson's class. There are fourteen students, including one white girl named Ashley. Ashley is much more boisterous than other white girls I've seen and is laughing and talking the whole time. She mostly talks with Randall, a black boy near her. Randall gets reprimanded several times during this, but Mr. Wilson, a white man, also sternly reprimands Ashley, which prompts the entire class to yell 'Oooh!' in unison. It seems that Ashley does not get scolded very much, at least not as much as Randall" (Field notes, January 31, 2001).

The social-class-based displays of individual white students influenced the discipline they received. Some white students, through their interactive style, choice of clothing, and friendship groups, seemed to signal to observers a type of "street," persona. This persona incorporated styles of dressing and speaking commonly associated with urban black youths, styles which I describe in more detail in chapter 6. Elements of this street persona included wearing baggy, oversized clothing and long, noticeable chains. It also included walking with a "strut," or rhythm, and speaking in a way similar to many African American students at the school, what many would call "black English" (Labov 1972). Interestingly, white students enacting this style were especially susceptible to discipline from white teachers, but not necessarily from black teachers.

One white student of this type was Jackson. Jackson was a large boy with light brown hair whom I introduced in chapter 1. Jackson, as the reader will recall, marked "White" on the student survey form I distributed, and in the "Other" space he wrote in "white chocolate." Jackson very much portrayed this "white chocolate" racial identity. He hung out with African American friends, used black English in his speech, and wore gold or silver chains outside his shirt. Through his dress and demeanor, Jackson enacted a tough, street-oriented interactive style. Black and Latino boys who projected a similar street style tended to be closely monitored and disciplined by adults. The more I observed Jackson, however, the more I noticed differences in how teachers and administrators reacted to him. Interestingly, these differences related especially to the teachers' racial background. White teachers tended to interpret and interact with Jackson more negatively, whereas African American teachers tended to ignore his transgressions or discipline him lightly. According to my observations and school records, Jackson did "get in trouble" quite a bit, but white educators seemed more concerned with him than black educators, such as in the following example:

> I get there just as the kids are moving to advisory (homeroom). Several adults are in the halls telling kids to get to class and tuck in their shirts. I am standing near Ms. Oates, an African American administrator. She tells a short black boy who walks by, "Get to class, and tuck in that shirt,

please." Then Jackson roams by wearing a blue headband with his shirt not tucked in. He does not have advisory in [this part of the school]. But Ms. Oates does not tell him to tuck in his shirt or get to his advisory. Ms. Oates then tells another black boy to tuck in his shirt and asks why he is over here and not in his advisory in [another part of the school]. She tells him to get to class. (Field notes, January 16, 2002)

In this example, Ms. Oates simply appeared unaware of Jackson and focused her disciplinary attention on black boys instead. An explicit part of the dress code, as I will analyze further in chapter 5, dictated that all students must tuck in their shirts. In this excerpt, as in many other instances, Jackson gets away with it. In the final year of my research, Jackson, along with several black boys at Matthews, began wearing headbands similar to those worn by many (mostly African American) professional basketball players at the time. Headbands fell under a gray area in the dress code, and the document I collected from Matthews delineating the dress code did not specifically mention headbands. However, I saw several black teachers and administrators tell black boys to take off their headbands or confiscate them. Jackson, by contrast, often wore his with impunity. Later the same day as in the field note above, however, I saw a white teacher reprimand him for it: "It is between classes and Ms. McCain, a white woman, is standing outside of her classroom. Jackson tries to enter the class initially, but Ms. McCain says "Uh-uh—wrong class—and get that headband off!" Jackson turns to go to his correct class, but does not remove his headband. (Field notes, January 16, 2002). Thus, while a black administrator had all but ignored Jackson's behavior earlier, this white teacher made sure to reprimand him for being in the wrong place and violating the dress code.

Jackson was one of the few white students I saw African American school officials reprimand at all, however. Many seemed to identify that he could engage in troublesome behavior, but still treated him with kid gloves, such as in the following example: "Ms. Rogers' class. Jackson is hanging out in the classroom before class begins, his shirt untucked as usual. He is getting some sort of note from Ms. Rogers, a black woman, to go to his next class (or to get out of this one—I'm not sure which). Ms. Rogers asks her student aide, a black girl named Rachael, to escort Jackson to his next class. She says, "Make sure he goes to class, 'cause he'll play all day if you let him" (Field notes, December 3, 2001).

White adults at the school, by contrast, often identified Jackson's behavior as more serious than African American adults did: "I am tutoring for the class of a white teacher named Ms. Jacobs, which is in the library that period. I notice that several kids are running around the library (which has Ms. Jacobs's class and another class in it) as I'm tutoring. The kids running around include Jackson, who is hitting some other kids with a rolled up notebook. The scene is somewhat chaotic, and the teachers seem unable to control all of the kids.

Mr. Newman, a black administrator, comes in at one point and looks menacing, but does not say anything to Jackson" (Field notes, May 10, 2002). I go over to Ms. Jacobs's room at the end of the period to drop off some information on the tutoring session. She thanks me and apologizes for the commotion in the library, which she seems somewhat upset about. She says, "Yeah, that kid in the gray sweatshirt [Jackson] wasn't even in either class—he was just roaming the halls!" I tell her I know him from other classes, and she continues, "Yeah, we called the front office and they never did anything about him!"

Black boys (and Latino boys) engaging in behaviors similar to Jackson's were often sternly reprimanded by black teachers and administrators. It appeared that, primarily because of his whiteness, black educators hesitated to view Jackson as a problem or punish him. White educators, by contrast, found Jackson far more disagreeable and unruly than black educators did.

The reluctance of African American teachers to discipline white students, especially through formal channels such as referrals to the assistant principal's office, is understandable considering the power whiteness undoubtedly represented to these teachers, even in a predominately minority context. A desire to avoid retaliation by white parents might have influenced black teachers to avoid disciplining white students. This perspective makes particular sense when considering the southern legacy of Texas—a legacy in which African Americans have been forced to use extreme caution in their interactions with whites. African Americans in Texas, similar to other southern states, have historically been expected to show deference to whites, with harsh consequences often resulting if they did not (Glenn 2002). The 1998 racially motivated murder of James Byrd, a black man, in the east Texas town of Jasper serves as a grim reminder that such consequences remain even in the post–civil rights era. Although no black teachers stated it outright, I suggest that the racially charged historical and contemporary context played a role in black teachers' apprehension to discipline whites.

Similarly, on a more local level, black teachers' perceptions of the school district administration appear to have played an additional role. As I stated in chapter 3, the Matthews attendance zone served the highest minority and highest poverty area of the Maplewood School District. Several African American teachers complained about the conservative and white-dominated leadership of the school district, which they claimed had not adapted to the racial diversity of students in the district, especially at Matthews. Mr. Caldwell, for example, called the district "a very racist school district" (Interview, April 24, 2002). This perception of racism imbedded in the district organization and hierarchy would understandably influence African American teachers to avoid confrontations with white students and their parents.

Perhaps coupling contextual understandings from local and extra-local levels, black teachers also perceived a broader institutionalized racism that benefited white students in general, including those at Matthews. For example, I asked an African American teacher named Mr. Neal if he thought the white kids at Matthews were like the other kids there in terms of their disadvantages. He replied, "No, because they [white kids] get the benefits of the system. I'll see these black boys around here and they are always thumping and hitting these black girls. But you won't see them thump a white girl. Why? Because they've learned that the system will be against them if they mess with a white girl" (Field notes, March 1, 2002).

I suggest that many African American teachers at Matthews viewed white students the way Mr. Neal suggests black boys did—as privileged by the system. This perceived institutionalized privilege, combined with an understandable apprehension of white retaliation, may have influenced black teachers to avoid much discipline of white students. Based on contemporary and historical cases of harsh retaliation against African Americans who criticized or "messed with" white people, the noncritical way African American teachers interacted with white students at Matthews makes perfect sense.

Conclusion

To sum, many white teachers at Matthews viewed white students as poor and their families as rather unfortunate. In my observations, white teachers did not react especially positively to these students. They tended to overlook white students academically, while focusing more disciplinary attention on them than African American teachers did. For many white teachers, white students' markers of social class appeared to hold a particular stigma (Goffman 1963), which influenced teacher-student interaction. White teachers remained especially aware of cues which marked these students as impoverished, inner-city residents. Hairstyles, methods of speech and interaction, and especially living in a predominately minority and low-income area seemed to shade the whiteness of many of these students for white teachers (see Hartigan 1999; Perry 2002). The whiteness of these students did not, in my observations, act as a form of privilege in the eyes of most white teachers. Instead, they viewed white students in this setting as somewhat anomalous and extended more positive attention to students of other racial groups.

This is consistent with the argument, elucidated in chapter 2, that many people, especially many white people, consider poor whites particularly aberrant and backward. Hartigan argues, for instance, that it remains popular for white people to invoke the term "white trash" to distance themselves from "whites who [have] disrupted the social decorums that have supported the hegemonic, unmarked status of whiteness" (1997, 317). At Matthews, white students and their families seemed to represent a disruption of these "decorums" through their proximity to urban African Americans and Latinos in residential location and interactive style. Many white teachers interpreted the unique social location of these white students and families as indicating serious poverty and misfortune. I propose that this teacher perception, which highlighted a presumed disadvantaged class background, influenced the less than positive way white teachers interacted with white students at Matthews.

Echoing the discussion of hegemonic whiteness in chapter 2 of this book, I should place these teacher perceptions in historical and cultural context. Many people have historically viewed poor whites in a unique way—as white trash. Beginning in the mid-nineteenth century, it became increasingly popular for people, especially white people, to discursively separate themselves from the white poor. Concern with poor, "feeble-minded" whites steeped among white elites in the United States during the eugenics movement of the late nineteenth century (Rafter 1988, 1992). Eugenically influenced beliefs were popular during this time primarily among middle- and upper-class whites, who feared that the proliferation of "inferior" (i.e., poor) whites threatened to corrupt the supposed purity of whiteness (N. Foley 1997). This history suggests that poor whites are often viewed with special repugnance because they threaten the hegemonic status of whiteness (Newitz and Wray 1997). Similarly, I suggest that residential location and stylistic sensibility, interpreted as outward markers of class background and disconnection from hegemonic modes of being white, can alter the perception and rewards of whiteness.

In contrast to white teachers, African American teachers at Matthews tended to describe white students there as middle class and reacted positively to them. I argue that for many black teachers at Matthews, the whiteness of white students represented high social status. They did not interpret the geographic location and social styles of these white students to indicate a disadvantaged background. Instead, African American teachers considered white students among the highest in the school in terms of income level, achievement, and self-discipline. This is not surprising when one considers the salience of race for most of these teachers. Their awareness of the impact of race appears to have influenced them to view white students as privileged in multiple ways. Many African American teachers appeared to assume that whiteness—even in this setting—represented educational advantage and status and carried with it the privileges of "the system," in the words of Mr. Neal. Interestingly, black teachers did not tend to describe themselves as part of this system that bestowed privileges on white students, even though they mediated these students' educational experiences. I propose that this may have obscured for black teachers how their own perceptions and actions might have actually helped construct white students' systemic benefits, particularly in terms of achievement and discipline.

I should not overstate the benefits African American teachers extended to white students, however. For example, I did not observe much depth in the relationships between black teachers and white students. In many ways, black teachers devoted more attention and mentoring to nonwhite students, especially African American students (see Quiocho and Rios [2000] and Antonio Goldsmith [2004] for the positive impacts of minority teachers on minority students). Although I frequently observed black students coming to black teachers' rooms during off periods to visit or to ask for help with an academic or emotional problem, I did not see this with white students and black teachers. While not necessarily forging an emotional bond with white students, many African American teachers just assumed they were good, well-disciplined students and treated them this way. The particular advantages for white students stemmed from these assumptions and manifested primarily in classroom interactions, not in conscious efforts to spend more time and energy on white students.

While social class indicators were strongly related to teachers' judgments and treatments of students academically at Matthews, perceived race actually served as one of the most important of these indicators. Whiteness symbolized a particular class background for students in this context, although the background it suggested differed according to the race of the perceivers. As I have mentioned, much previous research, in education and other areas, has attempted to separate race and class into independent effects, arguing that one has a greater impact than the other on an individual's chances of accruing social rewards. This chapter shows that in interaction at Matthews, race and class worked in concert, with the interpretation of one influencing the interpretation of the other. Further, how these concepts acquired their particular interconnected meaning—and treatment associated with this meaning—depended on the local context and the social backgrounds of those interpreting it. This suggests that perceptions of race and class can vary considerably, and these variations can influence particular patterns of advantages and disadvantages.[8]

Teacher perceptions of students relating to race and class have very important impacts and can affect student progress in academic areas such as grades, test scores, and ability-group placement (Alexander, Entwisle, and Thompson 1987; Muller, Katz, and Dance 1999; Oakes 1985, 1995; Oates 2003; Rist 1970). My evidence from Matthews expands this perspective to emphasize how students' race and class intertwine in shaping these processes and how teachers' race plays a vital role. The literature on teacher perceptions has not focused on how African American teachers perceive white students, nor on how white teachers perceive poor and working-class white students, particularly those physically and socially close to minority students. Through this omission, many have generally assumed that teachers tend to forge more productive academic relationships with students of their own race. My observations from Matthews suggest that teachers' race matters, but not in the ways typically supposed: white teachers might view white students they perceive as poor with some disfavor, whereas black teachers might extend advantages to these students in certain situations. The importance lies not in race as an essence, but in how race acquires meanings in different contexts and how people's racialized experiences shape their development and understanding of these meanings.

This chapter highlights the importance of interpretations of local history and geographic patterns on how teachers perceive the students they teach. These interpretations provided the guidelines through which educators approached and understood different groups of students at Matthews. The unique case of white students in this minority neighborhood and school has underscored this process, as white teachers tended to consider this group unfortunate because of *their* interpretations of the neighborhood, and black teachers tended to consider this group far less unfortunate because of *their* interpretations of the neighborhood. Thus, interpretations of race combined with interpretations of neighborhood history to shape student-teacher interactions. The particular interactions observed at Matthews perhaps reflect the particular residential patterns of that location. But because patterns of segregation and white flight continue in communities and schools nationwide (Reardon and Yun 2001; Reardon, Yun, and Eitle 2000), the impact of similar interpretations of local history could surface in more settings. How educators and others make sense of neighborhood history appears to shape interpretations and reactions to race and class in interesting and important ways.

The evidence from Matthews suggests that whiteness, and the particular advantages associated with it, are not monolithic. Local history, neighborhood composition, and the racial background of powerful gatekeepers (educators, in this case) may all work to mitigate or enhance white privilege. Whiteness relies primarily on context to gain its meaning, and on patterns of interaction associated with that meaning. Further, different people may develop different interpretations of whiteness and different reactions to it. These interpretations and reactions matter for how whiteness becomes stratified within itself, exalting some forms over others. The hegemonic, or most powerful, form often represents residential separation from nonwhites, economic success, intelligence, powerful social connections, and "normal" white ways of speaking and behaving. Marginalized forms represent deviations from these factors. Interestingly, black teachers at Matthews tended to place white students within the framework of the hegemonic form, probably because they highlighted the power whiteness affords to anyone with white skin. White teachers, in making sense of this unexpected minority of white students, placed them within a marginalized form of whiteness that deviated from the presumed typical and desired ideals of the hegemonic system.

This chapter shows how perceptions of whiteness can be differentiated by perceptions of social class. But did whiteness, overall, still result in certain educational privileges compared to nonwhiteness? In the next chapter I explore one schooling process that tended to centralize and privilege whiteness, particularly because it focused on the presumed inadequacies of students perceived as poor and racial/ethnic minority. This process lies in the school's disciplinary practices, which I have touched on in this chapter but not examined in detail for all groups of students. Indeed, as the next chapter will show, race and class, as well as gender, intersected to frame teachers' perceptions of student behavior and elicit different expectations for different students. This process overall subtly framed white students as harmless, gender-appropriate, and more easily compatible with school norms.

5

"Tuck in That Shirt!"
Race, Class, Gender,
and Discipline

Teachers commanded students to "tuck in that shirt!" virtually every day that I observed at Matthews Middle School. As I have mentioned, the school had a uniform dress code policy that required students to keep their shirts tucked in at all times. This created a constant battle between students, who despised this rule, and most teachers, who saw such rules as crucial to maintaining a sense of order in the school. Students often tried to avoid keeping their shirt tucked in through various strategies. Often, for instance, after returning from the bathroom, a student might conveniently "forget" to tuck their shirt back in. Or, a student might tug and pull on the shirt so much during the course of the day that it eventually hung over their waist—still technically tucked in, but not demonstrating the neatness for which the rule was intended. In the previous chapter, I examined how teachers perceived the numerical minority of white students at Matthews. This chapter focuses more explicitly on a particular *process* that tended to normalize whiteness and middle-classness in this predominately minority, working-class environment: school discipline. Although ostensibly trivial, I eventually saw the disciplinary policy and the conflicts it fostered as a key tension at the school, and one that reflects a larger debate over social mobility, inequality, and white privilege in education.

This debate does not just concern uniform dress codes. In broader terms, it concerns the struggle over bodily display and bodily discipline related to race, social class, and gender. Research in education has stressed the relationship of bodily display and behavior to advantages and disadvantages in schooling. As I discussed in chapter 2, one line of this research stems from the theorist Pierre Bourdieu and his concept of cultural capital. Cultural capital encompasses the set of cultural knowledge, skills, preferences, and styles that come from family and community background and can facilitate a person's success in various social fields, including education. From this perspective, middle-class and white students tend to be regarded as possessing more cultural capital (or more useful cultural capital) to contribute to their school success. Another line of research relevant to bodily display and behavior stems from the theorist Michel Foucault and his concept of bodily discipline. Discipline, in Foucaultian terminology, refers not just to "getting in trouble" in school, but to the entire purview of how schools shape, monitor, and regulate student activity. As noted in previous research, school disciplinary processes often identify working-class students of color as problematic (in need of discipline), while establishing middle-class white students as the implicit norm (A. Ferguson 2000). Matthews' instructions and regulations, as we shall see, exemplified such disciplinary regimes.

In this chapter, I analyze how educators at Matthews identified students deemed deficient in cultural capital, especially in terms of manners and dress, and attempted to reform these perceived deficiencies through bodily discipline. Although many school officials viewed this discipline as a way of teaching valuable social skills, I show that disciplinary concern differed importantly according to a student's race, class, and gender and that students often experienced their persistent and inconsistent regulation as confusing and alienating. Importantly, white students at Matthews tended to elude much discipline, and whiteness appeared to indicate possession of cultural capital in itself through an association with normal and appropriate comportment. In this way, whiteness served as an invisible but powerful "cultural resource," to use the words of Annette Lareau and Erin Horvat (1999, 42), although this was differentiated by teachers' perceptions of social class, as I examined in the previous chapter, and gender, as I will explore further in this chapter.

I utilize the concepts of cultural capital and bodily discipline here simply because they best explain the struggles I documented over dress and behavior at Matthews. Teachers at Matthews were very concerned with the students' dress and manners—important aspects of the set of cultural skills and knowledge that Bourdieu calls cultural capital. Based on this concern, teachers constantly regulated the ways that students spoke, dressed, and behaved (demanding tucked in shirts for instance), a process similar to what Foucault would call bodily discipline. I argue that these concepts, used together, can shed considerable light on how assumptions of cultural competencies and resultant disciplinary practices differ according to perceptions of students' race, class, and gender. These perspectives also illuminate a hidden curriculum that tends to frame white students (although importantly mediated by class and gender) as well mannered, "good" students, subtly centering hegemonic notions of whiteness.

For example, white boys at Matthews often escaped the type of strict discipline and monitoring typically aimed at black and Latino boys, even when, like Jackson, they enacted similar "street-based" styles and unruly behavior. Perceptions of race and gender in this case triggered some educators to interpret white boys as docile and appropriate and black and Latino boys as irascible and aggressive even when both exhibited similar behavior and dress. Thus, perceptions of cultural competency or deficiency based on race resulted in disciplinary practices that tended to privilege white boys in this case. As I discussed in the previous chapter, white teachers tended to monitor the transgressions of white students more closely than did African American teachers. However, because African American teachers composed a majority of the faculty of the school, this meant that white students overall avoided much discipline. Further, even for white teachers, black and Latino boys received the strictest and most persistent discipline. The students at the school whom teachers described as truly troublesome were nearly always Latino and African American boys.

This stemmed primarily from educators' preconceived notions of which students lacked cultural capital and required discipline. In this sense, Matthews somewhat unintentionally constructed some students as problematic and others as normative. The dress and behavior of white students overall, despite some variations according to class-based performance and gender, tended to be overlooked. Even white teachers, many of whom viewed white students in this environment as very unfortunate, directed most of their disciplinary focus on racial/ethnic minority students. In the arena of student dress and comportment—factors often related to perceptions of good students at Matthews—white students and those perceived as middle class were implicitly framed as standard and benign. Disciplinary practices thus constituted a key schooling process that furthered hegemonic notions of whiteness and white privilege.

The Importance of Dress

As I stated at the beginning of this chapter, hearing adults tell students to "tuck in that shirt!" was a daily, and virtually hourly, occurrence at Matthews. The phrase is peppered throughout my field notes, and although adherence to the dress code was not an initial concern of my study, I soon found it to be emblematic of the exhaustive focus on bodily discipline at the school. According to the principal, a survey of teachers conducted by the school just before I arrived found that dress code violations and discipline problems were among the top issues teachers wanted improved. Indeed, like other urban schools requiring uniforms, teachers and administrators at Matthews linked the dress code to student discipline and order in general (Stanley 1996). The school sent an information sheet entitled "Standard Mode of Dress" home to all students and their parent(s). This document states that the purpose of the dress code is to "ensure a safe learning environment" and "promote a climate of effective discipline that does not distract from the educational process." It describes the dress code and emphasizes in bold print that "baggy and over-sized clothing *will not* be

allowed" (emphasis in document). Students who deviated from this code, typically those who did not tuck in their shirts, were often spotted by adults and disciplined into compliance.

This nearly constant regulation of student dress and behavior bore striking
similarities to other studies exploring discipline in schools (e.g., A. Ferguson
2000; Martin 1998). The concept of "bodily discipline" employed by this
research examines how schools attempt to mold students, especially those perceived as lacking or resistant in some way, into embodying what school officials
consider proper comportment. Schools exercise this goal through persistent
discipline aimed at students' bodies, involving relentless surveillance and regulation of how students speak, move, and dress. All educational organizations,
particularly for younger students, feature some form of such discipline,
although some emphasize it more than others. Matthews certainly exhibited a
manifest, persistent focus on the regulation of its students, particularly regarding dress and behavior.

School officials at Matthews spoke of this discipline as constructive and
helpful for students. This sentiment surfaced especially in how educators at
Matthews attempted not only to restrict some forms of student dress, but also
to encourage others. Beyond simple adherence to the dress code, Matthews
emphasized teaching students how to dress "well." For example, the school held
what they called a "dress-for-success" day, when students were invited to dress
as one might for the "business world." Also, many teachers encouraged their
students to dress up when giving a presentation in class, and teachers at the
school were expected to dress up (often in suits and ties for men and dresses
and nylons for women), lending a tone of formality to the school. Matthews
devoted entire assemblies to instructing students on how to dress properly,
such as the following:

> The school has an assembly for advisory period. The point of the
> assembly appears to be to remind the students of how they should dress
> for upcoming events. Ms. Gilroy, a black assistant principal, first lectures
> the students on how they have strayed from the dress code recently and
> need to get back in line. "We need shirts tucked in and I don't want to
> see boys with earrings." Several kids laugh at this, but she isn't joking at
> all—this is all presented as if it were deadly serious. Next, she describes
> how the kids should dress on the upcoming "dress-for-success" day. "You
> need to dress like you would for a business. You may have something
> cute, but it may not be appropriate for what you would wear in a busi-
> ness setting." Next up to speak is Ms. Thomas, a white teacher who is in
> charge of the graduation ceremony. She tells the kids where and when
> the ceremony is and that they must be present in school that day to grad-
> uate. Then, she continues with a lengthy description of what the kids

should wear. She says there will be no cap and gown and emphasizes repeatedly that the kids should be in "Sunday dress," and "what you wear to church." Finally, another teacher gets up and continues the dressing theme to talk about the upcoming dance, again emphasizing "appropriate" clothing. (Field notes, May 11, 2001)

Thus, beyond the uniforms, the school sought to discipline the kids into wearing clothing considered appropriate on non-uniform school days and events. As Ms. Gilroy indicated in her disapproval of boys wearing earrings, instructions in how to dress well typically fell along gendered lines. Many teachers aimed an emphasis on etiquette and modesty toward girls (the school also had an etiquette club composed mostly of girls, for example). In terms of dress, this probably stemmed from the fact that school officials feared girls might wear revealing clothing that could be construed as overly sexual. Boys clothing, on the other hand, tended to be read, potentially, as more purposefully oppositional. Adults feared that boys, especially black and Hispanic boys, might wear something considered inappropriate to school and formal events, such as oversized pants that sagged below the waist. Several African American men and women at the school encouraged boys to dress like "gentlemen," even giving some practical advice such as not wearing white socks with a suit. In this sense, these boys appeared to educators to display "marginalized masculinities," interpreted as overly coarse and aggressive (Connell 1995). Educators aimed to reform these styles and behaviors into what were perceived to be more mainstream masculine forms. School officials viewed the gendered prescription of dress for both girls and boys as a central part of teaching the students appropriate manners. In this process, they distinguished street styles, which they deemed brash, from more appropriate, conservative styles of dress and behavior.

For example, the school had two popular student clubs, called the Proper Ladies and Gentlemen of Excellence, that, according to their statements of purpose, aimed to groom members into "gentlemen" and "ladies." Members of these clubs wore formal attire (suits for the boys and dresses for the girls) to school on the days of their club meetings. Field notes from my observation of a dual meeting of these clubs show their emphasis on how to dress and act in gender-appropriate ways:

After school. Ms. Adams, the faculty sponsor of the Proper Ladies, has a very strong and humorous personality. When she wants the kids, boys especially, to behave, she takes off her heeled shoe and shakes it at them. She begins the dual meeting by going over the proper attire for the girls in her group to wear at a private graduation ceremony for the two groups. She warns them, "Don't come in here with no hoochie-mama dress all tight up on your butt!" and demonstrates by hiking her skirt up and walking around with large, bold steps as the kids laugh. She continues to lecture the kids on attire and personal hygiene while they laugh: "Ladies, don't come with your hair all poofy—comb your hair or get a hairstyle at the beauty parlor." "Ladies, and this goes for you gents too, I don't want to have to smell nobody—make sure you smell good." "Boys, don't wear white socks with your suits. There is nothing that looks worse than white socks with a suit and dark shoes—and don't even think about wearing tennis shoes."

Ms. Adams instructs the girls on how to sit at the ceremony, which is mostly an instruction on how not to sit. Ms. Adams demonstrates what she calls the "hoochie-mama" way to sit with her legs spread open rather wide, one arm hanging off the back of the chair, and the other hanging between her legs. She then demonstrates the proper way to sit "like a lady," as she says, with her legs together and tucked back and to the side, and hands clasped on her lap.

Ms. Adams also instructs the girls to "make sure you are wearing a slip and panties!" This provokes raucous laughter, especially from the boys, who are suddenly more interested. Ms. Campbell, a teacher who assists Ms. Adams, says, "You laugh, but some ladies didn't do this a few years ago and they were in white dresses—now imagine what all you could see!" Ms. Adams then instructs the girls individually on what type of slip to wear depending on their skin color. (Field notes, April 12, 2001)

In addition to sponsoring formal events such as graduation ceremonies and dances, the clubs also took students on tours of area colleges. They implicitly connected proper dress and grooming to college life, particularly in fraternities and sororities. The club sponsors, two African American women and an African American man, sought to provide their student members with extensive knowledge of how to dress and conduct themselves appropriately in college or the business world. They seemed to assume, perhaps because most students at the school were from poor or working-class backgrounds, that many of their members lacked this knowledge—how to sit formally, for instance, or what socks to wear with a suit. Thus, while the clubs disciplined the bodies of their members, creating more acceptable embodiments of masculinity and femininity, they also attempted to transmit what they saw as a form of cultural capital, aiming to familiarize their members with the type of dress and conduct that could be linked to upward mobility.[1] Cultural capital can refer to something possessed inwardly, in the form of tastes and sensibilities, as well as something expressed outwardly, through dress, behavior, and speech (see, for example, Bernstein 1986; Heath 1983). Many adults at Matthews appeared to focus on this second aspect of cultural capital and attempted to mold students into exhibiting particular ways of dress and behavior.

Previous research suggests that cultural capital acts as a valuable commodity for students in schools, enhancing their educational achievement and attainment (Farkas 1996; Lareau 1987; Lareau and Horvat 1999; Lewis 2003b; Roscigno and Ainsworth-Darnell 1999; see Lamont and Lareau 1988 for a review). Students bring cultural styles stemming from their family and community background with them to school, and these styles aid some in school more than others. Working-class and minority students take certain knowledge, as well as ways of speaking, behaving, and dressing, from their community context. Their communities require such skills for survival and cultural participation. However, schools require a different set of skills and knowledge, which working-class and minority students are often seen to lack. Further, the forms of cultural skills and styles useful in working-class and minority communities often become impediments within the school context, hampering these students' access to education. Matthews composed an interesting place to explore this perspective because this school actively attempted to transmit cultural capital in the form of dress and manners to students.

Many adults at Matthews saw making students adhere to the dress code and use proper manners as a way of providing them with social skills, including those needed for future employment. An African American teacher named Mr. Kyle, for instance, said this: "They have to learn to follow the rules. Like coming to class late—I won't tolerate that. Or tucking in the shirts, . . . it's a rule and you have to learn to follow it. I teach them to say 'Yes Sir' and 'Ma'am.' It's a way to model good behavior, so that way they're not just book smart. If they go for an interview for a job, they've got to learn how to talk to someone. . . . If you know how to be respectful, you can get a job" (Interview, March 22, 2002). Thus, many adults thought that teaching students "the rules" of dress and manners, including adherence to the dress code, was an important way to prepare students for future success. Educators viewed their discipline of student's bodies, especially in appropriately masculine and feminine ways, as transmitting cultural capital—modeling the type of dress and conduct that could be linked to upward mobility.

However, prior research on educational inequality exposes many latent and negative impacts of disciplinary regimes, even when educators describe them as helpful or necessary. I observed some unintentionally detrimental results of discipline at Matthews. First, the constant emphasis on dress and manners appeared to detract from the time spent on instruction. I noticed, for instance, that teachers at Matthews emphasized manners and discipline most in lower-tracked "resource" classes, composed of students who were learning at a sluggish pace:

> Seventh-grade resource math, Ms. Anderson. The class appears very slow—they are still working on graphs and subtraction in the seventh grade. Ms. Anderson tells me they are two to three years behind grade level. The teacher has extremely good discipline for a resource class, but often the class seems more geared toward comportment than subject

matter. A black boy yawns, and Ms. Anderson tells him not to do that because it's rude. Soon after, she tells a black girl, Janice, to tuck in her shirt. At one point, Marcus, a black boy with an Afro hairstyle, asks Janice for a pencil. Ms. Anderson instructs Marcus to ask for the pencil "nicely." He complies and asks Janice quietly, "Please, can I have a pencil?" The one Hispanic girl in the class, who has not spoken all period, asks to use the bathroom sometime in the middle of the class. She goes, and when she returns, Ms. Anderson instructs her to tuck in her shirt, which is only partially tucked in. The girl sighs and tucks it in. (Field notes, October 10, 2001)

In this resource class, like others I observed, discipline in dress and manners often took precedence over the kids learning basic, essential skills such as subtraction. Resource classes appeared especially to emphasize behavior, which teachers assumed problematic with lower-tracked students, but this emphasis drained time that these kids urgently needed to catch up and master basic academic competencies.

Second, I noticed irregularities in the focus of disciplinary concern and the various forms this discipline took. Scholars have noted that a hidden curriculum of race, class, and gender often undergirds school discipline (Martin 1998; A. Ferguson 2000). Schools tend to regulate working-class and minority students more frequently, and differently, than others. I observed such a hidden curriculum of discipline at Matthews. School officials did not appear concerned with the dress and manners of all students in the same way. Instead, disciplinary action differed according to intersections of students' race, class, and gender.

Disciplinary focus at Matthews took three general forms, which I will discuss in detail. First, educators were concerned with "ladylike" behavior and dress, especially for African American girls. Second, educators were concerned with threatening and oppositional behavior and dress, especially for African American and Latino boys. Third, many school officials assumed that some students, particularly white and Asian American students, required little discipline in their behavior and dress. In what follows, I discuss each of these forms and then consider the impacts of such discipline through exploring the perspectives of students and teachers. For much of this chapter, I will not discuss white students or whiteness explicitly. Instead, I attempt to show how whiteness and middle-classness became the default categories of normalcy through the school's problematizing of students perceived as poor and racial/ethnic minority. As Margaret Andersen (2003) reminds us, critical studies of whiteness should not relegate people of color to the sidelines, but instead reveal how white privilege inextricably stems from nonwhite disadvantage. As we shall see, the disciplinary practices aimed at racial/ethnic minority students tended to frame these students as inappropriately masculine or feminine and divergent from school norms and expectations. These practices, I argue, subtly centered hegemonic notions of whiteness and middle-classness, constructing white privilege.

Acting like a Young Lady

Aside from "tuck in that shirt!" the most prevalent phrase in my field notes was some variation on "act like a young lady!" Adults invariably directed this reprimand at African American girls—I never recorded it directed at Latina girls, Asian American girls, or white girls (although members of these groups did receive other reprimands). Educators at Matthews appeared to perceive many black girls as inadequately feminine, which resulted in much monitoring and correcting of black girls' actions. Teachers and administrators often instructed black girls in how to sit and get up properly, dress appropriately, and speak quietly. The following excerpt illustrates how African American girls were instructed to act in gender-appropriate ways:

> As the students are working on Texas Assessment of Academic Skills (the state achievement test) worksheets, Brittany, a black girl wearing dark blue shorts and a white shirt, gets up from her desk to get a tissue. The action seems perfectly innocuous to me, but Ms. Taylor, a black teacher, sees something unacceptable in it. Before Brittany can get to the tissue box, Ms. Taylor makes her go back to her seat, sit down, and then get up "like a young lady." Brittany seems rather confused by this and seems about to protest, but eventually obeys with some huffing. She gets up much slower this time and with her legs closer together, looking at Ms. Taylor the whole time for assurance that everything is correct. Ms. Taylor says, "Thank-you, Brittany." And Brittany proceeds to get her tissue while still looking rather perplexed. (Field notes, March 21, 2001)

In a subsequent interview I conducted with Ms. Taylor, she explained why she considered it necessary to teach some girls ladylike behavior, as she did with Brittany: "I talk to them about how a lady talks and walks. I used to put books on their heads, so they would learn to stand straight and sit straight, with no slouching. I've had to say things like 'close your legs—ladies don't sit like that.' But there is a lack of parental involvement, and they are not taught these things. Some come in here as young ladies already, but some have to learn" (March 27, 2002).

Ms. Taylor's statement reflects an emphasis on persistent discipline as a way of molding students' bodies into appropriate representations of gender— training them to become "ladies." Because of perceived deficiencies stemming from their parents, Ms. Taylor saw it as part of her task as a teacher to mold some students into exhibiting this gender-specific behavior: "Some come in here as young ladies already," she emphasizes, "but some have to learn." Thus, according to Ms. Taylor, teachers had to recognize and identify which students did not possess the cultural capital of appropriately gendered behavior first, and then discipline them into learning this behavior.

According to my observations, the girls that adults thought needed to learn this ladylike behavior tended to be African American. I never observed white girls, by contrast, admonished for "unladylike" activity, even from white teachers. One black teacher named Mr. Neal told me in a conversation that black girls in particular required instruction in acceptable manners: "Mr. Neal talks to me about how important he thinks it is for black, urban youths to learn how to express themselves in acceptable ways, like through video and film. He tells me, "Like the black girls here—they lack social skills. The way they talk—it's loud and combative. They grow up in these rough neighborhoods and that's how they act to survive. We need to teach them more social skills because that's one of the big problems now" (Field notes, March 6, 2002).

Mr. Neal's statement echoes Linda Grant's (1984) finding that teachers tend to focus on improving the social skills of black girls. Other studies have argued that black girls and women in particular often grapple with demands that they must constantly display politeness and respectability (Collins 1998, 38–43; Horvat and Antonio 1999). My findings from Matthews indicate that, interestingly, this concern over the social skills of black girls stemmed from African American teachers as much, if not more so, as teachers from other racial backgrounds. Further, African American teachers appeared most interested in providing black girls with the training to improve these social skills.

However, many teachers, both black and white (as the reader will recall, the school had very few Latino or Asian American teachers), interpreted black girls as overly "loud" and aggressive. This was one of the main ways adults thought African American girls deviated from their model of ideal feminine behavior, and it often stimulated reprimands: "I am walking outside among the portable buildings that are used as classrooms while the school building is under construction. It is between classes, and the kids are running around to find their friends and laughing boisterously, as usual. A group of three black girls runs by Mr. Henry, a black teacher, laughing loudly. This upsets him and he scolds them as they leave: 'Hey! You need to act like young ladies!'" (Field notes, May 11, 2001). In this passage, Mr. Henry is offended not only by the volume of the girls' laughter, but also by the speed of their movements. He implies through his gendered scolding of this behavior that the girls could conduct themselves in a more acceptable and gender-appropriate manner if they slowed and controlled their bodily movements and spoke quietly.

In discussing the hidden curriculum of bodily discipline, Karin Martin (1998, 495–496) states that "this curriculum demands the practice of bodily control in congruence with the goals of the school as an institution. . . . [I]n such a curriculum, teachers constantly monitor kids' bodily movements, comportment, and practices." Martin goes on to show that the preschools she studied restricted the behavior of girls more than boys. Similar to these findings, I observed that school officials at Matthews restricted the movements of girls, encouraging them to exert greater self-control over their bodies and cover less physical space. While the children in Martin's (1998) study were predominately white, however, at Matthews adults directed these bodily restrictions primarily at black girls, providing white girls comparatively more freedom. Adults seemed to interpret the actions of black girls as overly aggressive and bold. They tended to read the behaviors of these girls as more stereotypically masculine than feminine and attempted to discipline African American girls into exhibiting behavior closer to stereotypical femininity, which involved restricting their movements, dress, and speech.

Interestingly, however, this concern with the gendered comportment of black girls did not seem to affect teachers' perceptions of them academically. While black girls were frequently disciplined, they were not viewed as particularly "bad." African American girls were overrepresented in pre–advanced placement classes, and teachers frequently described African American girls in regular classes as among their best students. In fact, stereotypically masculine behavior, such as the boldness many adults interpreted as loud, often seemed to benefit black girls in the classroom. As Mr. Wilson, a white teacher, said in describing some of the best students in his class, "The black girls up there I don't worry about; they can fend for themselves. They're loud, but they're a sharp bunch and do their work." Although many adults viewed training girls to act like young ladies as putting them on a path to upward mobility, their discipline of African American girls seemed to curtail some of the very behaviors that led to success in the classroom. White girls, by contrast, as I will discuss later in this chapter, did not tend to endure such bodily discipline and correcting. Whiteness appeared to make their femininity seem appropriate, and although teachers did reprimand white girls, such reprimands did not imply that something was wrong with their expression of femininity. As a result, these students were framed as standard—already possessing the skills and styles appropriate to their gender.

Symbolizing Opposition

In contrast to girls, adults saw many boys at Matthews as bad and occasionally threatening. This was particularly true for Latino and African American boys. In my observations, members of these groups were the most likely to get in trouble. Contrary to the corrections adults directed at girls, discipline of boys often entailed stern reprimands and referrals to the office for punishment. As I discussed in chapter 2, Ann Ferguson (2000) has compellingly documented how African Americans boys are often subject to strict, negative disciplinary regulation because of their presumed aggressive tendencies. I observed black boys at Matthews to be frequently reprimanded in classrooms, even when other students were also being disruptive, such as in the following example from the class of a white teacher named Ms. Klotz:

> Ms. Klotz reprimands a black boy named Oliver, who wears a large gold chain with a cross, baggy pants, and sports prominent gold teeth in the front of his mouth. He, another black boy named Dwayne, and a black girl had been throwing pens at each other. The girl got up to attack Oliver, and he fled while she chased him around the room. Interestingly, Ms. Klotz singled out Oliver, and not the girl, to scold for this disruption. . . . Eventually, Dwayne, who has his hair pulled back in a small, tight ponytail, wears a sweatshirt and baggy khaki pants, and has gold teeth like Oliver, is written up by Ms. Klotz for attempting to leave the room. I think it is just a threat, though, and Ms. Klotz does not send him to the office, but tells him to get back to work instead. Dwayne says he can't find his work, and Ms. Klotz appears frustrated with him. Ms. Klotz diverts her attention momentarily to tell Oliver to stop throwing pens and get to work. Meanwhile, Dwayne is professing his innocence to Ms. Klotz in the form of an impromptu rap: "Every day I wake up and pray, wake up and pray, don't ever smoke hay . . ." Ms. Klotz appears tired of Dwayne and instead attends to another student in need of help. Dwayne mostly hangs out for the remainder of the class period, talking and rapping, but not doing any work. (Field notes, April 11, 2001)

I observed Ms. Klotz disciplining both Dwayne and Oliver regularly, including sending them to the office. In this example, she appears to just give up on Dwayne without continuing to encourage him to do his schoolwork. She also singles out him and Oliver for reprimands over other possible candidates. A black girl was also involved in their mischief, but did not appear to be seen as the source of the problem by Ms. Klotz. Further, the same class contained a group of two white boys and an Asian American boy whom I also observed throwing pens at each other across the room (apparently a popular middle school pastime). I did not see any of these boys scolded by Ms. Klotz in this instance, or other in any other classes I observed.

The discipline directed at African American and Latino boys was strongly influenced by their presentation of self, however, especially through their choice of clothing, hairstyle, and response to authority (Goffman 1973; West and Fenstermaker 1995). In the example above, both Oliver and Dwayne, frequently disciplined students, wore baggy pants, gold teeth, and chains and, in Dwayne's case, enjoyed rapping, even when responding to teachers. In previous research on youths and education, Julie Bettie (2000, 2002, 2003) utilized the notion of "performance" to conceptualize categories of difference and inequality, especially social class.[2] This formulation of class as a mode of display is useful for considering how observers develop meanings of others in terms of social class. At Matthews these meanings were particularly important when kids displayed what I call a "street" persona. This persona, which included baggy pants, noticeable gold or silver chains, and rhythmic styles of walking and speaking, could often symbolize opposition to school. As with the example of Dwayne and Oliver, black boys displaying these styles appeared to get in trouble much more frequently than boys who did not display these markers.

Interestingly, however, educators at Matthews appeared to perceive a street style as particularly threatening when enacted not only by black boys, but also by *Latino* boys. Ann Ferguson (2000) has noted the strict discipline that schools tend to press on African American boys, perceiving them as overly aggressive. At Matthews, though, I saw that school officials considered many Latino boys as equally, if not more, dangerous and subjected them to constant surveillance and bodily discipline. Teachers interpreted Latino students who projected a street type of persona through their dress and behavior, similar to what I mentioned with Dwayne and Oliver, as indifferent toward school and often threatening. Some markers of this persona included overtly gang-related dress such as colored shoe laces, colored or marked belts, or a white T-shirt or towel slung over a particular shoulder. Other markers of this street style for Latinos were less directly related to gang involvement, however, such as baggy Dickies brand pants, shaved or slicked-back hair, or refusal to maintain a tucked in shirt.

Whether students actually had involvement in gangs or not, educators viewed styles interpreted as street-oriented as potentially oppositional. This interpretation is reminiscent of a story Angela Valenzuela recounts in her book *Subtractive Schooling*. Valenzuela (1999) describes a mismatch between styles of dress in a poor, Latino neighborhood and that neighborhood's high school. The school became concerned with student dress and eventually outlawed baggy pants. Valenzuela describes a Latina student named Carla who continued to wear pants that were slightly baggy, but also "neatly pressed"; school officials eventually scolded Carla for her "ganglike attire," which they interpreted as conveying opposition to the school (1999, 83). But Valenzuela explains that Carla merely tried to dress like everyone else in her community: "Far from trying to make a statement, she is doing her best *not* to stand out in her neighborhood" (1999, 83). Carla's dress, while normative in her neighborhood, acquired a connotation of opposition within the school's walls, causing educators there to assume Carla did not care about school.

Similar to the school's interpretation of Carla's "ganglike" opposition in Valenzuela's research, educators at Matthews remained particularly suspicious of Latino students and connections to gangs and oppositional values, using clothing style as the primary indicator. At Matthews, Latino boys (more so than

Latinas, as I will discuss) provoked fear from many teachers, especially when suspected of gang involvement. One white teacher, for example, referred to a group of Latino boys she called "gangsters" as "the type that would get back at you." Although many adults and students told me that most kids affiliated with gangs at the school were just "wannabe's" rather than full-fledged members, teachers viewed any gang-related students as potentially dangerous and disciplined them accordingly. Students suspected of being in gangs were almost always Latino boys and were monitored closely by adults, especially in terms of their dress:

> Mr. Pham, an Asian American teacher, is overseeing a class made up of students from different classes who have finished TAAS testing early. The kids are very unruly, and few heed Mr. Pham's directions for silent reading. During the course of this "class," Mr. Pham reprimands several Latino and African American boys, but no girls. Carlos, a Latino boy that another teacher told me is affiliated with the Crips, a large and popular gang, has been sent to the office. Towards the end of class he returns and, in a show of defiance, immediately untucks his shirt. Mr. Pham eventually notices and tells him to tuck it back in. Carlos complies somewhat, tucking half of it in. As the class draws to a close, Carlos walks by Mr. Pham and fakes like he will hit him. Mr. Pham seems to not notice amid all the other activity. (Field notes, April 26, 2001)

After class I talk to Mr. Pham about Carlos causing so much trouble. Mr. Pham says, "Yeah, well, he's in a gang. I won't back down to him, though."

Most students at Matthews resisted the dress code prescription to tuck in their shirt. However, teachers interpreted the resistance of Latino boys, such as Carlos, as particularly threatening and oppositional. This appeared to stem from adults' assumptions that Latino boys in particular were more likely to be involved in gangs than other groups of students. As Mr. Wilson told me, "The gang influence is bad among these Hispanics."

School officials often interpreted clothing as gang related when worn by Latino boys. Ms. McCain, a white teacher, expressed this view in an interview. I asked her, "How do you identify gang members?" She replied, "Like if one of my Hispanic boys is wearing all blue—blue shirt and blue pants . . . the Crips—they wear blue rag" (Interview, April 26, 2002). Students of many different race and gender backgrounds wore blue clothing at Matthews, occasionally all blue. Yet Ms. McCain implies that she interprets such clothing to indicate gang membership only when worn by Latino boys. The combination of race and gender with dress in this case could signal the difference between a potentially dangerous student and a harmless one.

Several Latino boys at the school were, indeed, involved with gangs, including the Crips, and announced this verbally as well as through their bodily displays. However, many adults viewed Latino boys in general as having the potential for gang involvement or violence, even if they did not openly display gang markers. For example, in another class I observed with Mr. Pham, he reprimanded a Latino boy who was wrestling with another boy. The Latino boy protested, saying he didn't think he was hurting the other boy. Mr. Pham told him to stop anyway and added, "One day you're gonna hurt someone and not know it and go to jail." This particular Latino boy did not wear any salient markers of gang affiliation typically used at the school. However, Mr. Pham still interpreted his actions as overly aggressive and warned the boy that they could one day land him in jail.

Discipline and surveillance were especially directed at Latino boys who projected various elements of a street persona. This persona did not necessarily include direct gang markers, but almost always included wearing baggy Dickies brand pants. Many Latino and African American boys preferred this brand of pants and shorts, usually wearing them oversized and low on their hips. The choice of Dickies by these students suggests a class-based, "tough" identity because the brand is primarily marketed as men's blue-collar work clothing (see Hebdige 1979 for a discussion of other styles of clothing and class identity). Many adults at Matthews, such as Ms. Boyd, an African American teacher, interpreted Dickies negatively: "You know how they wear these baggy Dickies pants and stuff—you know where that comes from? It's like how they dress in prison. A lot of them see their older brothers or whatever in prison and that's what they pattern themselves after" (Field notes, April 20, 2001).

For Ms. Boyd, Dickies represented oppositional values. She viewed students who wore this brand as modeling themselves after criminals. Interestingly, I almost never saw Dickies worn by white students, and only by a few Asian students. The brand was overwhelmingly preferred by black and Latino students, usually boys. This parallels Ann Ferguson's (2000) finding that school officials viewed many black boys as "bound for jail." My findings from Matthews expand this view to include Latino boys and highlight how something as simple as a style of pants can indicate potential criminality when worn by black or Latino boys.

Bodily display, especially clothing choice, had a major influence on how educators viewed and treated Latinos. Clothing choices could lead educators to interpret Latinos as middle class and, therefore, well behaved. The few Latino boys who wore Dockers brand pants, dark sneakers or dress shoes, and kept their shirts tucked in signaled to teachers that they were good students. One Latino student of this type was named Thomas. Thomas projected a middle-class, "schoolboy" type of persona through his Dockers pants, tucked in shirt, and parted hair. Although I heard him called a "little nerd" by some of his classmates, he received positive reactions from teachers in class. Thomas was rambunctious and did have a few referrals to the assistant principal's office.

However, these referrals were not for severe and persistent behavior, and teachers did not interpret Thomas's actions as threatening.

Thomas serves as an example of how Latino boys, largely through their dress and manners, could signal to school officials that they were conscientious students and came from middle-class backgrounds. This class-based display was important because teachers seemed to hold more polarized views of the potential class backgrounds of Latino students than they did for other students. Many told me that Latino kids at the school could come from either relatively wealthy, upwardly mobile backgrounds or very disadvantaged ones. I mentioned in the previous chapter how a white teacher named Ms. Phillips described the white students at Matthews as poor and noted that she thought most lived in rented apartments. Further in the interview, Ms. Phillips also explained that she thought many of the school's Latino students were middle class or at least stable working class, and in a better economic situation than most of the white students:

MS. PHILLIPS: I'm pretty sure most of the white kids who go here live in apartments and are poor like a lot of the other kids. Now, if you drive through the neighborhood just down from here—the one with all the houses—it's all Hispanic. A lot of the Hispanic families here are home owners.

EDWARD MORRIS: So the white kids here are poorer than a lot of the Hispanic kids?

MS. PHILLIPS: Yes.

Similar to Bettie (2000), I found that many Latino students actively "performed" class identity and membership, especially through their dress. A middle-class performance displayed the students' possession of cultural capital in the form of dress and grooming, and this mitigated the discipline they received. By contrast, any display of a working-class street style for Latinos could lead educators to perceive them as oppositional. This was true for boys as well as girls, but appeared less acute for girls. Latinas who displayed a street style could be disciplined and seen as bad, but not as dangerous as Latinos who displayed this style. Teachers suggested that, although they did view many Latinas as connected to gangs, they did not see them as "ringleaders" or instigators of trouble in classrooms, or as overly aggressive. Some teachers even tried to protect Hispanic girls from boys they suspected of gang activity:

Mr. Wilson's class. This is a relatively small class of fifteen students. The Latino kids in the class, who compose about half of the students, sit on the far side of the room, away from where I'm sitting. Three Latino boys and one girl sit towards the back of two rows of desks, and two other Latina girls sit at the front of these rows, with some space between them. The three boys in the back include Roberto, a boy I have seen hanging out with Carlos [mentioned earlier] and whom some teachers suspect to be involved with gangs.

After a warm-up activity with some class discussion, Mr. Wilson has the kids do worksheets. It takes awhile for the kids to get to work, but most eventually do, except for the Latinos in the back, who haven't even glanced at their worksheets. Mr. Wilson ignores them for the most part. After a brief lull in which most students are quiet, Roberto and the Latina girl in the back, who wears baggy Dickies pants and has her long dark hair tied back except for two strands in the front, start throwing pencils at each other. Mr. Wilson threatens to write a referral for them. He generalizes this to the entire group in the back, telling the three boys they are going to need to talk to the assistant principal if they keep this up. He also informs the girl that she "maybe" needs to go as well. "You come here to play and not do your work, and then you get smart with me," Mr. Wilson says to one of the boys. The boys finally do some work toward the end of class.

After class I talk to Mr. Wilson. He tells me that he tries to separate the Hispanic boys in the back of the class from the two Hispanic girls at the front who, he says, want to do their work. "I try to give them as much positive reinforcement as possible," he says, "so they don't get under the influence of those boys." (Field notes, October 3, 2001)

As in this example from Mr. Wilson, teachers at Matthews did not tend to perceive Latinas as very troublesome. Mr. Wilson did not focus his attention on the Latina girl who was also throwing pencils with the boys and described the boys to me as the primary bad influence in the class. Teachers could view Latina girls exhibiting a street style as oppositional, but they did not see this as the tendency for Latinas in general. By contrast, they did view many Latino boys as inclined to opposition and having the potential to influence others in that same way. In this sense, masculinity appeared to magnify the street style for Latinos, attaching more of an aura of aggression and hostility to boys enacting this style than girls.

Self-Discipline and Benign Resistance

The hidden curriculum of discipline at Matthews meant that while groups such as black girls and Latino boys endured much surveillance and correcting, adults allowed other students comparatively more freedom, appearing to consider them already acceptable. This occurred especially for Asian American and white students. Interestingly, members of these groups who exhibited a street style received some reprimands, but not in the same harsh and persistent way as black and Latino students who displayed this style. Further, the form of discipline differed for white and Asian American students: I almost never saw these students disciplined in terms of *dress or manners*, even when I observed clear violations.[3]

School officials appeared to view Asian students at the school through the lens of the "model-minority" stereotype of high academic achievement and discipline (see Lee 1994, 1996). I never saw Asian American girls disciplined for behavior or dress—in many ways these girls exemplified the educators' ideal self-disciplined student. I rarely observed school officials discipline Asian American boys. Behaviors that adults frequently rebuked African American and Latino boys for (e.g., getting out of their seat without permission, being loud) often went unnoticed when engaged in by Asian American boys. Further, some Asian boys exhibited almost identical behavior and dress to Latino boys considered dangerous and gang affiliated, but they continued to be seen as good students.

One Pakistani student named Roshan, for example, dressed in a street-based style, including wearing baggy Dickies pants. Roshan could be quite disruptive in classes and received some discipline, but educators did not perceive him as very threatening, and I never saw him referred to the assistant principal's office (for serious infractions). Roshan often dressed in all blue and, I learned, had some leanings toward gangs:

> I am tutoring a group a group of boys that includes Roshan and two Hispanic boys named Arturo and Ramon. They have not done anything on their project yet, so I try to get them started writing some things down. Roshan asks why I am at the school, and I say I am volunteering to tutor and that I'm doing a research project at the school for college. Roshan then tells me that Arturo is in a gang and I should put that in my report. Ramon clarifies that Arturo is not really in a gang, but is just a wannabe. Ramon then asks me if there are gangs in college. I say no, chuckling a little. Ramon informs me that Arturo is going to get jumped after school by a rival gang, and Roshan confirms this. Ramon then tells me an important twist to this story: *Roshan* is involved with this rival gang, even though he and Arturo are both friends. (Field notes, April 15, 2002)

Thus, even when Asian American boys such as Roshan exhibited particular markers associated with gang affiliation, and in his case actually did have some involvement in gangs, educators still did not view them as threatening, potential gang members, especially compared to Latino boys.

Adults, particularly African American adults, rarely disciplined white girls or boys, although, as with Latino boys, this was strongly mediated by race and class-based performance. As I have mentioned, several white students at the school presented a working class or street type of identity, which included urban, hip-hop-based styles of clothing and speech. Although I very rarely saw these white students wear Dickies pants, some wore gold or silver chains outside their shirts, similar to those worn by many black and Latino students at the school, and spoke using expressions and a cadence similar to that of many African American students at the school, what many might call "black English" or "ebonics" (Labov 1972). White students affecting this persona tended to receive more disciplinary action than other whites.

One white student of this type, as I have mentioned before, was Jackson. Although I tried not to focus too much on this one kid, something about Jackson's style and personality fascinated me. In most situations he tended to exhibit a rather aggressive and cocky demeanor, displaying his toughness to other students through his disregard for most school rules. I became intrigued by how Jackson managed to avoid discipline when he displayed tough behaviors and styles, while other students, especially Latino and black boys, tended to receive stricter and more regular discipline for the same kinds of behavior. For example, although Jackson often wore his pants or shorts well below his waist and rarely tucked in his shirt, I never saw him scolded for it. He did get in trouble frequently for other reasons, however; and as I have mentioned, Jackson was one of the few white students black teachers would reprimand, although he always seemed to elude more serious consequences for his behavior. In a class where students were expected to give class presentations for individual projects they had worked on, Jackson and a black teacher named Ms. Lewis had the following exchange:

> After a few presentations at the beginning that Ms. Lewis seemed satisfied with, the rest have not pleased her—many students had multiple misspellings and failed to follow directions. Ms. Lewis is particularly angry with Jackson for his. She has already scolded him and moved him away from the class for causing a disruption. I notice, as he moves, that Jackson is wearing a large gold chain on the outside of his shirt and that his shirt is not tucked into his long baggy shorts. No one has told him to tuck it in. As Jackson starts his presentation, his clothes contrasting with many of the other students who have dressed up for their presentations, he tells Ms. Lewis, "I ain't finish." Ms. Lewis tells him to do it anyway. He attempts to, but has not done most of the things she asked for. Ms. Lewis scolds Jackson for this and seems fairly angry with him. However, Jackson resists her by talking back and raising his voice, saying, "I *told* you I ain't finish yet." Ms. Lewis, growing more agitated, responds, "But why did you tell me it was done last week when you weren't doing anything?" Jackson tries to mount a weak defense: "It was—I just had it somewhere else." Ms. Lewis tells Jackson to see her after class but, interestingly, when the end of class comes she forgets about it, and he goes free. (Field notes, November 14, 2001)

Teachers often reprimanded Jackson like this for not doing his schoolwork or being insolent. However, as in the example above, Ms. Lewis does not monitor or correct his clothing or mannerisms (she does not tell him to tuck in his shirt, for example). Nor does she pursue further, presumably stricter, discipline by talking to him after class or referring him to the principal's office. Most school officials did not appear to perceive Jackson as particularly bad or threatening. In fact, although some teachers watched him closely during assemblies, he was allowed to walk around rather freely and stand near the teachers at the same time they often warned other students to "get in your seat!" or "tuck in that shirt!" In fact, Jackson, despite his foibles, even served as an office aide in the final year of my fieldwork—a position granted only to students considered especially responsible and conscientious! Thus, Jackson's whiteness seemed to make his technically deviant (according to school rules) dress and behavior appear harmless and benign to many educators. Even white teachers, who tended to consider Jackson more recalcitrant than other teachers did, did not really view him as a threat—certainly not compared with many black and Latino boys displaying a street style.

The same class with Ms. Lewis contained another white student who spoke in a style similar to many black students at the school and hung out with many black friends. This student was a girl named Lisa. As I discuss further in chapter 6, Lisa often wore her dark hair in styles similar to those of many black girls at the school, such as in cornrows, she tended to hang out with black girls, and she spoke in a rhythm similar to her black friends. Teachers occasionally monitored and regulated Lisa's comportment, such as when she gave her presentation in Ms. Lewis's class:

> Lisa, who has her hair styled like many of the black girls in a sort of bun on top of her head, and is dressed up, goes next. The teacher, a black woman named Ms. Lewis, again tells the class how important it is to "look nice" when doing a presentation for a job. She gives Lisa quite a bit of coaching, including making her take off her jacket: "You do not wear a jacket giving a presentation for a job unless it is part of your outfit." Lisa reluctantly takes the jacket off. Then Ms. Lewis tells her, "Take your hand off your hip and stand up at the front—don't slouch." Ms. Lewis also asks why Lisa's parent didn't come (students were given extra credit if they brought their parent[s] to see their presentation). Lisa says she doesn't know. She then starts her presentation, which she goes through quickly. She speaks in a slight southern/black cadence—similar to most of the black students at the school, but also somewhat similar to the white students—sort of in-between. (Field notes, November 14, 2001)

Lisa certainly received bodily discipline in this instance, which differed from what I observed with other white girls. The "coaching" of Lisa's behavior parallels what I witnessed with many black girls and appears as an attempt to instill Lisa with knowledge of how to conduct herself in a business setting. However, this discipline differed from that directed at the black girls discussed before in that the adult did not label Lisa's actions specifically unladylike. Ms. Lewis, like most of Lisa's teachers, did not seem to assume she really lacked knowledge of how to act like a young lady. Although Lisa dressed and acted in ways virtually indistinguishable from many black girls at the school, adults did not interpret her behaviors as overly bold or aggressive. Lisa's whiteness, however non-stereotypical, seemed to indicate adequate femininity in itself.

As I have discussed, the type of discipline directed at white students depended largely on educators' racial backgrounds. With street-oriented African American girls, black teachers expressed more of an interest in teaching them the social skills to become young ladies. White teachers also reacted more sternly to girls who exhibited a street type of identity, but, interestingly, this did not result in warning these girls to act like a young lady. Some girls who portrayed this style, such as Lisa, did not receive much discipline from white or black teachers, although this was difficult for me to gauge because Lisa did not have many white teachers. However, another girl, named Melissa, who exhibited a street-based persona and whom I will discuss more in the next chapter, was often disciplined, and white teachers appeared to see her as more of a problem. I observed Melissa several times in Ms. Taylor's class, for example; Ms. Taylor was very interested in discipline and gender-appropriate conduct, especially for girls. I did observe Ms. Taylor reprimand Melissa a few times, but far fewer than for black girls in her class and never in the context of unladylike behavior that needed to be reformed. Mr. Wilson, a white teacher, reprimanded Melissa frequently in his class. He even pointed her out to me as a troublemaker one day and stated that she was failing his class (Field notes, May, 1, 2002). However, he did not describe Melissa's behavior as specifically unladylike. Thus, although differences emerged between teachers in their monitoring and assessments of white students, teachers in general did not frame white students as inappropriately masculine or feminine, especially compared to students such as black girls.

In her study of the disciplinary experiences of black children, Ann Ferguson states, "The closer to whiteness, to the norm of bodies, language, emotion, the more these children *are* self-disciplined and acceptable members of the institution" (2000, 72). In my observations, students such as Jackson and Lisa performed identities that deviated from stereotypical whiteness despite their white skin and categorization of themselves as white on a survey form. Because these students lived in this working-class, predominately minority urban neighborhood, they reflected and aligned themselves with their experience in this context, which produced an alternative projection of whiteness. Kids such as Jackson and Lisa embodied marginalized forms of whiteness, deviating in style and manners from the central, hegemonic, expected ways of being white. However, while this performance tended to slightly differentiate these students from other white students in terms of discipline, their whiteness still afforded them less concern and monitoring from teachers than that directed at most African American and Latino students, especially in manners and dress. As I discussed in the previous chapter, this differed somewhat depending on the teacher's racial background, which suggests that white teachers and black teachers had different measurements of how close white students in this context were to "whiteness." The hegemonic model of whiteness itself, however, remained in tact, and disciplinary procedures privileged those students most closely perceived to resemble it.

Consequences of Disciplinary Control:
Marginalization and Centralization

I have discussed how disciplinary practices at Matthews tended to differ according to students' race, class, and gender. But what are the impacts of this discipline for students? Research suggests that strict social control from school officials can unintentionally engender resistance from students, which causes the schools to perceive them as deserving even greater discipline (McNeil 1986). This cycle can perpetuate disengagement from school. When directed at historically marginalized student groups, such discipline may only perpetuate their marginalization and inequality within the educational system. At Matthews, black and Latino students were monitored most closely, which implicitly constructed other students, even street-oriented white students such as Jackson and Lisa, as less problematic. Such discipline itself, especially when strict and persistent, often provoked student resistance, which made the dress code, and policing of dress and manners more generally, appear ineffective. Ironically, this only convinced teachers that kids they perceived as recalcitrant required even more discipline.

Most teachers at Matthews supported the concept of a dress code and saw it as crucial to creating a sense of order in the school. Many actually thought that the main problem with the dress code was in its lax enforcement. However, a few teachers did not favor strict discipline in dress and manners. A white teacher named Ms. Scott, for example, said this when I asked why she thought so many adults insisted on making the students tuck in their shirts: "Because it's an easy battle. You might not be able to get them to sit in their seat and do their work, but you can make them tuck their shirt in. It's an easy way for teachers to assert their authority over the kids and make it look like they have control" (Field notes, February 1, 2002). Ms. Scott implied that teachers who did not have enough control over their students to make them do schoolwork could project a façade of control through regulating student clothing. Similarly, some teachers I observed made their students tuck in their shirts before going to lunch, while ignoring untucked shirts in their own classrooms. These findings emphasize how important teachers considered the visibility of student compliance with clothing rules and echo Foucault's assertions that "in discipline it is the subjects that have to be seen. Their visibility assures the hold of power that is exercised over them" (1995, 187). Students displaying tucked in shirts symbolized and embodied the control and order sought by the school.

In contrast to adults, virtually all the students I talked to at Matthews expressed displeasure with the dress code, especially the policy of keeping shirts tucked in. Most complained that the dress code made them physically uncomfortable and stifled their ability to express creativity. For example, I tutored Daniel, a Latino boy whom I mentioned in chapter two, on a persuasive paper he was writing against the school policy of maintaining a tucked-in shirt. I asked him why he thought adults cared so much about making the kids tuck in their shirts. He replied, "Because they think it makes us look like we're educated." When I asked him why he opposed that, he thought for a while and finally stated, "Because it doesn't matter what you look like to be educated; it's all up here [points to his head]." In contrast to adults at Matthews, Daniel viewed regulation in dress and manners as unnecessary and asserted that mental development itself should be the primary form of cultural capital that teachers transmit to students.

Student displeasure with the dress code often translated into resistance. This resistance, especially untucked shirts and baggy pants worn low on the hips, symbolized defiance to the school for many teachers. Mr. Simms, the white teacher who characterized white students at Matthews as "trailer trash," described baggy pants in the following way: "We've tried to get them to wear pants that fit around their waist, but that hasn't really worked. That baggy style with the pants hanging low came from the black community and the prisons—they use it as a way to defy authority" (Interview, May 8, 2002). Mr. Simms, similar to Ms. Boyd, claimed that the baggy style came from prison. But unlike Ms. Boyd, he also located its origins in "the black community," specifically connecting it to race. Although he thought this style originated with black prisoners, in other conversations I had with Mr. Simms he pointed out Latino kids who also used baggy pants as a mode of defiance. Thus Mr. Simms, along with other school officials, interpreted the race- and class-based street styles of black and Latino children, in particular, as purposely oppositional. Many educators seemed to think that purging these styles from the school would also purge the opposition.

Adult-student conflict over school and cultural standards of dress and behavior is exceedingly complex and probably reflects a mixture of misunderstandings as well as a dynamic of control and resistance. If students interpret the school as strict and uncaring, they could utilize clothing and behavior in ways that purposely oppose its authority. Youths, especially working-class youths, might use certain styles of speech, behavior, and dress to signal their resistance to middle-class norms, which they experience as oppressive (D. Foley 1990; Hebdige 1979; Willis 1977). Dick Hebdige's (1979) study of British sub-cultures, for instance, describes clothing as a particularly important form of class-based youth identity. Many working-class youths wear certain clothing, according to Hebdige, to challenge the "symbolic order" of bourgeois institu-tions. A similar form of style-based challenge, which I observed to be prevalent at Matthews, exists in the contemporary United States with hip-hop fashions such as oversized baggy pants (Dickies at Matthews), conspicuous gold chains and jewelry, and hooded sweatshirts to name a few. Although often misunder-stood and linked to gang activity, prison, or aggressiveness, I suggest that such styles often just reflect a youth identity that includes relatively innocuous resistance to adult, mainstream norms.

Similar to what Valenzuela (1999) found at the school she studied, most youth I talked to at Matthews wanted to wear baggy pants and untucked shirts not specifically to oppose the school, but because they described this dress as normative for youths in their neighborhood. Certainly these styles reflect some amount of resistance to adult norms, and perhaps white middle-class norms more generally. But adults at Matthews did not tend to perceive such styles as relatively innocuous rebelliousness, particularly when worn by black and Latino students at the school. This parallels other research finding that these styles can acquire a threatening tenor of opposition particularly when worn by minor-ity youths, especially black and Latino boys (Anderson 1990; Patillo-McCoy 1999). Meanwhile, white boys such as Jackson at Matthews also displayed a street style, resisted the dress code and many rules of behavior, but educators tended to interpret his and other white students' resistance as relatively benign, thereby framing whiteness, even in this alternative form, as safe and normative.

Disciplinary regimes and assumptions about cultural capital can frame some students as problematic and inadvertently push them away from school-ing, while framing others as "normal" and incorporating them within the school fabric. We know that, on a national level, some groups of students tend to engage and remain in school while others tend to disengage and often drop out. Latino boys, for example, have the highest high school dropout rate of any major racial/ethnic and gender group in the United States, at 32 percent in 2001 (U.S. Department of Education 2001). White boys, by contrast, have among the lowest dropout rates, at 7 percent—over four times lower than the rate for Latino boys (U.S. Department of Education 2001). Interestingly, at Matthews, educators tended to discipline Latino boys much more persistently and strictly than white boys. In my view this did not help to bond Latinos to the school. Based on these observations, I suggest that how educators interpret students' presumed cultural capabilities or deficiencies and attempt to reform them through bodily discipline can compose a key factor in influencing their attachment to school or alienation from it and, thereby, a key factor in reproducing hegemonic white advantages.

Indeed, the restriction of certain styles of dress at Matthews perplexed many African Americana and Latino students most subject to surveillance and discipline and led many to see the school as an alien, unfairly punitive institution. For example, I tutored an African American boy named Derek, who wore baggy Dickies pants and his hair in cornrows, on a position paper he was writing on school uniforms. Derek, a somewhat shy and thoughtful kid, explained to me why he was against the uniform policy during a tutoring session:

> I sit with Derek in the library, and he tells me his reasons why he is against uniforms. As I talk to him, I learn that he feels strongly about this and is not just making up reasons for the exercise. One of his reasons is that the kids already have clothes and buying extra uniform clothes makes it more expensive. Another is that the uniforms create a prison-like atmosphere in the school. He writes that you could compare the students to prisoners because of the control the school uses with uniforms and timetables: "They [prisoners] wear uniforms; we wear uniforms; they have a certain time to eat; we have a certain time to eat."
>
> I ask Derek to explain his point that the uniforms make kids feel like prisoners. He explains, "It's 'cause like everyone is wearing the same thing like in prison." I ask what specifically is bad about that. He responds, "Because it's like we did something wrong, but we didn't do anything. Prisoners are there because they did something wrong. We're just here to learn, we didn't do anything wrong, but it's like we're being punished." (Field notes, December 10, 2001)

While adults such as Mr. Simms saw the restriction of certain styles of clothing and behavior as eliminating prisoner-like defiance, Derek interpreted this discipline as creating a prison-like atmosphere in the school. Ironically, Mr. Simms and Derek seem to agree in their view of him being like a prisoner. However, in Mr. Simms case this view stems from a stereotypical assumption that guides disciplinary practice, and in Derek's case it stems from being a target of such practice. Foucault (1995) argues that disciplinary institutions such as schools and prisons intend to produce individuals who internalize discipline and regulate themselves. Similarly, the disciplinary practices aimed at students at Matthews, based on often stereotypical assumptions about their lack of conformity, seemed to produce students who internalized these very assumptions. Because some adults interpreted certain dress and behaviors as oppositional or inadequate and sought to discipline them away, students subject to this discipline often came to see themselves as oppositional or inadequate.

Conclusion

Schools teach children many lessons. These lessons often transgress the formal elements of overt curricula and instruct children on how to speak, what to wear, and how to move their bodies. Schools use persistent and subtle discipline to produce students who will embody this appropriate conduct. At Matthews, this form of discipline was so lauded by teachers and administrators it verged on becoming part of the overt curriculum. Many school officials helped implement and regulate dress and manners out of an expressed, genuine desire to help students.[4] Left hidden, however, were the assumptions of which students needed this discipline and in what form. Because educators aimed the hidden curriculum of bodily discipline at African American and Latino students, particularly those who did not display middle-class markers, this framed white (and Asian) students, along with students perceived to be middle class, as appropriately integrated within the framework of the school. This further meant that the behaviors and expressions of these students were not constantly regulated and corrected, giving them little reason to see the school as unfairly punitive and making much of their rebelliousness appear innocuous.

In this chapter, I have explored how race combined with gender and social class to form the assumptions officials used to guide their disciplinary practices (see Collins 1990, 1998). Although importantly modified by interpretations of social class through street styles, whiteness remained a normative category, implying appropriate behavior. Blackness, by contrast, seemed to indicate aggression and forcefulness. When combined with gender, this influenced perceptions of masculinity and femininity, leading adults to see black girls as inadequately feminine, for example. This was true not only with skin color, but also with self-presentation. Adults viewed students adopting a street persona as potentially dangerous and oppositional. They monitored this persona more closely with African American and Latino boys, however, whose race and gender alone already seemed to indicate their potential for dangerous resistance. When adopted by white and Asian American students, a street type of persona elicited some discipline, but appeared less menacing to many educators. Even when affecting this style, white and Asian American boys were often seen as harmless, and white and Asian American girls as well-mannered.

As I have discussed previously, interpretations of social class stemmed from educators' perceptions of students' styles as well as their understandings of the neighborhood and residential situations of student groups in this neighborhood. Class perceptions appeared to influence educators' views of Latino students in particular because many thought some of these students could be from middle-class home-owning families. Educators saw Latino students who manipulated their outward appearance to suggest such a middle-class background as good, well-mannered students, even when they exhibited unruly behavior. However, educators had very polarized views of Latino students, who could also be considered some of the worst and most dangerous students. My observations suggest that, in general, school officials viewed Latino boys as acutely oppositional. This perhaps stemmed from popular culture characterizations of urban Latino boys as threatening gang members (Fregoso 1993). While many Latino boys at Matthews were indeed involved with gangs, many were not. Yet all endured adult assumptions that, because of their race and gender, they had the potential for danger and should be monitored and disciplined accordingly. Overcoming this assumption required displays of cultural capital from Latino boys in the form of dress and manners not required of other students, especially white and Asian students, whose race often seemed to represent cultural capital in itself (see Lareau and Horvat 1999).

Whiteness and Asian-ness, although partially qualified by performative display, appeared to indicate docility, and normative masculinity and femininity. How educators interpreted a street-oriented performance from these students was important, however, and indicative of how this persona could signal class background. Interestingly, this street style appeared to tarnish the perception of docility and normativity of white students for white teachers more so than for black teachers. In this sense, white teachers appeared to approach this style as indicative of a lower-class-based, oppositional persona when enacted by white students, while black teachers appeared to view it more as artificial posturing. Whiteness, and the privileges attached to it, could be modified by such perceptions of gender and social class. But even alternative embodiments of whiteness did not carry the same stigma as a Latino boy walking with a strut and baggy pants or a black girl talking out of turn in class.

Such race, class, and gender assumptions actually worked to subvert the goal of many educators at the school to provide students with the skills to gain upward mobility. Many students targeted for disciplinary reform came to see themselves as incompatible with school norms. Like Derek, they appeared to internalize the discipline aimed at them, and while for some this led to self-regulation and complicity, for others it produced resistance and disengagement from school. As I will revisit in the concluding chapter, these findings question the efficacy of persistent discipline in dress and manners, especially when targeted according to race, class, and gender. Rather than creating opportunities for advancement, this practice only seems to bolster perceptions of poor and minority girls and boys as flawed in some way, and it has the potential to push many away from schooling. This hidden curriculum reveals quite an opposite view and treatment of white students. At Matthews most adults interpreted these students as normal, if not ideal. By not enduring the same constant monitoring and correcting experienced by their black and Latino peers, these students were afforded more freedom to learn and explore. Although their class-based displays did incur some monitoring, particularly from white teachers, these students generally received the privilege of adults not perceiving them as potentially problematic.

This chapter, along with the previous chapter, has concentrated on the perspective of adults vis-à-vis kids: their perceptions of students and schooling processes. We have seen how white students in this predominately racial/ethnic minority environment provoked different interpretations and reactions from educators based largely on how they perceived the class background of these students. Based on understandings of the neighborhood surrounding Matthews and the personal style of the students, some adults interpreted these atypical white students as embodying alternative, marginalized forms of whiteness. At the same time, even those white students exhibiting street-based personas did not provoke the same degree of concern, correcting, or apprehension (from white or black educators) as African American and Latino students displaying a street style. Although meanings of race and whiteness were altered according to class and gender at Matthews, the "benefit of the doubt" afforded to white students through disciplinary processes remained. However, as I mentioned in chapter 2, it is important to avoid portraying kids as just passively molded by schooling processes. What role did white students themselves play in deviating from hegemonic notions of whiteness or complying with and reinforcing them? How did students of color react to white students and participate in constructions of whiteness in this predominately nonwhite context? I intend to answer these questions in the next chapter, which explores understandings of whiteness in the peer culture of Matthews.

6

"White Chocolate": Meanings and Boundaries of Whiteness in the Peer Culture

When I began my fieldwork at Matthews Middle School I intended to study how race shaped students' academic experiences, especially for white students. I planned to base this study primarily on my observations of classroom interactions at the school. It initially seemed clear what would happen when I entered the school to begin this research. I would simply identify the race (and gender) of the students and the teachers in certain classes and record how they acted and reacted to each other, a fairly straightforward process in most studies I had read. However, none of my readings on race, education, or observational methods fully prepared me for what I observed. When I entered my first classroom at Matthews, an advanced placement course with a terrific teacher and impressive students, I looked over the classroom to identify students in terms of their "race"—but saw only multiple shades of brown.

The students of this class, which I later understood to be black, white, Latino, Asian American, and multiracial, at first appeared almost indistinguishable to me in appearance, speech, clothing (as the reader will recall, the school had a uniform dress code), mannerisms, and friendship groups. Because of my research focus, I intended to identify white students in particular at the school and follow their academic experiences. I learned that first day, however, that the initial part of this process would be more difficult than I had supposed. To my complete and perhaps naive surprise, I had trouble determining who exactly was white! Of course, this merely substantiates the argument for the plasticity of race and racial distinctions in different contexts, as I discussed in chapter 2. But even with this knowledge, I could not anticipate the complex ways whiteness was enacted and interpreted by students and teachers, both white and nonwhite, in this setting.

In this chapter, I show how white and racial/ethnic minority adolescents in the predominately minority setting of Matthews collaborated to develop unique meanings and parameters for whiteness. As discussed in the previous chapters, many teachers at Matthews tended to connect whiteness to the possession of social skills and manners, self-discipline, intelligence, and a relatively economically privileged background. These assumptions about whiteness often resulted in certain forms of advantages for students considered white, particularly in classroom interactions and discipline. However, as I explore in this chapter, the students tended to have a different interpretation of whiteness. Although students accepted some of the same assumptions about whiteness as many teachers, what one might consider "stereotypical whiteness" had little currency within the kids' culture. This compelled all students at Matthews, including white students, to avoid being seen as "white" by their peers.

Because of this, I found that white kids at Matthews consistently enacted styles, consciously or unconsciously, that distanced them from normative or stereotypical whiteness—so much so that I had difficulty initially distinguishing many of them as white. White students, along with their African American, Latino, and Asian American peers, constructed unique meanings for being white in this setting, meanings that transformed this racial category and blurred the boundaries between white and nonwhite. Further, whiteness was identified, exposed, and linked to few advantages in the peer culture of the school. I did observe instances, however, where students seemed to stereotypically associate whiteness and white students with certain forms of power and knowledge. In general, however, new possibilities emerged in this peer culture for a form of whiteness that did not rely on the exclusion or subordination of others.

This alternative form of whiteness represented a deviation from the hegemonic form for which many white people strive and with which they are familiar. In this way, many white kids at Matthews embodied a way of being white that resisted the dominant model of whiteness, which is steeped in racial exclusion. They did this intentionally, by seeking friendships and mirroring the styles of their minority peers. But they also did this somewhat unintentionally, just by being a part of the predominately black and Latino, working-class, urban context of Matthews. These white kids, along with their African American, Latino, and Asian American friends, constructed interesting and unexpected racial meanings that moved beyond the rigid, hierarchical understandings of race employed by many adults.

Kids and the Social Construction of Whiteness

My observations from the peer culture of Matthews not only confirm that whiteness is a social construction, but also explore how this concept gets constructed. As I have mentioned, the "racial formation" perspective suggests that race functions less as an inherent essence possessed by individuals and more as something groups create, maintain, and alter (Omi and Winant 1994). The basis for hegemonic whiteness, I have argued, rests on society maintaining and accepting this particular form of race, often achieved through whites keeping social and spatial distance from racially defined groups (Lewis 2001; Lipsitz 1995). But what happens to the social construction of whiteness when it is does not attain this separation? As work by John Hartigan (1999) and Pamela Perry (2002) suggests, in such circumstances whiteness loses its hegemonic status, becoming challenged and exposed. This may lead both white and nonwhite people in predominately minority contexts to construct unexpected meanings for being white.

Indeed, I observed such unexpected meanings at Matthews. It was often extraordinary to witness how these kids would talk about race and whiteness in this context. They were able to stretch and manipulate these concepts in ways that I suspect few adults, particularly those interacting in racially segregated settings, could imagine. However, this should come as no surprise to scholars of children and youths, who have often pointed out that kids espouse very plastic notions of race, class, and gender (e.g., Chin 2001; Bettie 2003; Moore 2002; Thorne 1993).

Elizabeth Chin (2001), for example, gives an interesting account of racial boundary transgression in her analysis of play among black girls in a poor, predominately black community. Chin finds that these girls did not play with any of the variety of "ethnically correct" dolls available in darker skin tones—probably because these were too expensive. Instead, these black girls played with white dolls but manipulated them in ways that made them appear more "black." For example, they braided the dolls' long "white" hair into cornrows, a hairstyle also worn by the black girls themselves. Chin argues that through this manipulation, these girls transformed whiteness: "By doing this, the girls bring their dolls into their own worlds, and whiteness here is not absolutely defined by skin and hair, but by style and way of life" (2001, 163). These girls looked past the characteristic of skin color in understanding race and assigned more importance to context and style in demarcating race and whiteness.

During my fieldwork at Matthews, I also saw black hairstyles on white heads, similar to Chin's research. However, these hairstyles were not on the heads of dolls, but on the heads of white kids themselves. Further, the incorporation of nonwhite style went beyond hair—many of these white students consistently spoke and interacted in primarily nonwhite (stereotypically) ways. This reflects the power that nonwhite kids, especially African Americans and Latinos, had in establishing racial meanings in the Matthews' student culture. Whiteness did not remain invisible or desirable in this culture. Thus, white kids tended to distance themselves from it. Upon observing black hairstyles on white dolls' heads, Chin asks, "What has happened to the boundary between white and black?" (2001, 162). After my observations at Matthews, I expand this question to ask, What happens to the boundaries between whiteness and non-whiteness when white youth wear "Latino" makeup or speak using "black English." I suggest that these boundaries are transformed and given new meanings, but only partially—some stereotypical notions of race and whiteness persisted, even in the predominately minority context of Matthews.

"You're White!" Meanings of Whiteness for
Racial/Ethnic Minority Students

Racial/Ethnic minority students, especially African Americans, dominated the peer culture of Matthews. The cultural forms that students at Matthews preferred emblematized this dominance. For example, in a survey the yearbook students conducted on student favorites, rap and rhythm and blues (R and B), two predominately black musical idioms, were preferred by 84 percent of students (only I percent of students, by contrast, preferred rock and roll). These forms of musical expression also dominated school assemblies—even an assembly intended to get the students pumped up to take the TAAS exam included kids rapping on stage about performing well on the test (which appeared to quite effectively get students engaged). Only occasional "multicultural" assemblies would feature other cultural expressions less popular with most students, such as Indian students performing traditional dances. And, indeed, even Asian and other students appeared to prefer rap and R-and-B music. For example, an Indian student at one multicultural assembly I observed performed an interesting and creative rap accompanied by Indian music in the background.

African American, and to a lesser extent Latino, students had the power to decide what was most desirable or "cool" ("tight" in the kids' vernacular) among kids at Matthews. This typically included hip-hop music and its corresponding influence in movies, clothing, and speech. Because a student who did not like these musical styles and influences could be ostracized from the larger peer group, kids attempted to prove to others their affinity for them: "Library observation. An Asian American girl and an African American girl are talking about a project their class is doing on music. The African American girl asks, 'What kind of music are you doing?' The Asian American girl responds, 'Classical [*pauses briefly*]—I didn't pick it. If it was up to me, I'd choose hip-hop'" (Field notes, March 30, 2001).

Predominately white cultural forms such as country music and styles, by contrast, lay at the least desirable end of the coolness continuum. Students associated hip-hop with African Americans and country music with whites: "As I'm looking on Ms. Phillips's computer at a project she's working on, I overhear a conversation between Gary, a white boy, a black boy named Tony, and a black girl named Vanessa. Tony and Vanessa have been teasing Gary for most of the time I've been near them. Tony asks Gary if he likes country music. Gary in turn asks Tony, 'Why would you think that?' Vanessa replies before Tony can answer, 'Because—you're white.' Gary admits that he likes some country music but stresses that he does not care for it that much" (Field notes, May 8, 2002). Because he was perceived as white, Gary had to prove that he did not like country music, which most students ridiculed. The connection between whites and country music was rather prevalent at Matthews. For example, a history classroom I observed displayed student work on a multicultural project, in which students described characteristics of the following groups: African American, Asian American, Hispanic American, and Anglo American. Under the Anglo American category, some students had written, "[They] like country music." In the peer culture of Matthews this signified a woeful lack of coolness.

Behaviors and preferences commonly associated with whiteness held little currency in the peer culture of Matthews, for white students or racial/ethnic minority students. This was true of predominately white forms of popular culture, such as country music, as well as whiteness more generally. In fact, black and Latino students often used the word "white" as an insult. This bears similarities to Amanda Lewis's observations from a predominately minority elementary school, where she comments that "the label 'white boy' was used disparagingly in the yard" (2003b, 57). While Lewis describes this in relation to minority students, I observed the insult "white" directed at white students as well as minority students.

Similarly, my observations at Matthews provide some support for Signithia Fordham and John Ogbu's (1986) controversial contention that high-achieving African American students (and, to some extent, Latino students) often endure criticism from their peers for "acting white" (see Ainsworth-Darnell and Downey 1998 for a contrary view). According to Fordham and Ogbu, the black peer culture often equates academic success with "selling out," associated with a loss of racial, cultural, and community identity. Because of peer pressure, some high-achieving black youths may even refuse placement in advanced classes, even though guidance counselors might urge them to take these classes (Fordham 1988). Hence, this perspective links black underachievement in many instances to the adoption of a black racial and cultural identity. However, I found that Matthews' students did not connect being white to high achievement specifically but used it as a more generalized insult, typically directed at students perceived as "nerdy." Whiteness in this sense connoted more of a stylistic sensibility—a way of behaving and interacting—than a mode of achievement per se, although the two were often linked. I observed few high-achieving students at Matthews being criticized for their *achievement*, while I observed many low-achieving students whom others teased for nerdy behavior (see Tyson 2002 for a similar view).

Minority students who strictly observed the schools' uniform dress code—wore tighter-fitting clothing (for boys) and pants at their waist—could be accused by others of being white. These students also rarely got in trouble and tended to interact with authority figures in a very polite way:

> I sit in Mr. Pham's class, which today is composed of a hodgepodge of students from various classes who have finished the Texas Assessment of Academic Skills test (the state achievement test) for that day. As students come in, I notice Anisha, a black girl I saw in my first classroom observation at Matthews. She appears to be a good student and takes pre–advanced placement courses. I notice that Anisha is acting differently than I've seen her in other classes, where she is usually very polite. Here, she is chewing gum loudly and conspicuously (which is against classroom rules) and talking back to Mr. Pham, who is trying to manage the confusion of controlling these various students.
>
> A few black boys I don't recognize start antagonizing Anisha and question her behavior. One says, "Why are you trying to act like that? You're white!" (Although Anisha has somewhat lighter skin than these boys, from my perspective she looks clearly African American, and this was her designation on her survey form as well as school records.) Anisha seems insulted by this categorization and responds loudly, "I ain't white!" To which one of the black boys fires back, "You ain't black!" Anisha cannot think of a quick come-back to this, and the boys' laughter drowns out her delayed attempt at a protest. Mr. Pham then breaks up the group and the particular topic of conversation ends. Anisha doesn't seem too despondent and continues talking to those around her for the rest of the period, not doing the silent reading Mr. Pham is encouraging. (Field notes, April 26, 2001)

Although Anisha did take pre-AP courses and this probably factored into the boys' criticism of her, they more directly used her comportment as the basis to accuse her of being white. The boys identify that Anisha is acting in a way she usually does not, and they expose this inconsistency, claiming that she typically acts white. In this sense, they frame whiteness as Anisha's usual behavior—adhering closely to school and classroom rules, being very polite to authority figures, and not doing cool things such as breaking minor classroom rules. Anisha's visceral response indicates how most kids interpreted "being white" negatively and worked to avoid this particular peer assessment.

Although most research on "acting white" refers primarily to African American students, I observed students of all racial groups at Matthews framing whiteness as unappealing, primarily because of its association with being nerdy. Many Latino students in particular often worked to avoid their peers calling them white:

Ms. Jacobs, a white teacher, moves Felix, a rather boisterous Latino boy, to the other end of the room. Once moved, he continues to talk to the students around him, calling everyone "Ese" (which roughly translates to "dude"). Felix eventually turns to a Latino boy in that corner of the room named Jose, who takes English as a Second Language (ESL) classes and wears his pants high on his hips and rather high over the tops of his shoes. "You're white," Felix says simply to Jose (Jose has close to the same skin tone as Felix, which was fairly light). "I'm not white," Jose responds. "I'm Hispanic." "No, actually," he continues, "I'm Mexican." Felix responds, "Yeah I'm Mexican, too—I'm mixed." "Me too," Jose says. The conversation ends there and the boys both seem to come away satisfied to consider each other "mixed." (Field notes, October 31, 2001)

In this example, Felix does not ostensibly accuse Jose of being white because of high achievement (Jose did not take pre-AP classes, as Anisha did). A more apparent reason was Jose's light skin tone and rather nerdy behavior and dress. Jose certainly did not reflect the cool modes of dress at Matthews, which necessitated wearing pants at least slightly below the waist and at least slightly oversized so they bunched up at the feet. Taking ESL classes might have also increased Jose's lack of cool in the eyes of Felix (see Olsen 1997; Valenzuela 1999). Similar to Anisha, Jose resists the accusation that he is white—claiming other racial categories before deciding, with Felix's help, on mixed.

"Mixed" served as a rather popular racial designation for students at Matthews, especially Hispanic students. On my survey, several students with Spanish surnames chose none of the listed categories and simply wrote "mixed" in the "Other" space. This designation allowed kids such as Felix and Jose, whose relatively light skin color might allow them to pass for white in certain contexts, an identity that in some sense transcended extant racial categories. Judging from Jose's insistence that he was certainly not white, however, it seemed that this identity primarily distanced kids from whiteness who might otherwise be mistaken as white. Latino kids, as well as African Americans, viewed being seen as white negatively and tried to avoid it. The mixed identification reflected a strategy partly rooted in this avoidance.

Thus, racial/ethnic minority students, especially African Americans, largely determined the meanings and parameters of race among kids at Matthews. Things commonly associated with whites and whiteness held little popularity in this peer culture. Many black and Latino students scrutinized how other students presented themselves and determined whether or not this presentation was white, which they typically associated with nerdy and uncool, or "hatin'," behavior. Black and Latino students were not supposed to act white in this way. By extension, and as discussed in the next section, white students could not act too white either.

"White Chocolate": Establishing Distance from Whiteness

White students at Matthews engaged in certain interactive strategies (although not necessarily consciously) to distance themselves from whiteness. Often, this worked well enough that I, as a researcher, struggled to decide whether or not they were white. The first classroom I entered at Matthews, which I discussed at the beginning of this chapter, had one such student, a girl named Lisa, whom I have mentioned in previous chapters. I began classifying Lisa as white after some observations but soon switched this to a multiracial designation after she began wearing her dark hair in tightly braided cornrows, which made her look similar to many African American girls at Matthews. I eventually distributed to all students at the school a survey form that asked them to select their racial identity, as I described in the first chapter. Lisa selected just "White" on this survey, and this matched her classification in school records. Thus, I began classifying her as white.

This story is less indicative of the process of discovering Lisa's "real" race and more indicative of the ways students like Lisa performed and managed how they presented themselves racially. This, rather than their ancestry, *became* their race, in a sense, for themselves and many others. This is not to say that students and teachers did not still identify students such as Lisa as white (or that she did not identify herself this way, as evidenced by her survey response). But the styles of interaction she used lent a unique meaning to her whiteness. She typically wore her hair in cornrows, as I've described, and on school dress-up days or before school dances she often wore her hair artfully styled in a sort of bun on top of her head. This hairstyle was similar to how several African American girls wore their hair on those days and differed from many Hispanic girls and most other white girls, who typically wore their hair down on these occasions.

Lisa spoke using a distinct cadence and accent that sounded to me virtually indistinguishable from the way many black students at the school spoke. Lisa's speech pattern included many double negatives, frequent use of the word "ain't" and many elements of "black English" (Labov 1972; Dillard 1972; Smitherman 1977, 2000). However, I did not hear her use some of the more distinguishing features of black English often used by many African American students at the school and described by Labov (1972).[1] Her southern accent was slightly thicker than many of her African American peers, but the quick cadence of her speech closely resembled that of black students. Lisa hung out primarily with African American girls and occasionally with Latina girls. She participated in the cheerleading squad, which consisted primarily of African American girls except for Lisa and one Hispanic girl.

As I have mentioned, I find it helpful to characterize Lisa (and other students I describe below) as "performing" a particular racial identity. The concept of performance corresponds closely to Goffman's (1973) theory of self-presentation. Goffman (1973) argues that we manage our appearance, speech, gestures, and expressions as much as possible to convey particular impressions to others. Recent work on "performative" identity (Bettie 2000, 2002; see also West and Fenstermaker 1995) utilizes Goffman's theory of how people act out race, class, and gender identities through interaction, but qualifies this by recognizing that such performances do not always result from conscious or instrumental decision making. This appears applicable to Lisa because, while she enacted an almost exaggerated black style, she did not really alter this style depending on the situation. For example, she spoke the same way to white and black teachers, and to me, a white outsider, as she did to her friends and other students. Her style seemed less consciously affected than simply reflective of her way of life in this poor and working-class racial/ethnic minority community. Although this style was inflected with elements commonly associated with African Americans, it also projected a tough, street-based persona that in some ways related to neighborhood context and class background more than race per se.

Because many aspects of Lisa's self presentation could be, perhaps stereotypically, associated with black urban youths, she conveyed some distance from whiteness. This clouded the perception of her race for me, an outsider, but also for teachers at the school such as Ms. Garza, who responded with the following when I asked her about Lisa's race: "I think that she is white—she's not black. . . . I can't tell sometimes, though. At the start of the class I thought she was Hispanic. But I think she has some European, maybe English blood. It looks like it in her features, and her last name . . . sounds like an English name" (Field notes, April 2, 2002). Ms. Garza's admission that she "can't tell sometimes" indicates how she had to work to understand Lisa's race, tenuously deciding on white because of her facial features and last name. Perhaps because Lisa's hair, speech, and mannerisms closely resembled those of black girls at the school, she appeared not quite white to Ms. Garza. Lisa's light skin precluded her from being seen as African American, so Hispanic presented another likely choice. However, teachers determined which kids were Hispanic based largely on last name, and Lisa did not have a Spanish surname. Thus, Ms. Garza described her as white, almost by default.

This street-based style was not restricted to Lisa. As I have mentioned, a white boy named Jackson also exhibited interactive styles similar to many black students at the school. Jackson wore his brown hair very short, almost shaved, hung out primarily with black friends, and spoke in a way similar to many black students at the school. He also dressed in a way that closely matched his African American friends, preferring long baggy shorts, high-top sneakers with ankle-length socks, a long gold chain proudly displayed on the outside of his shirt, and, in the final year of my fieldwork, a headband. From my early observations, I perceived Jackson as white primarily because of his light complexion and hair. But

Jackson's choice of racial identification on my survey form exemplifies how he saw himself as rather distant from whiteness. As I have mentioned, on this form he marked his race as "White" but in the "Other" space wrote in "white chocolate." Through this clever identity choice, Jackson appears to signify a form of whiteness blended throughout with a "chocolate" or black essence. He, like Lisa and many other white students at Matthews, constructed a type of whiteness that resided at the margins of this racial category, very close to blackness.[2]

The psychoanalytic theorist Franz Fanon (1967) and contemporary psychologists such as Beverly Tatum (1999) argue that because of the dominance of white culture, many black people internalize the notion that whiteness is more desirable than blackness. At Matthews, where black culture was dominant, I saw the opposite—many white kids seemed to view blackness as desirable and sought to avoid whiteness. Many white students at Matthews appeared to view themselves in ways similar to the inner-city white respondent in Hartigan's study, who claimed that "we're all colored" (1999, 116). Like in central Detroit, whiteness in the peer culture of Matthews could not separate itself out and occupy an unspoken, dominant position. Thus, expressions of whiteness were subject to disruptions and challenges in this peer context, rather than the maintenance of hegemonic preeminence.

White students who did not project an identity that distanced them from stereotypical whiteness tended to be marginalized in the Matthews peer culture. Gary, for example, mentioned earlier, did not perform a more nonwhite or street type of identity like students such as Lisa and Jackson did (which probably exacerbated suspicions that he enjoyed uncool country music). Gary did not pepper his speech with phrases characteristic of black English and tended to hang out with a small group of Asian American, Latino, and other white students more than African American students. While he seemed to have a tenuous connection to many other (especially black) students, Gary frequently wanted to talk to me (a white male adult) and invite me to his classes. Lisa and Jackson, by contrast, attempted to have as little to do with me as possible. Gary told me that he did not like Matthews very much because he thought it was "kinda crazy here" (Field notes, April 5, 2002), and he added that his family would soon move to a more suburban area. Thus, in many ways Gary disassociated himself from the African American–dominated peer culture at Matthews, which identified him more with stereotypical whiteness. His interactive style and attitude stood out rather than blending in, like Jackson and Lisa, and this seemed to provoke teasing from other students.

Intersections of Whiteness, Class, and Gender

Matthews' students constructed various meanings of whiteness for white and minority students. This process was not isolated to race per se, but worked through constructions of class and gender. As I mentioned before, the street style exhibited by many white students projected a class- and neighborhood-based persona as much as a race-based one. Indeed, I call this style a "street" style precisely to emphasize its urban and working-class connotation, independently of any particular racial connotation. However, the urban aspects of this style (perhaps stereotypically) influenced how some teachers, along with myself, interpreted the racial background of white students. Additionally, this style allowed white students to distance themselves from whiteness in the eyes of their peers. Thus, although infused with racialized elements, a street style also worked through class elements (especially in the form of urban, streetwise postures and attitudes) to alter the projection of race and whiteness.

Meanings of whiteness also worked through gender at Matthews. For instance, as Mary Waters (1999) notes, accusations of "acting white" carry a gendered connotation (see also Fordham 1988). For boys, acting white is often associated with not being adequately masculine. Behavior interpreted as nerdy and obsequious for boys also tends to be seen as "gay," feminine, and childlike (see Willis 1977). At Matthews, because kids associated such nerdy behavior with being white, this meant that, for boys, establishing distance from whiteness also corresponded to proving masculinity. This placed white boys at somewhat of a disadvantage in terms of masculinity. White boys who presented themselves in ways interpreted by students as white, such as associating with mostly white and Asian students, adhering closely to classroom rules, and wearing their hair in longer bangs, also tended to be seen as gay or childlike. One white boy who fit this description, and wore Dockers brand pants and his light brown hair parted on the side with relatively long bangs, was teased and called "Home Alone" by other students, a reference to the child actor Macaulay Culkin. Home Alone was virtually the only white boy in the school who wore his hair in this way (as opposed to very short or shaved). To other students, including Dwayne and Oliver, whom we met in chapter 5, this appeared to indicate a stereotypically white and also innocent persona:

Ms. Klotz's class. A black boy named Dwayne has been scolded several times by Ms. Klotz during the class. He is currently rapping and occasionally exchanging punches with another black boy sitting near him named Oliver. Eventually, Dwayne's attention turns to a relatively quiet group of white and Asian American boys sitting in front of him. Dwayne calls to one of the white boys, one who has his hair in long, light brown bangs, "Hey, Home Alone, how old are you?" Home Alone, who appears used to responding to his common appellation, answers, "Twelve," somewhat hesitantly. Dwayne says, "Twelve—damn boy, you young. I'm gonna be driving my car soon and you gonna be chasing me on your bike!" Dwayne pedals his feet for emphasis and laughs. Home Alone laughs briefly and then returns to his work. Dwayne diverts his attention from

Home Alone and continues hitting and play fighting with Oliver, especially as the class is about to end. The group of boys with Home Alone, by contrast, does not hit each other once. (Field notes, April 11. 2001)

Dwayne interprets Home Alone as young and innocent. This perception implies a less mature, boyish, form of masculinity. To avoid such an association with less potent masculinity implied by whiteness, white boys had to demonstrate toughness and a streetwise persona. To be sure, proving a tough masculine identity remained important and necessary for boys of all racial groups (I observed boys of all racial groups called "gay" by other boys, for instance). But because students associated being white with the nerdy behavior also associated with weaker masculinity, this meant that white boys in particular had to prove their toughness. White boys who established distance from whiteness and attained popularity in the boys' peer group also demonstrated physicality and aggressiveness. Jackson, for instance, frequently punched other boys and enjoyed playing a game where he would purposefully walk into other boys in the hall, knocking them off stride while sarcastically apologizing. Perhaps because of such displays, other students did not tease Jackson through critiques of his whiteness or masculinity. Home Alone and Gary, by contrast, failed to prove their toughness to other boys. I rarely saw them engage in the punching and play-fighting rituals popular among most boys.

For girls, the nerdy behavior associated with being white did not necessarily call their femininity into question. Although girls in general did not desire such labels, whiteness or even nerdy-ness for girls could still be seen as feminine. Perhaps because of this, black and Latina girls appeared less conscious of acting white than did their male counterparts (see Waters 1999). Interestingly, however, African American girls in particular tended to monitor and critique *white* students who acted or sounded nonwhite in their estimation. This critique ironically resulted in some white students, particularly girls, being exposed as white. In contrast to Hispanic and black students, white girls accused of being white were not necessarily perceived as nerdy. Instead, African American girls appeared to call these students white when their nonwhite performance became too exaggerated.

A white girl named Melissa, for example, performed a street type of identity similar to Lisa's, including use of black English and wearing her hair in cornrows. Melissa, however, gained less acceptance among African American students and hung out primarily with Latino students, wearing the dark lip-liner and eye makeup preferred by Hispanic girls whom teachers described to me as "gang bangers." On several occasions I observed African American girls call Melissa "white" like an insult:

Mr. Wilson, a white teacher, is going over test questions with the class. Melissa is sitting right in front of me, next to Christina, a Hispanic girl.

She has been talking to Christina during the entire class. Mr. Wilson has reprimanded her once, but she continues to talk. Eventually, Dominique, a black girl who has been answering most of the questions, shouts at her across the room, "Shut up you *white* girl!" (emphasizing "white" with some distaste). This momentarily quiets Melissa, and she frowns and makes a loud "tsc" sound indicating her disapproval at this apparent insult. But Melissa does not openly challenge Dominique and instead turns to Christina and mutters what sounds to me like "I ain't white." (Field notes, April 15, 2002)

Dominique seems to identify that the last thing Melissa wants to be called is white. As with Lisa, I originally classified Melissa as multiracial because she presented herself in non-stereotypically white ways. Unfortunately, she did not return a survey form to me, but the school records had her classified as white, and this matched what teachers considered her race to be. As the example above suggests, students also saw her as white. Despite this, however, Melissa appeared to resist a white label as much as possible. In the example above she, like Anisha and Jose, interpreted being called white as an insult and tried to avoid this characterization.

Melissa's street-based performance appeared to backfire in the peer culture of Matthews, especially with African American girls. These girls perhaps perceived her nonwhite style as inauthentic, or perhaps too divergent from whiteness. From my perspective, Melissa's interactive style differed little from Lisa's, but Lisa seemed to gain more acceptance from black peers. This may have stemmed from the fact that Lisa took primarily pre-AP courses, while Melissa did not. Pre-AP students were a smaller, closer-knit group than regular students, which may have allowed Lisa more acceptance. As I describe below, black students in regular classes did sometimes make fun of Lisa's style. But while Lisa typically passed without being teased or indicted for being too white or too black, Melissa could not always achieve this balance.

Perhaps, especially because Melissa took regular classes, her street style evoked more of a social-class-based, rather than race-based, performance. Rather than moving her persona away from whiteness, Melissa's street performance may have only indicated a lower-social-class position. Indeed, I observed African American girls expose her not only as white, but as a lower embodiment of whiteness: "When the kids are coming back from lunch, I see a black girl in the hall yell to Melissa, 'Get to class, white trash!' Melissa responds, 'You trippin'!' The other girl laughs at Melissa as Melissa walks to her class" (Field notes, May 1, 2002).

Melissa was one of the few white students at Matthews that I observed other students directly call "white trash." In using this term these students symbolically identified Melissa as white but emphasized that this was a degraded or "trashy" form of whiteness. I suggest that Melissa's gender made her especially vulnerable to this label. Her enactment of a street-based style compromised her projection of femininity, especially to black girls, leading to a perception of her as trashy. White boys enacting a street style, by contrast, tended to be received more positively in the peer culture, probably because this style established them as tough and appropriately masculine.

"I Ain't Never Heard a White Girl Say That!" Transforming Racial Meanings

While many white students were teased or ostracized for acting too stereotypically white or too stereotypically nonwhite, many also gained acceptance among their peers. Although these white students typically performed a nonwhite identity, they did so with enough aplomb to skirt racial boundaries and transform what other students expected from a person with white skin. One cannot discount the influence of popular culture in guiding students to accept more street-oriented embodiments of whiteness. For instance, as mentioned above, most Matthews students considered rap their favorite music; but they also listed Eminem, a *white* rapper, as their favorite musical artist. Eminem, who grew up in the predominately black city of Detroit, gained notoriety at the time of my fieldwork for his controversial lyrics as well as his appeal to both white and black hip-hop fans (see Rich 2002). He was very popular among many students at Matthews, across all race and gender groups (many black girls, for example, carried binders with pictures of him pasted on the front). Eminem presented an urban, streetwise image of whiteness to popular culture, and this may have enabled many students at Matthews to enact and accept similar versions of whiteness locally.

These street-oriented versions of whiteness altered meanings that typically maintain the boundary between white and nonwhite. Black English serves as a clear example of this. When white kids use black speech nearly as prevalently as black kids, as many did at Matthews, this confounds how neatly one can still distinguish between white and black methods of speech. White kids who spoke in black ways, such as Lisa, provoked surprise from many black kids:

> I am observing in an elective class which has several students I know from other classes, including Lisa and two black girls named Danielle and Tanae. When the students return from lunch, Danielle and Tanae, along with two other black girls, are looking at a magazine. Lisa, who is sitting at the same long table one seat away from the girls, leans over and asks them something about one of the pictures in the magazine. Whatever Lisa said causes the four black girls to erupt in laughter, and they begin to tease Lisa for it. One says, "I ain't never heard a white girl

say that!" Another says, "She talking all black!" Lisa seems kind of embarrassed by this, her face looks rather red, and she turns away to talk to some Hispanic girls from her pre-AP classes. (Field notes, April 2, 2002)

I heard black students make similar comments in other classes about white students saying things that "sounded black." As in the excerpt above, black students perceived this as humorous, but also somewhat astonishing. By identifying that Lisa, a white girl, was talking black, these black girls appear to draw an essential distinction between how white people and black people talk. However, at the same time they do not ridicule the lack of authenticity of Lisa's speech, but seem surprised that it so closely resembles black speech. Although this episode caused Lisa some embarrassment, the girls do not suggest that Lisa failed to speak appropriately. Rather, they simply express their amazement that a white girl had spoken in a way they previously associated only with African Americans. Thus, for these girls at least, Lisa seemed to transform some of the expected behaviors associated with whiteness.

In her study of kids from six to twelve years old at two summer camps, Valerie Moore (2002) shows how these kids established interesting definitions and boundaries for race. One of these summer camps had a multiracial composition of campers and a "cultural awareness" focus. At this camp, Moore argues that kids "often complicated the usual ways our culture categorizes and evaluates race category membership" (2002, 68). In chapter 2, I described the black boy at this camp who insisted that the white counselor he admired was not really white. Campers in Moore's research, while very aware of race and race membership, nevertheless creatively manipulated racial boundaries and criteria. Similarly, kids in the predominately minority setting of Matthews created unique meanings and boundaries for racial categories. Much of this related to whiteness. The "mixed" designation popular among Latino students is one example of this creativity, as is Jackson's creation of "white chocolate." Both categories, while seeking distance from whiteness, also stretch and manipulate it into nonstandard and non-hegemonic forms.

Many white students at Matthews defied the rules of behavior and categorization ordinarily associated with whiteness, and with the help of minority students they "created their own sense of race" (Moore 2002, 69). This sense of race often transcended fixed categories: "I'm observing in an elective class, where things are pretty casual because it's close to the end of the school year. I'm hanging out with Anisha and Evette, two black girls who take pre-AP classes. John, a popular white boy who also takes pre-AP classes, comes over while we're talking. Anisha puts her arm around him and announces to me, 'This is John; he's my brother.' Evette, a light-skinned black girl, says, 'No—he's *my* brother because we're both white and black'" (Field notes, May 8, 2002).

John chose only "White" on his survey form but performed somewhat of a street type of identity. John enacted this identity in a similar way to Jackson, wearing oversized pants and shirts, a long gold chain, and speaking with a rhythm similar to African American students at the school. He tended to mute his presentation more than Jackson did, however, often wearing his chain inside his shirt and not using black English as liberally. John was probably the most popular white student at Matthews. His popularity among many black students corresponds to Evette's characterization of him as "white and black." Because of her close friendship with John, whom she and Anisha call their "brother," she constructs his race as something beyond just whiteness or blackness. She identifies that John has white ancestry but appears to suggest that his actions and friendships with black students give him an honorary blackness. Evette relates John's combination of black and white to herself, who, despite being classified as African American in school records, undoubtedly had whiteness in her ancestry as well.

Students at Matthews interpreted race and whiteness in a way that did not necessarily relate to visible physical characteristics. Like Moore (2002) and Chin (2001), I find that minority kids at Matthews connected being white more to structural position, style, and methods of interaction than skin color or other physical identifiers. For example, I observed kids call adults they perceived as possessing power and knowledge white, regardless of skin tone:

> I learn at the front desk that they are rehearsing for a mock trial in Mr. Caldwell's class. There are some local lawyers and law students that will be helping to organize the trial. I get to the classroom and talk briefly to Mr. Caldwell, and then he leaves to get the "lawyers," as everyone in the class refers to them, from the front office.
>
> The kids are excited about having the lawyers come, and they go into a sort of frenzy after Mr. Caldwell leaves. They post Andre, a tall black boy, as a lookout in the hall. Soon after, Andre runs in the room and announces, "I think the lawyers are here—Mr. Caldwell is in the hall with a bunch of white people walking with him!" The students rush to their seats and try to stay quiet as they eagerly await the arrival of this "bunch of white people."
>
> The lawyers arrive and, surprisingly, only two out of the four are noticeably white. There is one brown-skinned woman walking in front who, to me, looks clearly Latina, and I learn later she has a Spanish surname, and one black woman with an African or West Indian accent. (Field notes, February 27, 2002)

Based on skin tone, from my perspective, this group of lawyers was not all white. However, Andre appears to frame this group of lawyers as white not because of physical features, but because they held powerful positions as lawyers. Further, all of them dressed the part, wearing business dress suits (all four were women), which undoubtedly enhanced their projection of status. The methods of dress and speech exhibited by these women, whatever their skin color, represented the structural power these kids called white. For kids at Matthews, blackness or brownness represented the ways of dressing, interacting, and speaking common to their neighborhood, and whiteness represented something distant from this, often connected to the wealth and power typically absent from their residential context. These lawyers did not come from the neighborhood and did not present themselves in a way these kids associated with blackness or brownness, so this made them white.

Because of this flexible, contextualized notion of race, white students who lived in the neighborhood and attended Matthews did not necessarily represent the power and difference associated with whiteness. This gave white students at the school more of an opportunity to disassociate themselves from stereotypical, dominant whiteness, which set the foundation for interracial friendships. Through such interracial friendships, alternative possibilities for race and whiteness emerged. White kids such as John, Lisa, and Jackson gained recognition in the peer culture primarily through their association with racial/ethnic minority kids. This eroded much of the power from whiteness and opened more possibilities for cooperation and trust. White students, in the unique situation of a minority at Matthews, valued and connected with nonwhite things and nonwhite people. This resulted in constructions of whiteness that did not have to oppose or subordinate nonwhiteness. Thus, white and minority students often saw themselves as similar in status, background, and preferences, which enabled many cross-racial friendships. As represented by Evette's articulation of "black and white," these friendships challenged the very notion of racial distinctions and racial hierarchy.

Lingering Stereotypes of Whiteness

This should not suggest that kids at Matthews completely discarded the stereotypical baggage associated with whiteness, however. Racial/ethnic minority students at Matthews still equated whiteness with structural power, knowledge, and money. This especially surfaced in how kids reacted to adults, including myself:

> Mr. Caldwell's class. The class is working on their final practice before putting on a mock trial. I sit next to a black boy named Ricky, who asks me if I'm a law student. I tell him no, that I'm doing a research project at the school. Ricky is obviously bright, and he asks if I'm an anthropologist because I study people. I say I'm a sociologist, which is similar. He then switches the topic entirely and asks me if my parents are rich. I say that

> they are middle class and ask him why he thinks they are rich. He says,
> "Because they're paying for college and everything." I tell him that I'm
> paying for all of my education and mention that I'm married and also
> work as a teaching assistant. He responds, "Oh," but then continues his
> previous line of questioning, asking, "So, do your parents have like a real
> big house and stuff?" (Field notes, April 4, 2002)

In this excerpt, Ricky assumes that my parents are "rich" and they are paying for
my education. Even after I tell him that I am funding graduate school myself, he
seems enthralled with the idea that my parents are wealthy and own a big
house. I typically wore slacks and a tucked-in polo shirt to Matthews because
school administrators encouraged rather formal dress from adults. However, I
do not think my clothing exuded much wealth. In fact, I dressed much more
casually than most male teachers at the school, who often wore suits. Rather,
my white physical features, especially combined with my position as a relative
outsider to the school and neighborhood, seemed to guide Ricky's assumption
that I came from a wealthy background.

As discussed above, because the white students at Matthews lived in the
same general neighborhood as the other students, and attended school with
them, they did not as clearly represent this powerful form of extrinsic whiteness. However, racial/ethnic minority students did identify these students as
white, and this label still appeared to trigger some stereotypical assumptions
associated with whiteness. For example, in my observations Hispanic students
and especially African American students often perceived white students as
bookish and intelligent:

> I am observing in a class after TAAS testing, and the teacher wants the
> students to read silently. Clay, a white boy with closely cropped hair that
> is highlighted on top, sits with a Latino boy named Oscar. They are look-
> ing at some sort of magazine or catalogue that features stereo equip-
> ment. A black boy named Sean sits immediately in front of them. Sean
> has been practicing drum beats on his desk and occasionally looks back
> at Oscar and Clay, who are buried in their magazine. Eventually, Sean
> turns to Clay and comments somewhat critically, "You look like the type
> that would be reading a magazine. You always looking at something—
> reading." Clay looks at him and laughs briefly and then returns to the
> magazine. (Field notes, April 26, 2001)

Sean comments that Clay looks like "the type" of person that reads often.
Although a Latino boy also sat with Clay, reading the same magazine, Sean
directed his comment at Clay, singling him out as bookish rather than Oscar.
(Sean also did not make this comment to either an Asian boy or another Latino
boy, who at the time were both reading books in front of him.) I observed Clay

to be an average student who took regular classes and was not particularly fond of reading. He did enjoy looking at magazines featuring stereo equipment, but many boys at Matthews, both white and nonwhite, did as well. In this case, Clay's whiteness in particular seemed to accentuate his bookishness in the eyes of Sean.

As did Janet Schofield (1989) in her ethnography of a multiracial school, I also observed many African American students seeking out academic help from white students. In the library one day, for example, I observed a black boy named Alan pressing a white boy named Kevin to work on a science project with him, saying, "We should work together; we can get all kinds of stuff that way" (Field notes, October 3, 2001). I observed Kevin to be a conscientious but average student who took regular classes, and Alan to be the same way, but more outgoing. Other minority students in the class worked industriously on their projects near Alan, but he seemed especially interested in working with Kevin, a boy with whom he did not ordinarily associate. Kevin declined Alan's offer, and Alan eventually gave up on the idea, not asking anyone else in the class if they wanted to collaborate on the project.

Although Kevin demurred to collaborate with Alan in this example, other white students enjoyed positioning themselves as academically knowledgeable when minority students asked them for help. I observed a white girl named Kara, for example, and a black girl named Beth discussing tutoring in a pre-AP class. Beth asked Kara for help with the class, and Kara immediately framed herself as an expert academically, proclaiming that she would "tutor" Beth, saying, "So you can make A's like me!" (Field notes, February 20, 2002). Kara then proceeded to announce to the teacher and the other students returning from lunch that she would now act as Beth's tutor, which seemed to slightly embarrass Beth. In each of these examples, African American students sought out the few white students in their classes for help academically. Nonwhite students performed as well, if not better, in each of these classes, but these students still appeared to consider the white students to possess a unique academic acumen.

Many teachers tended to reinforce the link between white students and certain forms of knowledge. As I discussed in chapter 4, many teachers, especially African American teachers who composed the majority of the teaching staff, responded favorably to white students in academic situations. These teachers called on white students frequently in class, gave them positive feedback on their academic skill, and described them to me as exceptional students. In assuming that white students possessed certain academically oriented skills and knowledge, minority students at Matthews perhaps only followed the lead of these adults, as well as a larger culture that connects whiteness to powerful attributes such as intelligence, technological skill, and upper-class status (see Van Ausdale and Feagin [2001] for an account of how children learn and enact this culture of racial hierarchy). Thus, while students at Matthews performed and accepted many innovative, non-superior embodiments of whiteness, they also reinforced some stereotypical assumptions about race that bolster white dominance. While whiteness had few advantages for making a kid appear cool in the peer culture of Matthews, it could make a kid appear smart and knowledgeable.

I would like to emphasize, however, that I find only limited evidence for this association with whiteness and academic skill among the students, and it is impossible for me to take the instances described above and attribute these interactions solely to race. While many teachers did seem to reinforce this link in classroom interactions, some did not. In addition, the tracking structure of Matthews did not entirely reinforce a link between whiteness and academic preeminence. Research by Pamela Perry (2002) indicates that white students more often take higher-tracked classes even when these students compose a numerical minority at the school (see also Oakes 1985, 1995). Perry argues that, especially with the very visible characteristic of race, the racially skewed tracking process at the school she examined implicitly constructed white and Asian students as normative and ideal students because they dominated the higher-tracked classes. At Matthews I found that white students were overrepresented in higher tracks according to school records: white students composed 8 percent of the enrollment in pre-AP courses and 4 percent of the student body. However, this did not result in pre-AP classes composed predominately of white students because the school did not have enough white students to dominate these classes. The school also made a concerted, laudable effort to attract and retain African American and Latino students in pre-AP classes. Because of these factors, academically advanced courses, like all courses at Matthews, had mostly African American and Latino students.

Thus, although white students were more likely to be enrolled in pre-AP courses at Matthews, they did not predominate in these courses, which did not really convey a sense of white normativity or academic dominance at the school. While many teachers did frame white students as academically skilled, the overall structure of the school in terms of advanced courses did not emphasize a salient link between whiteness and academic ability. By extension, students at Matthews may not have fully internalized such a link. However, the vague stereotypes associating whiteness with intelligence and academic success continued to linger. These had the power to create a sense of disconnection, rather than commonality, among white and nonwhite kids at Matthews.

Conclusion

In this chapter I have explored how youths understood, enacted, and responded to whiteness at Matthews Middle School—a situation where whites were not numerically dominant. In this situation, most white kids associated themselves with styles and friends that were predominately nonwhite. This partially transformed many expectations and boundaries that typically distinguish white from nonwhite. Being white in this setting referred more to stylistic sensibilities, cultural preferences, and friendship groups than physical characteristics. Because students at Matthews interpreted this whiteness somewhat negatively, this compelled white kids to incorporate styles of interaction commonly associated with racial/ethnic minority youths and, most importantly, forge friendships with minority peers.

Because students at Matthews interpreted the forms of dress and behavior they called white as somewhat alien to their neighborhood context, this allowed some white kids to be seen as not really white (white and black, for instance), providing common ground for these friendships. White students at Matthews often performed a whiteness that, like white chocolate, blended with minority youths in this predominately poor and working-class neighborhood. Most did not segregate themselves from minority students, but aligned themselves as similar in many ways. This suggests that when whites are disconnected from structural processes that tend to provide them with advantages, such as attending higher-performing, mostly white schools or being shepherded into higher-level ability groups (see Lewis 2001; Oakes 1985), they do not separate themselves socially from racial/ethnic minorities; and this can foster interracial friendship and tolerance (see also Allport ([1954] 1958).

Gender and social class complicated this process of racial blending, however. For boys, acting stereotypically white was linked to being a nerd, which was associated with not being maturely masculine. This meant that white boys especially needed to prove their masculinity through performing a tough, street-based style. White boys exhibiting this style gained more acceptance among peers, especially other boys. For white girls, including those who exhibited a street style, it seemed more difficult to fit in. A white girl performing a street style could be viewed as blending in racially, but could also be viewed as inadequately feminine and trashy. For both girls and boys, the street-based performance, inflected with race-based elements, shaded their whiteness. For boys such as John, however, this tended to enhance their projection of whiteness to peers, while for girls such as Melissa this could degrade it. Thus, the students' perceptions of race, class, and gender interacted and influenced their perceptions of each other, which had an impact on how these youths developed ideas about whiteness and negotiated friendship boundaries.

While many white students at Matthews were still often assumed to stereotypically possess certain academically oriented skills, I did not find such a link to be pervasive among the students. (I observed no minority students, for instance, asking Jackson for academic help!) Although I did not observe these students from a very young age, research with young children (e.g., Connolly 1998; Van Ausdale and Feagin 2001) suggests that children learn stereotypical notions of race as they become socialized into a larger racist culture. Such stereotypes pertain to the hegemonic model that equates whiteness with intelligence, success, distinction, and unspoken power. Matthews' students lived on the cusp of internalizing these stereotypes, on one hand, and constructing their own unique ideas about race, on the other. Perhaps such stereotypes will gradually crystallize in these youths as they have more contact with larger structural and cultural forces that place high value on whiteness. Perhaps many minority students from Matthews will, unfortunately, come to associate academic achievement with whiteness and white students, and many white students will, unfortunately, begin to segregate themselves from minority students. At the time of my research, however, students at Matthews created many innovative, nondominant notions and embodiments of whiteness.

Despite the impact of a larger culture that links whiteness to power and knowledge, my observations at Matthews show that when whites do not have numerical dominance, and institutional mechanisms do not separate white students from other students, new relationships based on race are negotiated. This results in new forms of whiteness that do not have to rely on exclusion or domination to take their shape. Such unexpected forms of whiteness have the potential to disrupt the taken-for-granted, hegemonic ideal of being white. The youths at Matthews Middle School suggest new possibilities and challenges for whiteness in our increasingly multiracial society; this sets the stage for the final chapter of this study.

7

Conclusion

Assumptions and expectations about "normal" white behaviors and ways of life pervade our culture and social institutions, including our schools. Whiteness is rarely connected to concepts such as poverty, the inner city, gang activity, and nonstandard English. In this book, I have explored what becomes of whiteness when white people have a physical and social connection to African Americans, Latinos, and Asian Americans and display the behaviors and sensibilities typically associated with these groups, especially African Americans. The white students I came to know at Matthews defied the assumptions and expectations of whiteness through their unique location in a predominately minority school and, in many cases, their genuine regard for nonwhite people and nonwhite styles. The current normative, dominant form of whiteness in our society is built on attaining social and spatial distance from nonwhites. But the white students at Matthews symbolically (and often actively) challenged this hegemonic form of whiteness. In this conclusion, I discuss how and why these white youths might represent a disruption to white dominance and racial hierarchy. Using the notion of whiteness as a hegemonic system, I also elaborate on how perceptions of race, class, and gender as interconnected concepts shape the understandings and material results of whiteness. Finally, I discuss the challenges and possibilities for ending the reproduction of racial distinctions and inequalities in our schools and other social institutions.

We have seen that white youths at Matthews distanced themselves from whiteness, often blurring racial boundaries. But we have also seen how racial stereotypes and advantages tied to being white lingered in this environment. Intersections of whiteness with social class composed an important part of this process. Teachers' perceptions of and reactions to white students differed based on their interpretations of social class, read primarily through street styles and residential location. For teachers at Matthews, understandings of students'

social class could cloud the projection of privilege through whiteness. In chapter 4, I examined differences in teachers' perceptions of white students and
noted that white teachers were more likely than black teachers to discipline
white students (although still not to the extent of black and Latino students)
and interpret them as academically unremarkable. I argued that the different
way African American and white educators interpreted the class background of
white students, based largely on their understandings of community and school
context, influenced these divergent reactions. White teachers interpreted these
students as poor, which in the teachers' discourse indicated a student likely to
struggle, whereas black teachers interpreted these students as middle class,
which generally connoted a "good" or capable student. Interpretations of class
background appeared to either enhance or diminish the advantages of whiteness, but such advantages overall, as witnessed in white students receiving dis-
proportionate higher-track placement or end-of-year graduation honors, for
instance, remained largely in tact.

Chapter 5 further examined the advantages whiteness retained at
Matthews, focusing on school discipline. I described a hidden curriculum of
bodily discipline at Matthews, in which race, class, and gender interrelated to
influence adult perceptions of which students required discipline in dress and
manners and in what form. This hidden curriculum afforded white youths more
freedom and also constructed them as unproblematic and quietly central, not
requiring the reforms aimed at many nonwhite youths. Students, in general,
who displayed a "street style" tended to receive stricter and more persistent discipline. This style, along with race, appeared to especially influence adult perceptions of masculinity and femininity, as I examined through the examples of
black girls, such as Brittany, framed as inadequately feminine and Latino boys,
such as Carlos, considered dangerously masculine. In contrast, adults tended to
interpret white students, even those portraying a street style, as appropriately
masculine and feminine and viewed their actions indifferently, as acceptable
and benign.

Chapter 6 shifted the perspective from the standpoint of teachers to the
standpoint of students. This showed how kids at Matthews created progressive,
fluid concepts of race and whiteness, concepts which differed somewhat from
the views of adults. Similar to adults, these youths constructed understandings
of whiteness through class and gender, but they tended, ostensibly, to view
"being white" negatively. While whiteness could represent power and privilege
academically, it did not appear "tight" or desirable in the culture of peer relationships, for white youths or nonwhite youths. White kids such as Jackson and
Lisa at Matthews distanced themselves from stereotypical whiteness, developing unexpected ways of being white, largely through their close physical and
emotional connection to African American, Latino, and Asian American
friends. Although such variations existed in being white, many kids at

Matthews still associated whiteness with typical, hegemonic stereotypes connecting it to wealth, power, intelligence, and academically inclined manners. Interestingly, however, they appeared to do so especially in connection to forms of whiteness viewed as external to their neighborhood, demonstrating a much stronger connection, and non-stereotypical interpretation, of white students viewed as their friends and neighbors. Chapter 6 also showed that despite the lingering positive stereotypes of whiteness, many white kids at Matthews (with the guidance of their minority peers) embodied progressive, alternative ways of being white. Such embodiments of whiteness suggest modes of resistance to the current, hegemonic racial hierarchy and invite some further discussion.

Alternative Embodiments of Whiteness

Research and popular culture have critiqued the now-popular tendency for many suburban white kids to borrow cultural forms originating from African Americans, especially hip-hop styles of dress, speech, and music (see Bettie 2003; Perry 2002). These kids are, perhaps correctly, questioned for appropriating black, urban styles while having few actual interactions with black people and, in many cases, still holding stereotypical ideas about race. The situation of white students at Matthews was very different, however. These students were not trying to "act black" because of a fleeting desire to find difference and excitement. Rather, the street styles they presented reflected their reality growing up in an urban, working-class, predominately minority neighborhood. In this sense, they represented an alternative version of whiteness. They constructed this alternative not just through the ways they talked and dressed, but primarily through having consistent interactions with nonwhite people throughout their daily lives.

Alternative embodiments of race can elicit confusion and suspicion from those interpreting them. Kids such as those at Matthews, who often have flexible notions of race and racial distinctions, see little reason why alternative embodiments of whiteness cannot exist. But for adults, who have developed more fixed (and perhaps jaded) notions of race, such representations of whiteness often do not make sense. Perhaps they do not because adults have been more fully incorporated into a world based on racial difference and white dominance. Fluid notions of racial categories and racial meanings in general and, in this case, alternative projections of whiteness in particular threaten to disrupt such a world.

Research on men and masculinity provides a clue for why this might be the case. Masculinity, similar to whiteness, often functions as a dominant, unstated norm. Masculinity is also complicated by race and class intersections (as well as others, such as sexuality), similar to how whiteness is complicated by gender and class (among other categories). Further, based largely on these differences, multiple embodiments of masculinity exist at the same time, just as multiple versions of whiteness simultaneously exist. As I reviewed in chapter 2, Robert Connell (1995) argues that only one ideal form of masculinity—what he calls the "hegemonic form"—dominates in any historical or spatial context (see also Gramsci 1971). Other versions of masculinity (currently in the United States, those that are not white, middle or upper class, or heterosexual) become marginalized. The most marginalized and denigrated forms of masculinity tend to be those that most closely resemble femininity. As Christine Williams states, masculinity, especially in its hegemonic forms, acquires its entire shape and meaning by proving itself to be "different from and superior to femininity" (1995, 120). Thus, men who reflect and enact "feminine" qualities represent a powerful threat to the hegemonic status of masculinity.

Similarly, whiteness seems to predicate itself on physically and ideologically separating from nonwhiteness and implicitly maintaining superiority over nonwhiteness. This is accomplished through assumptions or ideologies that tacitly position a certain form of whiteness—a certain way of talking, interacting, living—as the standard in society. It is also accomplished through structural processes that separate white people from nonwhite people and through this provide greater advantages to white people. Continued residential segregation serves as one obvious example of this. Maintaining spatial distance from nonwhites has solidified white dominance for years and can be linked to racial disparities in education, employment, and health among other outcomes (e.g., Massey, Condran, and Denton 1987; Massey and Denton 1993; Oliver and Shapiro 1995). In education, similar forms of racial segregation between schools, as well as within schools through ability grouping, can perform similar tasks of separation and exclusion.

White people who do not clearly reflect ideas of white dominance or participate in processes of nonwhite exclusion represent not only an aberration, but an "internal threat to whiteness" itself (Newitz and Wray 1997). These whites, such as the many white students at Matthews, defy the assumptions and processes that perpetuate hegemonic whiteness. I suggest that the primary way they do this is through having social and spatial proximity to nonwhite people, especially African Americans, who continue to be the most segregated group from whites (see Reardon, Yun, and Eitle 2000). This close relationship with those considered racial/ethnic minority "out-group" members means that such white people contradict the regimes of superiority and exclusion that have formed hegemonic whiteness. By extension, they disrupt the structure of racial distinction and racial hierarchy more generally. White kids who live in inner-city neighborhoods and reflect the styles of these neighborhoods challenge the assumptions of many adults who have internalized the notion of rigid, basic, and inequitable boundaries between "white" and "black."

Interpretations of Race, Class, Gender, and Neighborhood

The exceptional position of these white people, as poor and working-class urban dwellers, means that they do not fit as easily into schemata that quickly relate race to social class and neighborhood. I have argued throughout this book that we need to move away from positioning race, class, or gender as distinctive effects and instead look at how they influence and alter each other in everyday life. Using race, whiteness in particular, as a starting point, I have attempted to emphasize the importance of how people perceive and develop meanings of this concept through understandings of gender and social class. This process shapes how people identify those considered white and react to them in certain contexts. These meanings and perceptions formed the basis from which students of various race, class, and gender backgrounds were treated at Matthews. White students in this predominately poor school did not necessarily have the advantage of race and the disadvantage of class; rather, race and class in the lives of these students fundamentally altered each other and stemmed from people's perceptions of both at once.

Interpretations of the neighborhood acted as a trigger for how race was perceived vis-à-vis class in this context. This neighborhood and local-historical context, along with the urban, class-based street styles performed by white students, altered interpretations of their whiteness, which influenced the reactions they received from teachers and other students. How these groups *interpreted* whiteness—through class (and gender)—shaped the extent to which race became advantageous or disadvantageous for white students at Matthews. These interpretations of whiteness were not monolithic, but changed depending on the perceivers and the circumstances. Based on this evidence, it appears that being white can consist of very different boundaries and very different meanings in various situations. These boundaries and meanings influence how a person's bodily display will be articulated into a race, class, and gender location and the patterns of treatment and material results this particular location will evoke within an organization. People perceive and understand race, class, and gender in localized and context-specific ways—these concepts interact and change the meaning of each other, and the ways they do so depend heavily on local, institutional histories and procedures, in addition to larger political and media-based discourses. This has important implications for the future of "whiteness" because local contexts and individuals may not reflect and benefit from the hegemonic norm, and they can produce resistance to the racial hierarchy.

As I have stated, many white students at Matthews embodied alternative forms of whiteness that did not rely on separation from and denigration of non-whites. The particular educational context and processes at the school bolstered this integrated form of whiteness. White students perhaps did not have a "critical mass" of other whites through which they could separate themselves from others, nor did they have a racially segregated tracking system that encouraged this separation. These structural factors laid the groundwork from which white students in the setting of Matthews could embody critiques of hegemonic whiteness. It is within such critiques, I suggest, that we can find potential for non-normative and non-exclusive forms of whiteness that challenge white dominance. These critiques are not necessarily based on hairstyle or musical preference, but on white people sharing close contact and experiences with African American, Latino, and Asian American people in schools and neighborhoods.

The Continuing Advantages of Whiteness

The ultimate goal of racial equality was complicated and distant even in the unique environment of Matthews, however. Culturally based assumptions linking whiteness to advantages endured in this setting and tended to aid white students academically. White skin in this context, although shaded and altered by class and gender, still often represented harmlessness, normative masculinity and femininity, knowledge of manners and etiquette, and, in many cases, academic ability. Even those who professed a "color-blind" perspective (white teachers, in particular) silently reproduced the central, normative status of white students by focusing disciplinary and reformative attention on African American and Latino students. Even as white students worked with their nonwhite friends to construct new, potentially progressive embodiments of whiteness, they provoked far less concern and monitoring than their African American and Latino peers when displaying virtually identical street styles. Whiteness was substantially modified through social class in this context, but not really restricted. White students appeared to have more options than nonwhite students for how they could construct their identity and still fit with school norms of behavior and achievement (see Waters 1990). White students could enact street personas without being interpreted as truly dangerous by most teachers and could follow school rules without being accused of "acting white" by peers. Assumptions—from both white people and nonwhite people in this setting—that linked whiteness to a nonthreatening, rule-abiding essence that matched school norms undergirded these generous parameters for white behavior.

Although I have argued that white teachers reacted more negatively to white students than black teachers did, I do not want it to be misinterpreted that black teachers bear the primary responsibility for buttressing the advantages of whiteness in this setting. I have mentioned the informal mentoring African American teachers provided for many African American students. Additionally, in my observations black teachers spent considerably more time teaching students about racism and confronting issues of race head-on. White teachers were more likely to take a color-blind perspective and avoid discussing racial issues in classrooms. As several scholars have argued, color-blindness often represents a "modern" form of racism and white privilege that pretends racial discrimination no longer exists in widespread structural form (see, e.g., Bonilla-Silva 2001; Lewis 2001; Winant 1994). Further, although white teachers did tend to discipline white students more than black teachers did, white teachers still disciplined black and Latino boys more than any other students (see A. Ferguson 2000). Thus, most white teachers certainly participated in constructing black and Latino students as more problematic than whites and positioned whiteness as normative. In my analysis of black educators I identified some ways they might also have collaborated in this process. In my view, this extends our understanding of white advantage beyond something based in racial attitudes, which implicates individuals, to something based in structural processes, which implicates customary ways of thinking and acting imbedded in organizations.

An example of the imbeddedness of white and middle-class privilege at Matthews lies in the school's intention to transmit cultural capital through discipline in dress and manners. Although not an explicit part of the curriculum, this practice pervaded much of the teacher-student interactions. The school seemed to follow the lead of scholars such as Lisa Delpit, who suggests that schools should teach poor and minority children what she calls the "codes of power," or "ways of talking, ways of writing, ways of dressing, and ways of interacting" that relate to the white middle or upper classes and often lead to social success (1995, 25). My observations suggest inherent problems with this approach. By attempting to transmit these forms of cultural capital to students, educators and schools inevitably identify certain students as lacking, deficient, or resistant. The value of cultural capital is necessarily defined by those in power, and this means that in an American context schools will identify nonwhite, poor, and working-class kids as problematic. This only solidifies the cultural hegemony of middle- and upper-class whiteness. Further, because whiteness itself can often be linked to cultural capital and appropriate behavior, even poor and working-class white students may evade the discipline and reformative focus directed at their African American and Latino peers.

Because many cultural styles relate to the body and bodily display (ways of dressing, interacting, etc.), schools must use persistent bodily discipline to reform these "problematic" students. Such discipline may in fact work to produce compliance. It may, for instance, transform energetic, curious girls into ironic paragons of docile, ladylike control and silence. However, it might also produce and identify misfits. These students are likely to see themselves as incompatible with the school, disconnect from it, and possibly disrupt it. Reformative disciplinary regimes, imbedded in institutions through the hidden curriculum, may lead poor and racial/ethnic minority students in particular to

internalize a view of themselves as defective or oppositional, which can provoke alienation and resistance to schooling. This subverts the entire goal of
providing students the tools for upward mobility and only serves as one more
tool to substantiate and justify white and middle- and upper-class dominance.
Discipline, in a general manner, is a necessary part of an adequate learning
environment. Discipline targeted according to race, class, and gender, on the
other hand (even if well intended), may only serve to reproduce these inequalities and centralize hegemonic notions of whiteness.

Concerns about cultural styles of dress and bodily discipline also relate to
the policies of dress codes and uniforms in schools. I argue that uniform dress
codes, when enacted in public schools almost exclusively in working-class,
urban environments, can make these institutions appear punitive rather than
caring. Because working-class and minority youth prefer and have developed
styles of dress deemed inappropriate by most dress codes, irregular enforcement of dress codes by race, class, and gender seems likely, and this uneven
enforcement can accentuate feelings of incompatibility with schooling. Interestingly, the uniform dress code at Matthews fulfilled neither of its stated inten-
tions. It did not mask poverty—students as well as teachers still identified
certain students as poor and others as wealthy, and this affected interactions
with these students. Nor did the dress code stifle the representation of gang
affiliation. Students constantly invented new ways to announce their gang
predilection, creatively out-maneuvering the dress-code strictures. Teachers
themselves also contradicted this intention of the dress code by identifying
markers of supposed gang affiliation (two of which related to race and gender
in and of themselves), despite the students' wearing uniforms.

While dress codes may work effectively in private schools, students attending these schools are mostly white and middle to upper class and have chosen
to attend. The kids in such schools do not typically fall under stereotypes that
they lack social skills or have oppositional attitudes. In such settings, this policy
(although it may still irritate students) does not carry the same sense of forced
restriction and confinement that it might for poor, disproportionately minority, urban kids. These kids see that predominately white public schools, some
of which may be nearby, do not require uniforms. This stigmatizes impoverished, minority schools and students as problematic and in need of reform,
while most white students are once again positioned as appropriate and normative. Even with parental approval, mandatory uniform policies for poor and
minority kids can make schools, as Derek eloquently described, resemble prisons. Feelings of being targeted and unfairly punished could proliferate in such
an environment for students and impel them to resist education.

However, uniform policies in schools still have some potential benefits. In
many Catholic and other private schools, as I have mentioned, these appear to

work quite effectively, and students grow very accustomed to wearing a uniform while learning. These students have chosen to attend such schools, but even so, public schools may be able to borrow from their example. In schools where students all wear uniform dress and such policies are not enforced in an uneven way, kids can become less focused on appearance and more focused on learning. In such an environment, self-expression becomes not something purchased through commodities, but something enacted through personality. Uniforms in schools can mitigate the consumerist fascination that has engulfed U.S. society and encourage expression through thinking and doing rather than wearing and owning. However, as my evidence from Matthews shows, such a policy in public education should not be implemented only in urban schools perceived as unsafe and unstructured. Such localized initiatives only make predominately white schools seem standard and superior by contrast. Instead, all public schools should enact such a policy if any do. Wealthy suburban students could certainly benefit from a de-emphasis on commodity captivation just as much as urban kids. Moreover, students could be allowed some room to express themselves within uniform guidelines without being perceived as oppositional—the restriction of baggy pants, for example, seems pointless, particularly when so many youths prefer this style. Wide-reaching but flexible uniform guidelines would reduce the likelihood that any groups of students would feel singled out unfairly by such a policy.

While many overt or hidden policies, such as disciplinary regulation, contributed to marginalizing working-class and racial/ethnic minority students at Matthews and elevating hegemonic notions of whiteness, others did not. The tracking process at the school, in particular, did not manifestly position white students as separate from minority students and superior to them, as most tracking procedures do. Because this process did not stratify students by race, it did not present a salient reminder of white educational dominance. When whiteness is not positioned as organizationally dominant in this way, and not constructed as simultaneously central and exclusive, this obstructs the development of assumptions about whiteness that congeal this quality with achievement and education in general. Such an organizational context allows kids, who often have less rigid notions of race, to transform racial boundaries and meanings—negotiating new places and criteria for whiteness and nonwhiteness.

The racial composition of ability groups at Matthews resulted primarily from two sources: educators' efforts and the predominately nonwhite composition of the student body. Even with these factors, white students still took higher-level classes in greater numbers than their percentage of the student body would suggest. This indicates that the procedure of tracking or ability grouping across courses presents potential difficulties for racial equity and contact. Pamela Perry (2002) finds that inequitable tracking can present a visually apparent example of white academic superiority, even in predominately minority schools. Matthews' tracking system did not result in such a symbol of white advantage. However, if the school had only a few more white students overall, proportions suggest they would predominate in upper-level classes. Hence, whiteness, even in a working-class setting, can continue to symbolize intelligence, social skills, and harmlessness. Such stereotypical notions will linger only until social organizations and structures no longer reflect and reproduce them. These stereotypical ideas feed a tracking system that only reaffirms them by providing white kids access to a superior education in uneven proportions.

I disagree with arguments that tracking can be mended in a more racially equitable way (for example, Hallinan 1994). Even in the unique, non-magnet, predominately nonwhite environment of Matthews (in terms of students, teachers, and administrators), white students were still placed in higher-level classes in greater proportion than minority students. The only way to ensure that ability grouping does not project a cogent symbol of white academic dominance and impede minority students' access to the best possible education is to abandon this procedure altogether. Teachers can be retrained to utilize intellectual diversity in their classrooms and not anticipate classes divided between "good kids" and "bad kids." This would provide all students, regardless of race, class, or gender, a fair opportunity for educational success, foster greater interracial contact between students, and counteract the reproduction of stereotypes that connect being white to high academic ability.

Challenges and Possibilities

An innovative and unique racial structure was evident at Matthews, but kids there still showed signs of learning and inhabiting more fixed and stereotypical racial discourses. I can only speculate on what will happen as these white students begin to possibly internalize a view that their whiteness should afford them more opportunities and power than it seems to. This may occur as they enter other social institutions that reward a hegemonic form of whiteness—but not the form they embody—and implicitly encourage them to seize on their race to assert difference and privilege over their minority peers. In this way, the hegemonic process that solidifies white domination can elicit support from different, potentially resistant, white people such as many kids at Matthews. These students and others who embody internal critiques of whiteness through class or neighborhood location may abandon identifying with these modes of difference and instead consent to replicating white hegemony, even if they will be marginalized within this system.

The stories from Matthews Middle School suggest new possibilities and challenges for our schools and educators. This study reveals how whiteness maintains its advantage through excluding nonwhites as well as whites that disrupt its attempts to maintain preeminence. Educational organizations reproduce the inequitable privileges of this dominant whiteness through assumptions and practices that stereotypically link being white to cultural capital, self-discipline, and academic ability. However, such practices and assumptions need not control our school system. We must make real efforts to stop exclusionary practices in education that stem from segregation within schools and across schools. We must also work to value, rather than reform, nondominant forms of style, interaction, masculinity, and femininity. Through such efforts, educators and youths can work to change the reproduction of white middle- and upper-class privilege, perhaps paving the way for a more egalitarian future.

APPENDIX:
RESEARCH METHODS

In this appendix, I describe my research methods in more depth. In particular, I wish to discuss several issues that may have shaped my findings, relating to my access to the research site, my modes and strategies of data collection, and my social position as a white, middle-class, male researcher. Through this discussion, I also describe my relationship to the school and its teachers and students, without whom this study would not have been possible.

Data Collection

I typically spent two to three days a week at the school, virtually every week of the school year. The study proceeded, as I mentioned, over the course of two school years, beginning in the fall of 2000. I visited the school just three times during the fall of 2000 but started more frequent visits in 2001 until May of that year. These frequent visits continued in the 2001–2002 school year, ending in May 2002. During my initial visits, teachers and administrators seemed somewhat cautious around me. As I continued research, this gave way to astonishment at the consistency of my visits (one teacher commented when I walked in the front door after about three months of frequent visits, "You must love this school. You're here every day!"). And finally, around April of 2001 and for most of the 2001–2002 school year, teachers and students appeared to grow accustomed to my presence.

Much of my time at the school was focused on classroom observation. These observations did not follow a set pattern. Instead, I tried to randomize them as much possible, so I was able to observe an array of classes of different levels, different subjects, and different students and teachers. I observed before school and after school, including sporting events, ceremonies, and productions, in addition to classroom observation. As I have mentioned, I also volunteered as a tutor at the school. The classes and students I tutored varied, but focused predominately on helping with writing, at the behest of the school. Tutoring allowed me to converse with several different students (I tutored roughly fifteen students one-on-one and probably over forty in group settings and within classrooms), without formally interviewing them. Moreover, this provided me with a great opportunity to connect to students and teachers, as well as give back to the school, which I will discuss further toward the end of this appendix.

When not participating as a tutor, I typically took down notes in a small notebook from observations as they occurred. When helping in a class, or if I sensed that my note taking might appear obtrusive in a situation, I wrote down notes as soon as possible afterwards (see Emerson, Fretz, and Shaw 1995). I also wrote down conversations with teachers and students in classrooms as soon as possible after they occurred, usually in the school library, lunchroom, or my car. Upon entering classrooms, I introduced myself to teachers, explained that I was there to conduct research for my dissertation and the Annenberg Foundation, and asked if I could observe. I made it clear that they should not feel compelled to let me observe, and occasionally some would say that they "didn't feel like it" that day, which I respected. I generally contained my observations to classrooms or school-based activities. I do not use conversations I had with teachers or students outside of classroom situations, or any statement prefaced with "off the record," as direct data (see also Spradley 1979), although such conversations did affect my general thinking.

Following Spradley (1979), I collected quick, brief jottings of observations in my notebook at the site and later added detail to these when off site. Spradley suggests maintaining three notebooks as a field researcher, one for a brief "condensed" account of observations, another for an "expanded" account of these same observations, and a third to record thoughts, hunches, and issues encountered during the research process. I began research with the intent to use these three notebooks, but they began to overlap as I proceeded through my fieldwork, partly because I had a long commute to the school. I abandoned the third notebook early on and began to record thoughts, hunches, and issues within my primary field notebook under separate headings. This was simply easier logistically and allowed for a quicker recording of thoughts when they arose. Similar to Spradley's suggestion, though, I did continue to keep a condensed account in my primary field notebook and then expanded this account in a computer file.

I tape-recorded two educator interviews, but, because of the uneasiness this caused the interviewees, I wrote down the other interviews as I conducted them (I conducted fourteen formal interviews in all). I interviewed teachers of different experience levels (from first year to almost thirty years), racial backgrounds (approximately half were white and half were African American), and subject areas. The teacher interviews followed a semi-structured format. I used an interview guide but occasionally deviated from this guide to pursue topics of particular interest for which I did not have specific questions. I also altered this guide somewhat as I became more acquainted with the field, to pursue topics that were particularly meaningful in that setting. However, I did follow the same basic interview schedule with all interviewees, especially in the second year of my research, when I conducted the bulk of the interviews. I provided all interviewees with an information sheet/consent form, which explained the purpose of the study and their voluntary participation in it.

All interviews occurred in the teachers' rooms during their off-periods and lasted about one hour each. The teachers' rooms were not ideal locations for privacy, as many times students and other teachers interrupted briefly, but I hope these locations gave the teachers a more empowering feeling of being on "home turf." When unsure of a statement made during an interview, I asked the respondents for clarification. If I was ultimately unsure about the wording of a statement that was made to me in an interview or that I overheard when observing, I did not record this as a quote. Thus, while the quotes provided in this study are not verbatim, they are reasonably accurate.

Data Analysis

I analyzed my data in a similar way to the modified version of the "grounded theory" approach (Glaser and Strauss 1967) advocated by Emerson, Fretz, and Shaw (1995). Grounded theory stresses that a researcher should remain very open when analyzing qualitative data and allow connections and theories to emerge from the data themselves, rather than being imputed artificially by the researcher (Glaser and Strauss 1967). Emerson, Fretz, and Shaw (1995), by contrast, suggest that one should remain relatively open to making new discoveries from the data but caution that ethnographers cannot pretend to stand apart from the data they collect. Collecting ethnographic data, they contend, constitutes a dialectical process in which ideas developed through data collection shape the way subsequent data are collected. Thus, ethnographic data arrive in a way already patterned by the researcher's biases and interests, even if the researcher developed these in the field. This means that a researcher should approach analysis of these data with certain broad themes in mind.

I coded data in a "focused" way (Emerson, Fretz, and Shaw 1995), relating to key themes that I interpreted as important to race, class, gender, and academic experiences at the school. I entered the field with broad interests in race, class, gender, and schooling as they related especially to white students in this setting, and I narrowed this to more specific sub-themes (some of which were completely unexpected) after some time in the field. After data collection, I read through field notes and interviews manually, searching for examples that fell within these sub-themes and coding them as such. These themes correspond to the three main analysis chapters that appear in this study: teachers' perceptions and interactions with white students; discipline in terms of race, class, and gender; and students' perceptions and interactions regarding white students and "being white."

Methodological Issues

I gained access to Matthews Middle School through the Annenberg Foundation. As part of a large-scale school reform effort across the United States, including several schools in Texas, this foundation provided funding for reforms at Matthews and also facilitated my research at the school. The process of Annenberg reform in the school created a somewhat unique context and may have shaped the data I collected in a somewhat different way than if I had collected these data more independently. I explained to teachers and administrators that I was there to research the reforms as well as conduct my own research. Although I often explained that none of my findings would be linked to future Annenberg funding for the school, some teachers and administrators seemed cautious around me and hesitant to mention tensions at the school. This hesitancy subsided slightly as I gained more rapport with some educators at the school, but I sensed that it remained an undercurrent with others.

As part of the funding for this study, I traveled over one hundred miles to conduct research at the school. Because of this long commute, it was difficult for me to "hang out" with teachers, parents, and kids outside of school hours. I made it a point to attend as many after-school festivals, forums, and sporting events as possible, however, and made sure to arrive at the school before classes started as much as I could. I also volunteered as a tutor, and while I did this most often during school hours, sometimes I stayed after school for kids who needed extra help. Ultimately, though, I could not really enter the lives of my participants outside of the school walls, as so many excellent ethnographic studies in education have been able to do. The most critical hindrance for this study, I think, is that I could not get a complete perspective from parents at Matthews. I was able to talk to a few parents when they came to the school, but not many, and this study could be enhanced by incorporating their perspectives. However, to overcome these restrictions, I narrowed the research focus and questions of this study to pertain especially to interactions within the school. Interestingly, as I mention, this has actually been a somewhat neglected level of analysis in recent ethnographic work in education, with many studies focusing on student identity.

My study also differs from much of this ethnographic literature in that I did not attempt to gain access to students specifically. Bettie (2003), Perry (2002), and Valenzuela (1999), for instance, describe how they presented themselves in the school environment, especially through their dress, to align themselves more with the students than the teachers. Because, for the purposes of this study, I was not concerned with understanding the perspective of the students exclusively, I did not attempt a similar strategy. This would have been impossible, furthermore, because the school encouraged adults there to dress formally (many men wore business suits, for instance), and I certainly would have alienated myself from many teachers by wearing jeans and a T-shirt. Thus, I attempted to find a middle-ground look that typically consisted of slacks and a tucked-in polo shirt (similar to what students at the school wore, but not in their uniform colors). As I have stated, I also served as a tutor at the school, which placed me more in the "adult" camp, but allowed me to talk and get to know the kids better as well.

I tried to signal to kids that I was not fully aligned with their teachers by making a point to not discipline them. Because of this, on many occasions I sat with kids while they freely discussed illegal activities such as drug deals. Since I did not actually see anything illegal, and their discussion was usually pretty minor anyway, I chose not to report anything although most teachers and administrators would have probably disagreed with this approach. Several times, teachers would leave their rooms and ask if I could monitor the kids. I accepted this charge, but refrained from any stern discipline in these situations, instead only warning the students that the teacher would soon return. I only really yelled at kids to stop doing something on one occasion, which I recount in my field notes:

> The teacher has very little control over this class and disciplines about as much as I do. The class is throwing pencils, erasers, and other paraphernalia across the room at each other. At one point an eraser hits me hard in the shoulder. I hear shouts of "ohhh!" from across the room, and I turn over there to ask who threw it. They won't fess up, so I tell them, "Stop throwing things across the room. I don't want to get hit again." This actually works for a limited amount of time, but soon a boy sets up shop on the other side of the room to throw things at his friends, and some projectiles go whizzing past my head again. I look at him and tell him that one better not hit me. He insists this won't happen. This is a strange situation, because I don't want to discipline, but I also want to preserve my own safety. I don't think the teacher even noticed that I got hit with an eraser. The teacher does come up to me later and apologizes for the students' behavior, saying, "This class is just pretty big and out of control. Rather than spend all my energy trying to contain them, I'm just going to ride the bronco 'till the end of the year and hope to hang on."

For the most part, though, I did not go around disciplining kids, and I think once they learned this they conducted themselves more freely when I was around. At the same time, because I acted as a tutor and helped out in many of the classes observed, I think the teachers also became accustomed to my presence and conducted themselves less cautiously around me.

To collect my data, I jotted notes into a small notebook I carried around in a shoulder bag. When I was tutoring in a class, or if I noticed that my jottings made a teacher nervous or distracted students, I wrote notes down directly following my observation period. When I began conducting interviews with teachers, I tape-recorded the first two interviews. However, I noticed that the tape recorder appeared to make the respondents nervous and hesitant. Their answers were brief and seemed rather guarded. Because of this, I wrote down interviews with the other respondents in a notebook while I conducted them. I then retreated to my car or the school library to add detail to my notes of these interviews based on my recent memory. This strategy may have sacrificed some accuracy, as I could not record everything teachers said verbatim. However, what was lost in accuracy was more than made up for in frankness. These interviews proceeded swimmingly compared with the first two and struck me as much more conversational.

Further, I eventually improved my speed of note taking, and I think I was able to capture what the interviewees stated in a reasonably accurate way. If a respondent said something for which I was not entirely sure of the wording, I did not record this as a direct quote, and I do not include it here in quotation marks (the same is true for field-note quotations). For the most part, though, especially with interesting statements, I either recorded them word for word on the spot, or could easily remember them when I added detail immediately afterwards.

My social location as a white, middle-class, male researcher undoubtedly influenced what participants told me at Matthews and what I observed. I often found myself to be the sole white person in classrooms and meetings I observed. This, coupled with my position as a researcher affiliated with the Annenberg Foundation, probably magnified my outsider status in many situations and influenced the interactions I observed, making them less than typical. This may have played an important role in shaping the data for this study, especially those excerpts that appear in chapter 4. There is reason to believe that my presence in the classroom might have influenced the findings of black teachers and white teachers responding differently to white students. Because I am white, African American teachers may have reacted more positively to white students in my presence and made sure to tell me of white students they considered good students. Similarly, white teachers may have downplayed their relationships with white students and embellished their positive perceptions of students of color in order to project to me an appearance of racial equity.

Further, my race, class, and gender background might have caused me to misunderstand, or just simply miss, the full meaning of many interactions and statements. For example, in chapter 5 I mention the gender-specific social clubs, called the Gentlemen of Excellence and the Proper Ladies, at the school. I did not know that such clubs, which often emphasize grooming, manners, and college attainment, were relatively common in the African American community, especially among the middle class, until a black colleague told me about this. This added an important context to my view of these clubs and much of the emphasis on dress and manners at Matthews. I first saw this focus as punitive, but after understanding this context I saw more of the strategy of teaching social skills that could lead to upward mobility.

My lack of fluency in Spanish probably formed the most apparent way I often failed to understand interactions and conversations. Students often conversed in Spanish and I had little notion of what they were saying. Further, this certainly impeded my access to these students because I could only communicate with them in English. My gender also undoubtedly attuned me more to the lives of boys at Matthews than girls. Because I was more knowledgeable about boys' clothing, for instance, I noticed more about the important divisions in dress among boys. Although I tried to remain aware of girls' styles as well, the reader will notice that I describe the boys' clothing in more detail. As with the teachers, I did not try to explicitly connect with either girls or boys. This was easier than I thought, as girls seemed just as willing to talk to me and ask me questions as the boys did. The tutoring also served as a boon in this regard because it gave me a chance to spend time with both girls and boys, although teachers more often matched me with boys.

I found that my social distance as an outsider in general decreased over time, as I became more familiar with adults and students at the school, and they with me. However, the biases of my background undoubtedly shaped the data I collected. In my view this does not render these data invalid, but just different from what a nonwhite woman, for instance, might have collected. No researchers can hope to match themselves completely with the infinitely variable social positions and backgrounds of their respondents (see Johnson-Bailey 1999), and the insistence that they should logically proceeds to what Robert Merton (1972) calls "methodological solipsism": the view that we can really only study and know ourselves. To overcome this epistemological egoism, I think researchers should allow themselves some methodological leeway in learning about the perspectives and experiences of outsider groups. This process might not yield the same information as that of an insider, but this does not mean the information is wrong, only that it stems from a different perspective. Because this book might reflect my biases and limited cultural knowledge as a white, middle-class, male adult, I have chosen to use most field-note extracts exactly as I recorded them, so readers can more easily assess them using their own perspectives.

During the process of observing in classrooms, I saw many ways in which I had an impact on those classrooms. As I mentioned, some teachers became nervous when I observed, and some students became distracted. Several times, especially when observing classrooms for the first time, students would ask the teacher something like, "Miss ——, why are you talking like that?" This suggested that these teachers acted somewhat differently, perhaps more formally, in my presence than they would have ordinarily. Sometimes teachers used my presence as leverage to improve their students' conduct. In one instance, recorded in my field notes, this put me in a rather awkward position:

> The teacher is losing more control over the class, and eventually starts yelling at them: "You need to be quiet now! You are acting so bad, and we have a visitor. Imagine what he must think of you!" (I can't stand it when teachers make remarks like this, and even worse, this prompted students to ask what I thought of them). One girl, who had been in trouble earlier in the class, asks me, "Do you think I've been bad, mister?" I kind of shrug at her, and then her friend from across the table asks much louder, "Mister, do you think I have been bad?" At this moment, the whole class gets silent and awaits my answer. I have to consider whether to take the teacher's side or the students' side. I try to offer a diplomatic answer: "That's for [your teacher] to decide, not me," I tell her softly, trying to not make an announcement for the whole class. This seems to appease both the teacher and the students, and everyone continues with their business.

Teachers often developed creative ways to explain my presence in the classroom when I was just observing. During one class, a student turned around during a lesson to ask me what I was doing there. The teacher, a black woman named Ms. Hawley, said, "Don't just turn around and ask him that. That's rude, and I'm trying to teach here. If you want to know, he's my brother!" Ms. Hawley and I shared a good laugh over this, and the kids laughed as well. But later some of them asked me quietly, "Are you really Ms. Hawley's brother?"

These examples show that I could distract kids somewhat when observing. To compensate for this I often volunteered to help out in classes, or I tried to not respond to students who were vying for my attention. Sometimes I accidentally slipped and acted in a way that might have disrupted students. This would happen most often when I would laugh at something when the teacher wanted a more serious atmosphere. For example, once when I observed in Ms. Taylor's class, she instructed the kids to get out their TAAS (Texas Assessment of Academic Skills exam) workbooks. A girl sitting near the front exclaimed, "Jesus—not TAAS again!" To which Ms. Taylor responded, "That's right. Pray to Jesus and maybe you'll actually pass TAAS!" I couldn't help but chuckle at this out loud, which was a mistake because it encouraged the students to laugh as well. Ms. Taylor, on the other hand, glared at them with a stern look, not wanting such levity at that moment. In some cases, however, my presence in the classroom may have actually helped students focus. When I asked Mr. Reed if my presence distracted the students in his class, he said he thought it actually encouraged them to concentrate more and behave more maturely because they wanted to impress me and I served as another adult in the room who was interested in their progress.

Comments such as this, and teachers and administrators thanking me for helping with tutoring, made me feel as though I did not create too much of a disruption or burden for the school. Matthews provided me with so much—educators and students there were almost always warm and accommodating to me—that I tried to make my presence easier for them and repay them however I could. For instance, I tried to buy candy or other items sold for school fundraisers whenever possible. The most rewarding way I tried to repay the school, however, was to volunteer as a tutor, as I have mentioned. I would often offer to help out in classes, and in the second year of my research I served a more structured role to prepare students, especially those that the school identified as needing extra help, for the TAAS test in writing. Students seemed to benefit from this one-on-one help, and teachers were often incredulous that certain students had written so much after I had worked with them.

I probably did little to help these students compared to what their teachers and many administrators did as part of a concerted effort to improve writing scores at the school. However, I was pleased to see that the passing rates for Matthews' students on the writing portion of the TAAS that year improved by nearly ten points—the largest gain of any test subject. The principal was even more pleased, but thought I played more of a role in this improvement than I think I actually did. In fact, as I recall in chapter 1, during the graduation ceremony at the end of the year she surprised me by honoring my help at Matthews in front of the entire school and all the students' families! I was certainly flattered by this, but also felt embarrassed and somewhat guilty. I did not really think I deserved such an accolade when educators at Matthews did so much more to help students than I did. I was flattered, however, to be recognized for helping at the school.

In the end, although I tried to help and give back, I inevitably act as author of this text and take the experiences created primarily by educators and students at Matthews to form my own arguments. Matthews Middle School is a wonderful school, filled with many dedicated educators and students. I sincerely hope no one reads this book and comes away thinking that Matthews is a "bad" school or that it is filled with misguided educators. However, for the purposes of this study, this school composed a site to critically analyze interactions in terms of race, class, and gender. I analyze certain meanings and processes at the school through this critical lens not to place blame on any individuals, but to interrogate a larger culture and practice of educational inequality that supersedes a single school or a single set of educators. This approach reflects the intellectual biases of my research interests (see also Bourdieu and Wacquant 1992, 39) and attunes me to the salience of race, class, and gender inequality at the school, but it is not meant as a sweeping commentary on the school as a whole. Ultimately, this study, like the study of any social setting, excludes many of the myriad stories existing at Matthews, some perhaps more inspiring than those I include here, others perhaps more disheartening. Thus, the stories told in this book bear the inevitable mark of my interpretation, which is just one of many and should be read as such.

NOTES

CHAPTER 1   INTRODUCTION

1.   This is a pseudonym, as are all personal and place names in this book, to protect confidentiality.

2.   I wish to clarify a couple of issues regarding terminology in this book. First, I will occasionally refer to adolescents as kids because that is how teachers often referred to them and how they often referred to themselves (see also, Thorne 1993; Moore 2002). Second, I will alternate between African American and black, Hispanic and Latino, and Asian and Asian American for readability and because educators and students at the school alternated between these terms. I also occasionally use the term "nonwhite" to refer to people of color. I do not intend for this term to re-center whiteness as the norm, but instead I use it for readability and to establish contrast.

3.   In focusing on the experiences of these few white students, I do not intend to ignore or marginalize the experiences of students of color, as Margaret Andersen (2003) warns that many studies of "whiteness" have the potential to do. In this research I take a critical view of white advantages, and I do not want this strategy to imply a re-centering of whiteness. For this reason, I describe and analyze the experiences of students of color as well as white students, and trace the continuing privileges of whiteness in this context. However, I do want to highlight and explore what becomes of whiteness when white people compose a distinct numerical minority.

4.   In this sense these whites are in a similar situation to distinct numerical minorities often called "tokens." Research on tokenism in occupations shows that historically disadvantaged groups such as African Americans and women tend to suffer psychological stress and difficulty in advancement when they compose a numerical minority in their jobs (Kanter 1977; Jackson, Thoits, and Taylor 1995). However, men, members of a historically advantaged group, tend to experience enhanced opportunities and prestige when composing a numerical minority in predominately female occupations (Williams 1995).

5.   This projection of white people declining in population in the United States requires some clarification. First, this assessment is based on the category referred to as "non-Hispanic whites," or people considered white who are not of Latin American background. Second, and somewhat related, this projection is based on the assumption that the existing boundaries of whiteness will remain the same and groups now considered nonwhite will not eventually merge into the white category. Given the past history of boundary changes in the white category, many commentators suggest this would be unlikely (see Warren and Twine 1997; Yancey 2003).

CHAPTER 2   UNDERSTANDING WHITE ADVANTAGES
             IN EDUCATION AND SOCIETY

1.   The comparison between white students in these two schools is somewhat sophistic,
      however, because the predominately minority school actually served as an arts mag-
      net school. This school might well have attracted white students who had progressive
      and liberal views of race and racial politics at the outset. We do not know if these stu-
      dents' attitudes in favor of affirmative action, for instance, stem primarily from con-
      tact with racial/ethnic minority youths or primarily from pre-existing political
      worldviews that allowed them to choose this particular school in the first place.

2.   I first discussed the concept of hegemonic whiteness, borrowing from Connell's
      (1995) theory of hegemonic masculinity, in my dissertation (Morris 2003). Since that
      time, others have also discussed this concept independently (Lewis 2004). Here, I
      flesh this concept out further, elaborating on what the theory of hegemony can tell
      us about whiteness.

3.   I agree with Demetriou's (2001) contention that, while Connell does well to theorize
      differences within masculinity, his distinction between hegemonic, marginalized,
      subordinate, and complicit masculinities is somewhat rigid. Thus, I do not categorize
      differences among whites in this exact way, but see hegemony as maintained inter-
      nally through a continual process of appropriating, as well as denigrating, various ele-
      ments of whiteness.

4.   For example, Connell (1995) emphasized changes in dominant versions of masculinity
      across time and space, and Gramsci (1971) viewed hegemonic configurations uniting
      various groups as specific to particular eras, referring to them as "historical blocs."

CHAPTER 3   MATTHEWS MIDDLE SCHOOL IN HISTORICAL
             AND CONTEMPORARY CONTEXT

1.   After I completed my fieldwork at Matthews, Texas changed TAAS to TAKS (Texas
      Assessment of Knowledge and Skills) and included testing in all grades from third to
      eleventh.

2.   The TAAS test differed substantially from grade to grade and from year to year. The
      large differences between seventh- and eighth-grade passing rates at Matthews par-
      tially reflect this differentiation.

3.   The actual tract identification numbers and tract areas changed in these two censuses,
      so I used the mapping programs available on the Census Bureau Web site (www.cen-
      sus.gov) to link the tracts from both censuses to the approximate school attendance
      boundaries. In both cases, some tracts included a small amount of area that lay out-
      side the school boundaries. In addition, as I note in the tables, the tracts are not pre-
      cisely comparable to each other across these censuses. However, tract A in 1990
      roughly corresponds to the same region of the Matthews attendance zone as tract A in
      2000. The main difference is that the 1990 tracts included more geographic area that
      spread outside of the Matthews attendance zone. Because of these shortcomings, the
      data I report here should be viewed as just a very rough means of comparison.

4.   I realize that a map depicting the census tracts I use with their actual identification
      numbers, along with the school attendance zone, would give this description sub-
      stantially more clarity and allow the readers to trace and judge its accuracy for them-
      selves. However, I have chosen to avoid this in order to ensure the confidentiality I
      promised to the school and my participants, which I discussed in chapter 1.

5. The 2000 census allowed respondents to select more than one race to describe themselves. The percentages I report here are for individuals choosing only one race out of the total number of respondents. I have placed those respondents who chose more than one race (N = 909) into a separate category. The most common race chosen by respondents reporting multiple races was African American.

6. This could, of course, be an artifact of the changes in census tract area, but the surrounding census tracts in 2000 show similar racial demographics, suggesting that the entire area made up of the 1990 census tracts demonstrated these same patterns of racial change.

CHAPTER 4   FROM "MIDDLE CLASS" TO "TRAILER TRASH"

1. See also the influential work of William Julius Wilson (1980, 1987, 1991), who has argued that, for African Americans at least, class is a more important factor than race in affecting life chances. Wilson traces a history of race relations in the United States from the antebellum period and argues that after World War II political and structural changes occurred that forged a transition from race-based to class-based inequality. Previous to this period, African Americans as a group suffered from oppression based on race, e.g., slavery and Jim Crow segregation. But the dismantling of state enforced racial exclusion brought about through the civil rights movement, and culminating in affirmative action policies, extended unprecedented opportunities to African Americans. Wilson has contended that only a few upwardly mobile black people were able to take full advantage of these policies, leaving behind a vast group of black poor. Thus, he states that discrimination based on race per se has declined in significance, having virtually no bearing on the economic situation of middle-class African Americans. Rather, in his view, the oppression experienced by most black people stems primarily from their class background, and this class oppression is especially egregious for the burgeoning and increasingly isolated black urban poor. Wilson's powerful argument has (perhaps unintentionally) encouraged a spate of either/or thinking regarding race and class in racial/ethnic studies.

2. Bourdieu delineates three main forms of capital, which provide social advantages to those who possess them: economic, social, and cultural. In addition to these, Bourdieu has also identified what he calls "symbolic" forms of capital. He defines symbolic capital as "capital—in whatever form—insofar as it is represented, i.e., apprehended symbolically" (Bourdieu 1986, 255; see also Bourdieu and Wacquant 1992, 119; Lewis 2003b). Thus, symbolic capital appears to exist, in Bourdieu's scheme, through display or representation of any of the other forms.

3. As I mentioned in chapter 3, this test covered a range of academic areas, and the Texas Education Agency publicly reports results (in percentage of students passing) from all schools by key student subgroups such as race, gender, and economic disadvantage. At Matthews, seventh graders took TAAS tests in reading and math, and eighth graders took TAAS in reading, math, writing, science, and social studies.

4. The foregoing discussion begs the question of which group of teachers was correct: Were the white kids mostly poor or mostly middle class? The reader will recall from chapter 2 that I unfortunately lack the economic background data on white students, data that could provide a more definitive answer to this; but one administrator did tell me that about half of the white students received free or reduced-price lunches. However, the point I am trying to make through this analysis underscores the importance of *perceiving* social class (whether "accurate" or not), and how these perceptions

influence reactions and treatment. I found it most interesting that white teachers and black teachers had such divergent views of class background, and I sought to assess how they interacted with these students rather than determine which group's views more closely matched that of official economic indicators.

5. Interestingly, Ms. Boyd taught seventh grade. She was also relatively new to the school when I interviewed her and did not teach at the school in 1999–2000, when the 2000–2001 eighth graders were in seventh grade.

6. White students composed 8 percent of the enrollment for pre-AP courses and 4 percent of the student body.

7. Alexander, Entwisle, and Thompson (1987) suggest that teachers' class origin is actually more important than their race in shaping reactions to students. Few teachers I talked to at Matthews, black or white, came from highly advantaged backgrounds, so it was difficult for me to explore this proposition. Race and class origin probably combined to frame teacher perceptions at Matthews, but I found the most obvious differences related to race.

8. This should not imply that perceptions tell the whole story, however. As Lareau (2002) compellingly demonstrates, social background also works within family life to influence how individuals approach institutions and gain institutional advantages. I merely suggest that perceptions of social background compose an additional key element in how race and class influence life chances.

CHAPTER 5   "TUCK IN THAT SHIRT!"

1. Gender-specific youth organizations such as these, emphasizing social skills, formal etiquette, and community service, analogous to college-level fraternities and sororities, are not uncommon in the African American community. During the time of my fieldwork, for instance, many predominately African American schools in the city hosted similar clubs.

2. Bettie (2000, 2002, 2003) distinguishes between how class is "performed," or how individuals actively manage themselves to project a particular notion of class (see also Goffman 1973), and how class is "performative," or how individuals unreflectively enact certain class-based styles and preferences. I find this notion of social class useful; however, I am less concerned than Bettie is with how individuals' perform an identity that diverges from their class-based origins and instead focus on the impact of performances on observers.

3. One could argue that this stems from the fewer numbers of whites and Asians at the school and that I was simply less likely to encounter discipline aimed at these students. However, I purposely observed more classes and interactions involving white students than other students. It is possible that I missed some of the discipline aimed at Asian students, but this is highly unlikely in the case of white students.

4. While certainly strict, Matthews' climate was not one of harsh and severe discipline, such as that described by Anyon (1997) in her study of a predominately African American urban school.

CHAPTER 6   "WHITE CHOCOLATE"

1. As Labov (1972), Heath (1983), and others have argued, "black English" includes phrases and logic that distinguish it from white southern speech. Lisa's speech often

exhibited patterns characteristic of black English. For example, Lisa used the word "be" to indicate habitual behavior and dropped the pronunciation of final letters of words, such as when I noted her say, "She be doin' her hair good, y'ao [you all]" when talking to friends about hair styling, or "hol' up [hold up]" to indicate to a teacher that she wanted to start a reading passage over. In another similarity to black English, her speech often exhibited the absence of a copula, or connecting word, such as in the following question posed to a teacher: "Why I gotta read it?" An example of black English that I did not hear Lisa use, but did hear from several African American students at the school, was use of the word "go" to mean "is," such as "here go some paper." Of the white students at Matthews, only Lisa and a few others used elements of black English regularly, but virtually all used it occasionally, especially among peers.

2.   The relationship of students like Lisa and Jackson to whiteness parallels the perspective of Dalton Conley, a white sociologist who grew up in a predominately minority neighborhood and aligned himself early in life with his nonwhite peers. In his memoir *Honky* (2000), Conley writes, "I've studied whiteness the way I would a foreign language."

REFERENCES

Ainsworth-Darnell, James W., and Douglas B. Downey. 1998. Assessing the Oppositional Culture Explanation for Racial/Ethnic Differences in School Performance. *American Sociological Review* 63: 536–553.

Alexander, Karl, Doris R. Entwisle, and Maxine S. Thompson. 1987. School Performance, Status Relations, and the Structure of Sentiment: Bringing the Teacher Back In. *American Sociological Review* 52: 665–682.

Allport, Gordon W. [1954] 1958. *The Nature of Prejudice.* Garden City: Doubleday Anchor Books.

Andersen, Margaret L. 2003. Whitewashing Race: A Critical Perspective on Whiteness. In *White Out: The Continuing Significance of Racism*, ed. Ashley W. Doane and Eduardo Bonilla-Silva, 21–34. New York: Routledge.

Anderson, Elijah. 1990. *Streetwise: Race, Class, and Change in an Urban Community.* Chicago: University of Chicago Press.

Antonio Goldsmith, Pat. 2004. Schools' Racial Mix, Students' Optimism, and the Black-White and Latino-White Achievement Gaps. *Sociology of Education* 77: 121–147.

Anyon, Jean. 1980. Social Class and the Hidden Curriculum of Work. *Journal of Education* 162: 67–92.

———. 1997. *Ghetto Schooling: A Political Economy of Urban Educational Reform.* New York: Teachers College Press.

Asante, Molefi. 1987. *The Afrocentric Ideal.* Philadelphia: Temple University Press.

Bankston, Carl L., III, and Stephen J. Caldas. 1996. Majority African American Schools and the Perpetuation of Social Injustice: The Influence of De facto Segregation on Academic Achievement. *Social Forces* 72: 534–555.

———. 2000. Majority African American Schools and the Family Structures of Schools: School Racial Composition and Academic Achievement among Black and White Students. *Sociological Focus* 33: 243–263.

Berger, Peter L., and Thomas Luckmann. 1966. *The Social Construction of Reality.* New York: Doubleday.

Bernstein, Basil. 1986. On Pedagogic Discourse. In *Handbook of Theory and Research for the Sociology of Education*, ed. John G. Richardson, 205–240. New York: Greenwood Press.

Best, Steven, and Douglas Kellner. 1991. *Postmodern Theory: Critical Interrogations.* New York: Guilford Press.

Bettie, Julie. 2000. Women without Class: *Chicas, Cholas*, Trash, and the Presence/Absence of Class Identity. *Signs* 26: 1–35.

———. 2002. Exceptions to the Rule: Upwardly Mobile White and Mexican American High School Girls. *Gender and Society* 16: 403–422.

———. 2003. *Women without Class: Girls, Race, and Identity.* Berkeley: University of California Press.

Bird, S. Elizabeth. 2002. It Makes Sense to Us: Cultural Identity in Local Legends of Place. *Journal of Contemporary Ethnography* 31: 519–547.

Blau, Judith R. 2003. *Race in the Schools: Perpetuating White Dominance?* Boulder: Lynne Rienner Publishers.

Blumer, Herbert. 1958. Race Prejudice as a Sense of Group Position. *Pacific Sociological Review* 1: 3–7.

———. 1969. *Symbolic Interactionism.* Berkeley: University of California Press.

Bonilla-Silva, Eduardo. 2001. *White Supremacy and Racism in the Post–Civil Rights Era.* Boulder: Lynne Rienner Publishers.

Bourdieu, Pierre. 1977. Cultural Reproduction and Social Reproduction. In *Power and Ideology in Education,* ed. J. Karabel and A. H. Halsey, 487–511. New York: Oxford University Press.

———. 1984. *Distinction: A Social Critique of the Judgment of Taste.* Cambridge, Mass.: Harvard University Press.

———. 1986. The Forms of Capital. In *Handbook of Theory and Research for the Sociology of Education,* ed. John G. Richardson, 241–258. New York: Greenwood Press.

Bourdieu, Pierre, and Jean-Claude Passeron. 1977. *Reproduction in Education, Society, and Culture.* London: Sage Publications.

Bourdieu, Pierre, and Loic J. D. Wacquant. 1992. *An Invitation to Reflexive Sociology.* Chicago: University of Chicago Press.

Bowles, Samuel, and Herbert Gintis. 1976. *Schooling in Capitalist America: Educational Reform and the Contradictions of Economic Life.* New York: Basic Books.

Brodkin, Karen. 1998. *How the Jews Became White Folks and What That Says about Race in America.* New Brunswick, N.J.: Rutgers University Press.

Chen, Anthony S. 1999. Lives at the Center of the Periphery, Lives at the Periphery of the Center: Chinese American Masculinities and Bargaining with Hegemony. *Gender & Society* 13: 584–607.

Chin, Elizabeth. 2001. *Purchasing Power: Black Kids and American Consumer Culture.* Minneapolis: University of Minnesota Press.

Chubbuck, Sharon M. 2004. Whiteness Enacted, Whiteness Disrupted: The Complexity of Personal Congruence. *American Educational Research Journal* 41: 301–333.

Collins, Patricia Hill. 1986. Learning from the Outsider Within: The Sociological Significance of Black Feminist Thought. *Social Problems* 33: 14–32.

———. 1990. *Black Feminist Thought: Knowledge, Consciousness, and the Politics of Empowerment.* New York: Routledge.

———. 1998. *Fighting Words: Black Women and the Search for Justice.* Minneapolis: University of Minnesota Press.

Collins, Patricia Hill, Lionel A. Maldonado, Dana Y. Takagi, Barrie Thorne, Lynne Weber, and Howard Winant. 1995. Symposium: On West and Fenstermaker's "Doing Difference." *Gender and Society* 9: 491–513.

Conley, Dalton. 2000. *Honky.* New York: Vintage Books, a division of Random House.

Connell, Robert W. 1995. *Masculinities*. Berkeley: University of California Press

Connolly, Paul. 1998. *Racism, Gender Identities, and Young Children: Social Relations in a Multi-Ethnic, Inner-City Primary School*. London: Routledge.

Cooley, Charles Horton. 1902. *Human Nature and the Social Order*. New York: Charles Scribner's Sons.

Cooper, Richard. 1984. A Note on the Biological Concept of Race and Its Application in Epidemiological Research. *American Heart Journal* 108: 715–723.

Dance, L. Janelle. 2002. *Tough Fronts: The Impact of Street Culture on Schooling*. New York: Routledge Falmer.

Dauber, Susan L., Karl L. Alexander, and Doris R. Entwisle. 1996. Tracking and Transitions through the Middle Grades: Channeling Educational Trajectories. *Sociology of Education* 69: 290–307.

Delpit, Lisa. 1995. *Other People's Children: Cultural Conflict in the Classroom*. New York: Free Press.

Demetriou, Demetrakis Z. 2001. Connell's Concept of Hegemonic Masculinity: A Critique. *Theory and Society* 30: 337–361.

Dillard, Joey L. 1972. *Black English: Its History and Usage in the United States*. New York: Random House.

Doane, Ashley W., and Eduardo Bonilla-Silva, eds. 2003. *White Out: The Continuing Significance of Racism*. New York: Routledge.

Dyer, Richard. 1997. *White*. London: Routledge.

Eckert, Penny. 1989. *Jocks and Burnouts: Social Categories and Identity in the High School*. New York: Teacher's College Press.

Emerson, Robert M., Rachel I. Fretz, and Linda L. Shaw. 1995. *Writing Ethnographic Fieldnotes*. Chicago: University of Chicago Press.

Fanon, Frantz. 1967. *Black Skin, White Masks*. New York: Grove Press.

Farkas, George. 1996. *Human Capital or Cultural Capital? Ethnicity and Poverty Groups in an Urban School District*. New York: Aldine de Gruyter.

Farley, Reynolds, C. Steeh, M. Krysan, T. Jackson, and K. Reeves. 1994. Stereotypes and Segregation: Neighborhoods in the Detroit Area. *American Journal of Sociology* 100: 750–780.

Feagin, Joe. 1991. The Continuing Significance of Race: Antiblack Discrimination in Public Places. *American Sociological Review* 56: 101–117.

Feagin, Joe, Anthony M. Orum, and Gideon Sjoberg. 1991. *A Case for the Case Study*. Chapel Hill: University of North Carolina Press.

Feagin, Joe, and Melvin Sikes. 1994. *Living with Racism: The Black Middle-Class Experience*. Boston: Beacon Press.

Ferguson, Ann Arnett. 2000. *Bad Boys: Public Schools in the Making of Black Masculinity*. Ann Arbor: University of Michigan Press.

Ferguson, Ronald F. 1998. Teachers' Perceptions and Expectations and the Black-White Test Score Gap. In *The Black-White Test Score Gap*, ed. C. Jencks and M. Phillips, 273–317. Washington: Brookings Institute Press.

Fine, Michele. 1997. Witnessing Whiteness. In *Off White: Readings on Race, Power, and Society*, ed. M. Fine, L. Weis, L. Powell, and L. Mun Wong, 57–65. New York: Routledge.

Fine, Michele, L. Weis, L. Powell, and L. Mun Wong, eds. 1997. *Off White: Readings on Race, Power, and Society*. New York: Routledge.

Flores-Gonzalez, Nilda. 2002. *School Kids/Street Kids: Identity Development in Latino Students.* New York: Teachers College Press.

Foley, Douglas E. 1990. *Learning Capitalist Culture: Deep in the Heart of Tejas.* Philadelphia: University of Pennsylvania Press.

Foley, Neil. 1997. *The White Scourge: Mexican, Blacks, and Poor Whites in Texas Cotton Culture.* Berkeley: University of California Press.

Fordham, Signithia. 1988. Racelessness as a Factor in Black Students' School Success: Pragmatic Strategy or Pyrrhic Victory? *Harvard Educational Review.* 58: 54–84.

Fordham, Signithia, and John U. Ogbu. 1986. Black Students' School Success: Coping with the Burden of "Acting White." *Urban Review* 18: 176–206.

Foucault, Michel. 1995. *Discipline and Punish.* 2nd ed. Trans. Alan Sheridan. New York: Vintage.

Frankenberg, Ruth. 1993. *White Women, Race Matters: The Social Construction of Whiteness.* Minneapolis: University of Minnesota Press.

Fregoso, Rosa Linda. 1993. *The Bronze Screen: Chicana and Chicano Film Culture.* Minneapolis: University of Minnesota Press.

Gallagher, Charles A. 1995. White Reconstruction in the University. *Socialist Review* 24: 165–187.

Gamoran, Adam. 1992. Access to Excellence: Assignments to Honors English Classes in the Transition from Middle to High School. *Educational Evaluation and Policy Analysis* 14: 185–204.

Gilmore, Perry. 1985. "Gimme Room": School Resistance, Attitude, and Access to Literacy. *Journal of Education* 167: 111–128.

Giroux, Henry, and David Purpel. 1983. *The Hidden Curriculum and Moral Education.* Berkeley, Calif.: McCutchan.

Glaser, Barney G., and Anselm L. Strauss. 1967. *The Discovery of Grounded Theory: Strategies for Qualitative Research.* Chicago: Aldine.

Glenn, Evelyn Nakano. 2002. *Unequal Freedom: How Race and Gender Shaped American Citizenship and Labor.* Cambridge: Harvard University Press.

Goffman, Erving. 1963. *Stigma: Notes on the Management of a Spoiled Identity.* Englewood Cliffs: Prentice Hall.

———. 1973. *The Presentation of Self in Everyday Life.* New York: Overlook Press.

Goodman, Alan H. 2000. Why Genes Don't Count (for Racial Differences in Health). *American Journal of Public Health* 90: 1699–1702.

Gramsci, Antonio. 1971. *Selections from the Prison Notebooks.* New York: International Publishers.

Grant, Linda. 1984. Black Females Place in Desegregated Classrooms. *Sociology of Education* 57: 98–111.

Graves, Joseph L., Jr. 2001. *The Emperor's New Clothes: Biological Theories of Race at the Millennium.* New Brunswick, N.J.: Rutgers University Press.

Hall, Stuart. 1986. Gramsci's Relevance for the Study of Race and Ethnicity. *Journal of Communication Inquiry* 10: 5–27.

Hallinan, Maureen T. 1994. Tracking: From Theory to Practice. *Sociology of Education* 67: 79–91.

Haney Lopez, Ian F. 1996. *White by Law: The Legal Construction of Race.* New York: New York University Press.

Harris, David R., and Jeremiah Joseph Sim. 2002. Who Is Multiracial? Assessing the Complexity of Lived Race. *American Sociological Review* 67: 614–627.

Hartigan, John, Jr. 1997. Unpopular Culture: The Case of "White Trash." *Cultural Studies* 11: 316–343.

———. 1999. *Racial Situations: Class Predicaments of Whiteness in Detroit*. Princeton: Princeton University Press.

Heath, Shirley Brice. 1983. *Ways with Words*. Cambridge: Cambridge University Press.

Hebdige, Dick. 1979. *Subculture: The Meaning of Style*. London: Routledge.

Hedges, Larry V., and Amy Nowell. 1999. Changes in the Black-White Gap in Achievement Test Scores. *Sociology of Education* 72: 111–135.

Hill, Mark E. 2002. Race of the Interviewer and Perception of Skin Color: Evidence from the Multi-City Study of Urban Inequality. *American Sociological Review* 67: 99–108.

Horvat, Erin McNamara, and Anthony Lising Antonio. 1999. Hey, Those Shoes Are Out of Uniform: African American Girls in an Elite High School and the Importance of Habitus. *Anthropology and Education Quarterly* 30: 317–342.

Ignatiev, Noel. 1995. *How the Irish Became White*. New York: Routledge.

Jackson, Pamela Braboy, Peggy A. Thoits, and Howard F. Taylor. 1995. Composition of the Workplace and Psychological Well-Being: The Effects of Tokenism on America's Black Elite. *Social Forces* 74: 543–557.

Jencks, Christopher, and Meredith Phillips. 1998. *The Black-White Test Score Gap*. Washington: Brookings Institution Press.

Johnson-Bailey, Juanita. 1999. The Ties That Bind and the Shackles That Separate: Race, Gender, Class, and Color in a Research Process. *International Journal of Qualitative Studies in Education* 12: 659–670.

Kanter, Rosabeth Moss. 1977. *Men and Women of the Corporation*. New York: Basic Books.

Kenny, Lorraine Delia. 2000. *Daughters of Suburbia: Growing Up White, Middle Class, and Female*. New Brunswick, N.J.: Rutgers University Press.

Kirschenmen, Joleen, and Kathryn M. Neckerman. 1991. We'd Love to Hire Them, But . . . The Meaning of Race for Employers. In *The Urban Underclass*, ed. Christopher Jencks and Paul Peterson, 203–232. Washington, D.C.: Brookings Institution Press.

Kozol, Jonathan. 1991. *Savage Inequalities*. New York: Crown Publishers.

Labov, W. 1972. *Language in the Inner City: Studies in the Black English Vernacular*. Philadelphia: University of Pennsylvania Press.

Ladson-Billings, Gloria. 1994. *The Dreamkeepers: Successful Teachers of African American Children*. San Francisco: Jossey-Bass.

Lamont, Michelle, and Annette Lareau. 1988. Cultural Capital: Allusions, Gaps, and Glissandos. *Sociological Theory* 6: 153–168.

Lareau, Annette. 1987. Social Class and Family-School Relationships: The Importance of Cultural Capital. *Sociology of Education* 56: 73–85.

———. 2002. Invisible Inequality: Social Class and Childrearing in Black Families and White Families. *American Sociological Review* 67: 747–776.

Lareau, Annette, and Erin McNamara Horvat. 1999. Moments of Social Inclusion and Exclusion: Race, Class, and Cultural Capital in Family-School Relationships. *Sociology of Education* 72: 37–53.

Lee, Stacey J. 1994. Behind the Model-Minority Stereotype: Voices of High- and Low-Achieving Asian American Students. *Anthropology and Education Quarterly* 25: 413–429.

——. 1996. *Unraveling the Model Minority Stereotype: Listening to Asian American Youth*. New York: Teachers College Press.

Lewis, Amanda E. 2001. There is No "Race" in the Schoolyard: Color-Blind Ideology in an (Almost) White School. *American Educational Research Journal* 38: 781–811.

——. 2003a. Everyday Race Making: Navigating Racial Boundaries in Schools. *American Behavioral Scientist* 47: 283–305.

——. 2003b. *Race in the Schoolyard: Negotiating the Color Line in Classrooms and Communities*. New Brunswick, N.J.: Rutgers University Press.

——. 2004. What Group? Studying Whites and Whiteness in the Era of "Colorblindness." *Sociological Theory* 22: 623–646.

Lipsitz, George. 1995. The Possessive Investment in Whiteness: Racialized Social Democracy and the "White" Problem in American Studies. *American Quarterly* 47: 369–387.

MacLeod, Jay. 1995. *Ain't No Makin' It: Aspirations and Attainment in a Low Income Neighborhood*. 2nd ed. Boulder: Westview Press.

Martin, Karin A. 1998. Becoming a Gendered Body: Practices of Preschools. *American Sociological Review* 63: 494–511.

Massey, Douglas, Gretchen A. Condran, and Nancy A. Denton. 1987. The Effect of Residential Segregation on Black Social and Economic Well-Being. *Social Forces* 66: 29–57.

Massey, Douglas, and Nancy A. Denton. 1993. *American Apartheid: Segregation and the Making of the Underclass*. Cambridge: Harvard University Press.

McIntosh, Peggy. [1988] 1998. White Privilege and Male Privilege: A Personal Account of Coming to See Correspondences through Work in Women's Studies. In *Race, Class, and Gender*, ed. M. L. Andersen and P. H. Collins, 94–105. Boston: Wadsworth.

McIntyre, Alice. 1997. *Making Meaning of Whiteness: Exploring Racial Identity with White Teachers*. Albany: SUNY Press.

McLaren, Peter. 1986. *Schooling as a Ritual Performance: Towards a Political Economy of Educational Symbols and Gestures*. London: Routledge and Kegan Paul.

McNeil, Linda M. 1986. *Contradictions of Control: School Structure and School Knowledge*. New York: Routledge.

——. 2000. *Contradictions of School Reform: The Educational Costs of Standardized Testing*. New York: Routledge Press.

Mead, George Herbert. [1934] 1962. *Mind, Self, and Society*. Repr. Chicago: University of Chicago Press.

Merton, Robert K. 1972. Insiders and Outsiders: A Chapter in the Sociology of Knowledge. *American Journal of Sociology* 78: 9–47.

Moore, Valerie Ann. 2002. The Collaborative Emergence of Race in Children's Play: A Case Study of Two Summer Camps. *Social Problems* 49: 58–78.

Morris, Edward W. 2003. The Majority Minority: Academic Experiences of White Students in a Predominately Racial/Ethnic Minority School. PhD diss., University of Texas at Austin.

Muller, Chandra. 1995. Maternal Employment, Parental Involvement, and Mathematics Achievement among Adolescents. *Journal of Marriage and the Family* 57: 85–100.

Muller, Chandra, Susan Roberta Katz, and L. Janelle Dance. 1999. Investing in Teaching and Learning: Dynamics of the Teacher-Student Relationship from Each Actor's Perspective. *Urban Education* 34: 292–337.

Newitz, Annalee, and Matthew Wray. 1997. What Is "White Trash"? Stereotypes and Economic Conditions of Poor Whites in the United States. In *Whiteness: A Critical Reader*, ed. Mike Hill, 168–184. New York: New York University Press.

Noguera, Pedro A. 1995. Preventing and Producing Violence: A Critical Analysis of Responses to School Violence. *Harvard Educational Review* 65: 189–212.

Oakes, Jeannie. 1985. *Keeping Track: How Schools Structure Inequality.* New Haven, Conn.: Yale University Press.

———. 1995. Two Cities' Tracking and Within-School Segregation. *Teachers College Record* 96: 681–690.

Oakes, Jeannie, Adam Gamoran, and Reba Page. 1992. Curriculum Differentiation: Opportunities, Outcomes, and Meanings. In *Handbook of Research on Curriculum*, ed. Philip W. Jackson, 570–608. New York: Macmillian.

Oakes, Jeannie, Molly Selvin, Lynn Karoly, and Gretchen Guiton. 1992. *Educational Matchmaking: Academic and Vocational Tracking in Comprehensive High Schools.* Santa Monica: RAND.

Oates, Gary L. St. C. 2003. Teacher-Student Racial Congruence, Teacher Perceptions, and Test Performance. *Social Science Quarterly* 84: 508–525.

Ogbu, John. 1978. *Minority Education and Caste: The American System in Cross Cultural Perspective.* Orlando, Fla.: Academic Press.

Ogbu, John U. 1991. Immigrant and Involuntary Minorities in Comparative Perspective. In *Minority Status and Schooling: A Comparative Study of Immigrant and Involuntary Minorities*, ed. Margaret Gibson and John Ogbu, 3–33. New York: Garland Publishing.

Oliver, Melvin L., and Thomas M. Shapiro. 1995. *Black Wealth/White Wealth: A New Perspective in Racial Inequality.* New York: Routledge.

Olsen, Laurie. 1997. *Made in America: Immigrant Students in Our Public Schools.* New York: New Press.

Omi, Michael, and Howard Winant. 1994. *Racial Formation in the United States:From the 1960 to the 1980s.* 2nd ed. New York: Routledge and Kegan Paul.

Orenstein, Peggy. 1994. *School Girls: Young Women, Self-Esteem, and the Confidence Gap.* New York: Doubleday.

Orfield, Gary. 1996. *Dismantling Desegregation: The Quiet Reversal of Brown v. Board of Education.* New York: New Press.

Pattillo-McCoy, Mary. 1999. *Black Picket Fences: Privilege and Peril among the Black Middle Class.* Chicago: University of Chicago Press.

Perry, Pamela. 2002. *Shades of White: White Kids and Racial Identities in High School.* Durham: Duke University Press.

Pollock, Mica. 2001. How the Question We Ask Most about Race in Education Is the Question We Most Suppress. *Educational Researcher* 30: 2–12.

Quiocho, Alice, and Francisco Rios. 2000. The Power of Their Presence: Minority Group Teachers and Schooling. *Review of Educational Research* 70: 485–528.

Rafter, Nicole H. 1988. *White Trash: The Eugenic Family Studies, 1877–1919.* Boston: Northeastern University Press.

———. 1992. Claims-Making and Socio-Cultural Context in the First U.S. Eugenics Campaign. *Social Problems* 39: 17–33.

Rasmussen, Birgit Brander, Eric Klinenberg, Irene J. Nexica, and Matt Wray, eds. 2001. *The Making and Unmaking of Whiteness.* Durham, N.C.: Duke University Press.

Reardon, Sean F., and John T. Yun. 2001. Suburban Racial Change and Suburban School Segregation, 1987–95. *Sociology of Education* 74: 79–101.

Reardon, Sean F., John T. Yun, and Tamela McNulty Eitle. 2000. The Changing Structure of School Segregation: Measurement and Evidence of Multiracial Metropolitan-Area School Segregation, 1989–1995. *Demography* 37: 351–364.

Rich, Frank. 2002. American Idol: Eminem, for Everyone. *New York Times Magazine*, November 3.

Rist, Ray. 1970. Student Social Class and Teacher Expectations: The Self-Fulfilling Prophecy in Ghetto Education. *Harvard Educational Review* 40: 411–451.

Roediger, David R. 1991. *The Wages of Whiteness: Race and the Making of the American Working Class.* London: Verso.

Roscigno, Vincent J. 1998. Race and the Reproduction of Educational Disadvantage. *Social Forces* 76: 1033–1060.

Roscigno, Vincent J., and James W. Ainsworth-Darnell. 1999. Race, Cultural Capital, and Educational Resources: Persistent Inequalities and Achievement Returns. *Sociology of Education* 72: 158–178.

Sadker, Myra, and David Sadker. 1994. *Failing at Fairness: How Our Schools Cheat Girls.* New York: Simon and Schuster.

Schofield, Janet Ward. 1989. *Black and White in School.* New York: Teachers College Press.

Scwalbe, Michael, Sandra Godwin, Daphne Holden, Douglas Schrock, Shealy Thompson, and Michele Wolkomir. 2000. Generic Processes in the Reproduction of Inequality: An Interactionist Analysis. *Social Forces* 79: 419–452.

Smedley, Audrey. 1993. *Race in North America: Origin and Evolution of a Worldview.* San Francisco: Westview Press.

Smitherman, Geneva. 1977. *Talkin and Testifyin: The Language of Black America.* Boston: Houghton Mifflin.

——. 2000. *Talkin that Talk: Language, Culture, and Education in African America.* New York: Routledge.

Snyder, Benson R. 1971. *The Hidden Curriculum.* New York: Knopf.

Spradley, James P. 1979. *The Ethnographic Interview.* New York: Holt, Rinehart, and Winston.

Stanley, M. Sue. 1996. School Uniforms and Safety. *Education and Urban Society* 28: 424–436.

Stevenson, David Lee, Kathryn S. Schiller, and Barbara Schneider. 1994. Sequences for Opportunities for Learning. *Sociology of Education* 67: 184–198.

Tatum, Beverly Daniel. 1999. *Why Are All the Black Kids Sitting Together in the Cafeteria? And Other Conversations about Race.* 2nd ed. New York: Basic Books.

Thorne, Barrie. 1993. *Gender Play: Girls and Boys in School.* New Brunswick, N.J.: Rutgers University Press.

Tyson, Karolyn. 2002. Weighing In: Elementary-Age Students and the Debate on Attitudes toward School among Black Students. *Social Forces* 80: 1157–1189.

U.S. Census Bureau. 2000. Projections of the Resident Population by Race, Hispanic Origin, and Nativity: Middle Series 1999–2100. Summary File NP-T5. Retrieved from http://www.census.gov/population/www/projections/natsum-T5.html.

U.S. Department of Education. 1999. *Digest of Educational Statistics.* Washington, D.C.: U.S. Government Printing Office.

——. 2001. *Digest of Educational Statistics.* Washington, D.C.: U.S. Government Printing Office.

U.S. Department of Labor, Bureau of Labor Statistics. 2003. Median Weekly Earnings of Full-Time Wage and Salary Workers by Detailed Occupation and Sex. Retrieved from http://www.bls.gov/cps/cpsaat39.pdf.

Valenzuela, Angela. 1999. *Subtractive Schooling: U.S.-Mexican Youth and the Politics of Caring.* Albany: State University of New York Press.

Van Ausdale, Debra, and Joe R. Feagin. 2001. *The First R: How Children Learn Race and Racism.* New York: Rowman and Littlefield.

Warren, Jonathan W., and France Winddance Twine. 1997. White Americans, the New Minority? Non-Blacks and the Ever-Expanding Boundaries of Whiteness. *Journal of Black Studies* 28: 200–218.

Waters, Mary C. 1990. *Ethnic Options: Choosing Identities in America.* Berkeley: University of California Press.

———. 1999. *Black Identities: West Indian Immigrant Dreams and American Realities.* Cambridge: Harvard University Press.

Wells, Amy Stuart, and Robert L. Crain. 1997. *Stepping over the Color Line: African American Students in White Suburban Schools.* New Haven: Yale University Press.

West, Candace, and Sarah Fenstermaker. 1995. Doing Difference. *Gender and Society* 9: 8–37.

Williams, Christine L. 1991. Case Studies and the Sociology of Gender. In *A Case for the Case Study,* ed. J. Feagin, A. Orum, and G. Sjoberg, 224–243. Chapel Hill: University of North Carolina Press.

———. 1995. *Still a Man's World: Men Who Do Women's Work.* Berkeley: University of California Press.

Willis, Paul. 1977. *Learning to Labor: How Working Class Kids Get Working Class Jobs.* New York: Columbia University Press.

Wilson, William Julius. 1980. *The Declining Significance of Race.* Rev. ed. Chicago: University of Chicago Press.

———. 1987. *The Truly Disadvantaged: The Inner City, The Underclass, and Public Policy.* Chicago: University of Chicago Press.

———. 1991. Studying Inner-City Social Dislocations: The Challenge of Public Agenda Research. *American Sociological Review* 56: 1–14.

Winant, Howard. 1994. *Racial Conditions: Politics, Theory, Comparisons.* Minneapolis: University of Minnesota Press.

Yancey, George. 2003. *Who Is White? Latinos, Asians, and the New Black/Nonblack Divide.* Boulder, Colo.: Lynne Rienner Publishers.

Zinn, Maxine Baca, and Bonnie Thornton Dill. 1996. Theorizing Difference from Multiracial Feminism. *Feminist Studies* 22: 321–332.

Zuberi, Tukufu. 2001. *Thicker Than Blood: How Racial Statistics Lie.* Minneapolis: University of Minnesota Press.

INDEX

academic ability, 8, 56, 76, 89, 134; achievement, 67, 96, 111, 113, 128; and class,
61–62, 137–138, 139; and race, 126,
137–138; and white students, 38, 125, 126,
130, 138
Adams, Ms., 83–84
advantages of whiteness, 1–2, 5, 11, 15–31, 76,
108, 126, 129, 139; and class and gender, 6,
20–24, 63, 64–67, 130, 134–138; and education, 16–19; and hegemony, 19–20,
24–27, 103; perceived, 56, 60–61; reproduction theory, 27–30; and tracking,
137–138. *See also* whiteness
affirmative action, 19
African Americans, 44, 47, 84, 109, 131,
146–147; culture of, 50–51; and peer
culture, 110; and whiteness, 113, 129, 134.
See also blackness; race
African American students, 7, 48, 59, 71–72,
104–106; boys, 28–29, 83, 89–97; and discipline, 70–74, 80–81, 89–92, 95–100, 134,
135; girls, 39, 52, 69, 86–89, 114; and
whiteness, 112, 118, 121, 124
African American teachers, 56, 63; and discipline, 81, 85, 88, 96; opinion of
Matthews, 58–61; perception of white
students, 68–70, 75, 134–135
aggression, 89, 90, 95, 102, 104, 118
Ahmed (student), 49–50
Andersen, Margaret, 86, 151n1
Anderson, Elijah, 23
Anderson, Ms., 85–86
Anisha (student), 112, 121
Annenberg Foundation, 43, 142, 144, 146
apartments, 61, 63, 64, 94
Asian Americans, 47, 129, 134. *See also* race
Asian American students, 7, 66, 104–106,
110, 117, 126; and discipline, 86, 95–96;
and dress code, 93; and gender, 52, 70, 96
authority, 53, 90, 101, 112, 122–123, 128, 131.
See also power

Bad Boys (Ferguson), 28–29
Balcones City, Texas, 41–44, 48, 62
behavior, 80, 84, 101, 102, 105; and white-
ness, 111–113, 121, 127, 129
Best, Steven, 28
Bettie, Julie, 63, 90–91, 94, 144, 154n2

black English, 28, 71, 97, 110, 154–155n1;
used by whites, 114, 116, 118, 120–22
blackness, 21, 22, 104, 116, 122. *See also*
African Americans; African American
students
Blau, Judith, 17
Blumer, Herbert, 25
bodily display, 10, 79, 93, 133, 135
Bourdieu, Pierre, 27, 79–80, 153n2. *See also*
cultural capital
Boyd, Ms., 58, 66–67, 68, 93, 101, 154n5
boys, 28–29, 51, 80–81, 83, 89–100, 120, 127;
aggression of, 89–95; Latino, 70–74, 124,
130; and self-discipline, 95–100. *See also*
gender; masculinity
Brittany (student), 87, 130
Byrd, James, 73

Caldwell, Mr., 48–49, 59, 63, 122, 123–124
Campbell, Ms., 84
Carlos (student), 92, 130
centralization, 100–103. *See also*
marginalization
Chen, Anthony, 25
Chin, Elizabeth, 109, 122
Christina (student), 118–119
class, 6, 8, 13, 60, 63–64, 77, 154n7; and academic ability, 61–62, 137–138, 139; and
discipline, 79–81, 86; and dress code, 40;
and education, 20–24; and gender and
race, 10, 20–24, 31, 116–120, 129–130, 131;
and hegemony, 25–27, 56; and Matthews,
42, 44, 47–54; and neighborhood, 42, 44,
53, 133–134; and perceptions of students,
56; performed, 91, 94, 115, 119, 154n2;
plasticity of, 109; and race, 18, 19, 56–58,
127, 129–130; and reproduction theory,
27–30; and TAAS, 35–38; trailer trash, 23,
57, 65, 101; upper class, 125, 135, 139; and
whiteness, 6, 20–24, 63, 64–67, 130,
134–138; white trash, 119. *See also* middle
class; working class
Clay (student), 124–25
clothing, 71, 107. *See also* dress and dress
code; style
Cohen, Ms., 43–44, 53
college, 38, 84
Collins, Patricia Hill, 21

167

ABOUT THE AUTHOR

EDWARD W. MORRIS is an assistant professor of sociology at Ohio University, where he teaches courses in race and ethnicity and the sociology of education. He received his PhD in sociology at the University of Texas at Austin in 2003. His research has won outstanding dissertation and paper awards and appears in several journals.

CPSIA information can be obtained at www.ICGtesting.com
Printed in the USA
269367BV00001B/5/P

9 780813 537214